AS THEY WERE

As They Were

M. F. K. FISHER

Vintage Books
A Division of Random House
New York

First Vintage Books Edition. May 1983

Library of Congress Cataloging in Publication Data
Fisher, M. F. K. (Mary Frances Kennedy), 1908-
As they were.
I. Title.
AC8.F52 1983   081   82-40427
ISBN 0-394-71348-6 (pbk.)

Cover art is a detail from the Paul Cezanne painting,
"Still Life: Dish and Apples, 1873-1877."
Courtesy the collection of Walter H. Annenberg

For Norah, again and always

CONTENTS

AS THEY WERE

PREJUDICE, HATE, AND THE FIRST WORLD WAR

 Preface

In the sixties, my fine old house in St. Helena seemed hollow, with the children gone. I said, Mary Frances, now is the time to go to new places and find different views of things.

Friends kept the hearth warm and the animals happy, and other friends let me stay in their own places when they were away. It was a vivid period of slow wandering, very rich, like a carpet I had often trod before I realized that it was there.

One winter I went to Long Island to a house I knew well from several summer visits. It was on the dunes near Bridgehampton. There was a car, so that I could drive into the village for mail and food. I cashed checks at the liquor store next to the grocery. I liked the tough fellow there,

and when I went back after several months in Sag Harbor,
I liked him even more, because he laughed with real pleasure when he saw me, and said, "God, were we glad to get
you off the dunes and outta here!"

I knew why, because he was one of the volunteer fire-
men who would have risked their lives to reach the house
if they knew I was without heat or help. They did not
want to die, any more than I did, but ....

The story I wrote about that incident is called "The
Wind-Chill Factor," and the house I lived alone in, except
for rare weekends with its owner who came down from her
job in New York, was a deliberate contradiction of the
local wisdom: "natives" of that part of the Island build and
farm and work *inland*. Only ignorant summer people stay
along the blandly beautiful beaches, flirting in bland igno-
rance with hurricanes and such.

My house had been partly demolished in the last Big
Blow, but was solid again and partly "winterized," as was
then said, and my hostess and I agreed that I was indeed a
lucky person to face a cozy winter there. I holed in.

After what I reported in "The Wind-Chill Factor," I
knew that many more lives than mine depended on
whether my lights had gone off, those three or four wild
nights, and I moved to a one-room flat in Sag Harbor. I
had the parlor and bathroom of what had once been a
whaler captain's house, with a cursory kitchenette at one
end. I was warm and quiet, and worked steadily because
there was nothing else to do. Outside, everything was
mostly silence, because the snow stayed high for weeks at a
time, and it was arduous to shuffle down the narrow high
tunnels of sludge that led to the post office and the grocery
store.

Fortunately, right across from my lodging was a small
boozerie owned by a handsome Greek who was paraplegic
from a railroad accident. We talked nostalgically about

good wines, and I came to enjoy and even appreciate popular jug-stuff.

I never capitulated to the currently popular fizz wines, carbonated mixtures of fruit juices and dregs, but through the thin back wall into the apartment that had once been the captain's dining room I often listened to a young fisherman, laid off during the bad weather, drink himself worse than silly on something like Thunderhead or Tango-Tango and then commit conjugal rape on his very devout wife every Saturday night, so that she could not receive Communion the next morning, after her Saturday Confession. Ho-hum. Their baby, about six months old, wailed a lot. They lived in a somewhat smaller "parlor" than mine, and there was always that half-gallon jug handy, under the bed.

My Greek friend and I talked in a detached casual way about this.

"The Wind-Chill Factor" taught me that there is a difference between what is true and what one believes is the truth. I depicted the storm in as bare a way as I could, since it had happened only to *me*. During the strange ordeal, there was nobody else, to observe or even survive. It was a true catharsis.

For a few days, after it, I felt floaty and emptied. And I had to face the fact that all my vague plans to write about an earlier life were crude fabrications of a fertile and fairly articulate mind. I wanted suddenly to write about *my* first years, for some unknown pushing reason, and I saw, after the wind on the dunes, that nobody but a child can write what has just happened to him. It is almost impossible for an older person to report such things without coloring them, twisting, invading the story, to make a more vivid or more self-flattering report.

In Sag Harbor I was almost always alone, for the months I was there. I never felt *lonely,* though, because that is not my bent. Some might say my life was austere. With an occasional glass of California jug-rosé from the little icebox that hummed along in a corner of my room, I tried to go as far back as I could into the life I honestly believed I had lived when I was four, or even ten. It was a sweaty job, at times painful.

People in Whittier have been hurt by some of the story's candor (not many, nor much, I hope). But since the time on the dunes, and then in Sag Harbor, I know that I can never write polite tomfoolery again, if I ever did.

So ... this report about some first days is not much more than a proof that ghetto children can survive as happy people if they are part of a close loving family.

By *ghetto* I do not mean *slum,* which now seems to spell the word to many people. I mean a small community within a larger one, where people of a certain ethnic or religious kind are segregated, either by choice or by unwritten laws. Whittier itself was a ghetto of Quakers who founded the little town so that they could live apart from other white Christians. Within its quiet bounds were a few intruders like us: a handful of Catholics and Protestants, now and then a Jewish family to run the five-and-ten, never a black person. I wanted to call the book *Child of an Inner Ghetto,* but by the late sixties the term had apparently lost its real meaning to everybody but me. We lived happily in an enclave within a bigger enclave.

My father, Rex Kennedy, bought the Whittier *News* in late 1911. As I understand it, the little daily was in a dubious and even shady state, financially as well as socially. What is more, Father was an Episcopalian (roped and tied by his bride, after a rebellious Methodist upbringing). The town of less than 5,000 was a closed communal settlement of Quakers who had created it with pride and stress in the remote hills southeast of small sleepy Los Angeles. Only other Quakers were welcomed. Word on the local Rialto (the corner of Greenleaf and Philadelphia, where the bank was) said gently that the new young editor might possibly last a year ... (Forty-two years later Rex died there, respected and loved.)

We lived until I was about eleven in a roomy solid ugly good house on Painter Avenue, just a few feet on the "right" (North) side of the Philadelphia intersection. South Painter was as green and quiet, but the houses were smaller, and the people lived simpler work-lives. North Painter, in 1912, was where the banker and some lawyers and a retired colonel were.

My parents were innocent of such rules of prestige and protocol, but the house was for sale because the Myers family wanted a smaller place nearer Mr. Myers' department store on North Greenleaf.

There were four or five bedrooms upstairs, which my parents planned to fill with more children, and Father added a nice apartment downstairs for Grandmother Holbrook, who was his champion, financially and many other ways, against the world, his wife, and Outrageous-Fortune-in-General. It all worked well, as far as I can know, and gradually the debts got paid, and there were indeed new siblings. I was a very happy little girl.

And that is what I wanted to write about in Sag Harbor: the way it *was,* not the way I might have come to see it. I wish there were time to try again.

As I see it now, our non-Quaker family started out in Whittier with several strikes against us. When I was a child there, though, I was unaware of almost everything except

being sturdy and happy. I still have no idea of how much
and how often Rex may have been rebuffed and rebuffed as
editor of the *News*, as well as a known companion of men
who played poker, drank liquor, and even went to Mass. As
for my mother, she took out whatever social desires she may
have had—and they were indeed puny, for by nature and
training she was asocial—in working valiantly for the
Woman's Club and the small mission which later became
the Episcopal church, and in exchanging long cheerful letters with her Eastern relatives ... and in running a kind of
boardinghouse for anyone even remotely related to her. As
long as she lived, anyone whose uncle on his mother's side
had married a second cousin of Grandmother's sister-in-law
could and did come to stay with us for anything from a week
to several months, although it was a real ordeal for Mother
to ask two "other people" to dinner. Some of the relatives
were staid and stuffy, but there were fortunately a lot of
them who could safely be called eccentric or, now that my
candor cannot hurt my mother, downright crazy. They were
the leaven in the loaf, and only rarely did my father suggest
in a mild way that perhaps it would be nice to have some of
his own brothers or nieces around for a few days. I think he
knew that his wife's feverish need to open her house to her
own clan was a sign that she was, in truth, lonely in her local
world of polite but distant Quaker ladies.

Of course Anne and I knew nothing of all this. Painter
Avenue was a wonderful street, gummed over with tar
which melted deliciously during the first heat waves in May
and then settled into a cozy warm ooze which felt good on
our feet. And tar meant the steamroller, the most exciting
mobile object in my lifetime, until I heard my first and last
real calliope in about 1917. Probably the ground was
smoothed or scraped a little first. Then, awesomely, the

steamroller would rumble into view. We stood almost prayerfully on the front porch and then, as we grew older and bolder, on the sidewalk, and watched it move up and down our block. It was like a gigantic snail, but of course noisier, with a man up in its shell to wave now and then to us. It was faultless in the way it rolled the tar, our tar, into the flattened street bed. It always went forward, and perhaps did not even have a reverse gear: I am ignorant of anything but its irrevocable progress past our house, a jolly Juggernaut.

We stood as long as we were allowed, probably almost dozing on our feet, hypnotized by its enormous and ruthless behavior, but I am sure that our jaws were not dropped, for we had our backs to the house and were chewing on the tar that had been spread earlier that day, and strictly forbidden by both Grandmother and Mother, a double hazard.

Tar with some dust in it was perhaps even more delicious than dirty chips from the iceman's wagon, largely because if we worked up enough body heat and had the right amount of spit we could keep it melted so that it acted almost like chewing gum, which was forbidden to us as vulgar and bad for the teeth and in general to be shunned. Tar was better than anything ever put out by Wrigley and Beechnut, anyway. It had a high bright taste. It tasted the way it smelled, but better. And it was challenging, for unless we could keep up the heat and the juice and the general muscular involvement, it would flake off and turn our teeth a spotted betraying black . . . black as tar. Dangerous game!

One time after we had flagrantly and plainly cheated, Mother said coolly to me at the dinner table, after we had eaten the first course with propriety and were waiting to see what came next (for Anne and I had been too busy on the sidewalk that afternoon to quiz the kitchen), "Mary Frances,

I would like you to show your father your teeth." I steeled myself, and bared my little fangs at him. Things were still as church. Then Rex gave a great good laugh, and said, *"TAR!* Delicious! Best thing I ever chewed! But it looks awful on teeth!"

Later we did discuss the dubious sides of turning our backs, and the knowledge that we were cheating, and all that, but the reaction of my father made it easier for Anne and me to accept our capitulation to Obedience, and within a comfortable time the steamroller stopped its majestic smashing and we had a paved street, which made even ice chips less tasty.

Down on the corner of Philadelphia and Painter, near enough for us to see at night from the sleeping porch which we gradually had to ourselves as our parents started a new batch of children in another part of the upstairs, there was a big light strung over the intersection, and when a man had climbed up to it to clean it, he would drop out a long greyish tube of some kind of clay which made fine chalk. The sidewalks were sketchy in the town then, but we had a lumpy one going along our block, over the bulging roots of pepper and camphor trees. Later I found it hellish to skate on, but for hopscotch and artwork it was very good.

Across the street lived Old Lady Ransome, and her house still stands in its genteel green-and-white remoteness. Now and then my mother would put on a hat and gloves and go across to pay a call, and the two women would come out on the wide cement porch behind the hanging baskets of smilax ferns and perhaps wave to us. Anne and I went there only a few times, to carry Easter eggs or some such trifle, for Mrs. Ransome was crippled, and in pain.

Next door to her lived a series of people we never knew,

except that during the influenza epidemic in 1918 Mother made us stay in the back yard while two or three coffins were carried away from it, one of a young woman, perhaps not yet twenty, who had waved now and then to us as she walked downtown to work for a lawyer. We did not feel one way or another about the plague, probably, although it interested us that soon after that Father came home at noon and pulled off the gauze mask requested by the Red Cross and said something like, *"Bushwah!* I can't smoke in it. And my nose is too big."

Next to the sad unknowns across from us, for a magical few years lived the Smiths. He was a lawyer. She had enormous sunken dark eyes, and played the piano very well. I think she was the fairly rich daughter, with what in France would be called a dowry, of the owner of a department store in Kansas City or some such place. Gradually they had two little girls. All four of them were tubercular. The last I heard, at least three of them had died. Mr. Smith's family was very bitter about his having caught the terrible disease from her, and her family felt the same way about him, and Mother worried a lot about their dilemma, but Anne and I simply enjoyed them. We went on wonderful picnics, for one thing. And I remember sitting under Mrs. Smith's beautiful grand piano and holding on to one of its legs while through my body ran the force and delicacy of the music she knew and played well. I think now it was Schubert, Mozart.

On up the street lived the Maples. They were and probably still are important in Whittier, and I remember them as a handsome large family. They were intelligent and well bred, and went to local schools and then away to Western colleges. Mr. Maple was the banker. On the top floor of the large house, into which I never once stepped, lived Mrs.

Maple's mother, a small and apparently fearsome woman who looked down all day on the corner of Painter and Hadley from her high windows, but never waved or nodded.

I remember walking to the Bailey Street School when I was about five and a half years old, with the oldest Maple girl, Caroline, who was wearing her first long skirt. This was in about 1913, and it was plainly an important step for her to take. Two or three girls accompanied her enviously, still with skirts flapping above their shoe tops, perhaps nine inches from the ground. Much later in our lives I met Caroline a few times and liked her very much, but always felt some of my childhood awe of her having grown up that long before I did.

I was supposed to be a good friend of her little sister Josephine, but it never worked. Both of us tried for years to like each other, because our mothers thought it would be nice for one reason or another; we went to little parties, and had mutual friends, and remained consistently cold and disinterested.

Josephine had blond hair and was solidly built, as a child. She was rather malicious, I think, and I remember that once when I was tagging along shyly behind Red Sutherland, my first and only love in schools until I was well on toward marriage, Josephine in a small gang of my friends spread the word that I had blown a kiss to Red's back or head as he marched on bravely in front of me. This hurt me. I would have liked to blow a kiss to him, but would never have done so. It also insulted me: such a childish gesture, turned into such a lascivious one! I was no dolt, but rather a sensitive proud princess riding behind her knight, whether or not he cared. (He did not.) I felt defiled, no matter how naïvely.

The real thing I still have against Josephine, even now, although by now we well might like each other without cavil,

is that once she whispered meanly to a school friend about
my mother's looks. This I found, and still find, hard to for-
give, and it gave me my first ugly taste of real hate. It must
have been in 1918, because Mother was bending over my
new sister Norah in her pram at the bottom of the front
steps, where the baby lay in the sunshine. Skirts came to the
floor or more daringly the ankle then, for a woman of my
mother's age and social position, the first of which was about
thirty-seven and the second, precarious. She was probably
pregnant with my brother David, and her ankles were puffy,
and as I watched her tuck the soft white covers about the
baby I heard Josephine titter to my other school friend,
"Look at her big fat ankles." Ah, there was a flash of rage in
me, still felt!

It was the custom for the little girls of one or another
neighborhood to meet on the sidewalk in front of their
houses and walk to Penn Street School together, in a morning troupe that sometimes held fifteen or so, and I suppose
the boys did the same. We never rode bikes, except after
school and on Saturdays, and skates were out of the question
because of the chancy sidewalks. We walked.

That morning of the slur on my mother's beauty, I knew
we would stop for at least eight friends before we got to
Penn. For perhaps the first time in my life I was so conscious
of being angry that I knew I could not go with them, and
especially with the sly secure tittering traitor who had
mocked Edith Kennedy's ankles. Mother had suddenly become real and beautiful to me. I wanted to embrace her
wildly, which we never did in our family, especially in those
early days, and then run out onto the sidewalk and hit Josephine in her blond smug face until all her teeth popped out
and her skin turned black and her eyes died.

This would not do, plainly. Instead I gave a bang on the

side of the baby's pram, turned away roughly from my
mother's tender if preoccupied goodbye, and ran around to
the back of our house and down the alleys, alone all the way
to school. And I was swinging higher than anybody when
my own crowd came onto the playground before the bell
rang.

Across the street from the Maples, and down a block toward us, so that the house would be only a little north and
across from the low brown cottage so full of love and music
where the Smiths coughed and rotted, the Fays stayed for
several years. Mrs. Fay was very *grande dame,* and always
dressed formally for dinner, although they were poor as Job's
turkey, according to my mother. When my parents went
there, Mrs. Fay simply slung her train over one arm as she
carried in the vegetable dishes, I was told later with laughing
admiration. They did not even have a Hired Girl, and Mrs.
Fay washed her lone child Eleanor's long hair and pressed her
middy skirts' countless pleats.

Eleanor was very nice to us, and today might have been
called a baby-sitter, on the rare times when Rex and Edith
and the Fays would drive into Los Angeles in our Model T
for a dinner with wine at Foix's or Marcel's or the Victor
Hugo. My sister Anne and I never liked her much, one way
or t'other, but I cannot remember why, for she read to us
and was not sly or a tattletaler. Later the Fays moved away
and she was sent to a fashionable school, and occasionally we
heard that she had done things like make a debut (to what,
in Southern California?) and get married. Caroline Maple
kept in touch with her for a long time, and passed news
along to my mother, but it did not seem to move any of us.
The Fay we remembered, with varying degrees and for different reasons, was her father, Charles, always thought of as
Charlie.

All I can say now is that he was thin, not as tall as Father, and ineffably distinguished. He wore shabby hunting clothes the way most men dream of doing. He was from Boston, and I loved to hear him talk, although I don't think he ever addressed more than a remote greeting to me. Often he came in for a nip of sherry or beer or a rarer whiskey, before he went on up the street to change into his dinner clothes for the evening ritual of the thin fare he could provide, and I would listen with delight from a nearby room as his elegant high voice hung in the air. My parents were under his spell too, and when he was with them they spoke with more wit, more attention to their own fineness.

He and Rex often went hunting, during several years, and unloaded dead doves or quail from the back of the Ford, late at night. Rex always carried his own weapons, but said that Charlie did the shooting and he was bird dog. Then they stopped going away together, and it was most probably coincidence that about then the Fays left Whittier and never came back, but later I learned that Rex had refused ever to hunt again after a weekend with Charlie in Antelope Valley, where countless sportsmen stoned and clubbed the trusting little fawn-like beasts to death, and then sometimes stripped them of their skins, and mostly left them dead or dying, and went on clubbing and laughing and swigging from their flasks. Before that we had often eaten antelope when Charlie Fay brought us a piece, but from then on we never did, and as far as I can remember, this unwritten taboo covered all game like venison, bear, the occasional wild kid that still turned up in California hills. We did eat birds, but only when people gave them to us, and although my father never shot again, later he liked to go away on fishing trips, mostly for trout, so that he could be with men he enjoyed. (I know he and Charlie parted as friends.)

The only other thing I remember about the Fays, except that he was probably the first man I ever realized was attractive, is that between their small parlor and the dining room hung a curtain made of long strings of eucalyptus buds. I thought this was truly elegant. I think there were colored glass beads now and then on the strings of the scented little nobs, and I would have loved to wrap myself naked in the clicking tinkling spray that hung down with such mystery between the two small crowded ugly rooms.

We never had any such modish fripperies at home, if one overlooks an elaborate edition of *Sesame and Lilies* by Ruskin, and there were a couple of other local status symbols I pined for, but not too strongly, in those days. One was a brass vase, at least two feet tall, in which stalks of pampas grass would stand. This should be placed in a corner of the living room or perhaps in the entrance hall. If possible, the frothy weird seed pods or whatever they are should be tinted pale lavender and pink and yellow. I have no idea where I got this vision, for we went into almost no homes in Whittier. I can remember only Mrs. Fay's, Miss Brotherton's when I was learning anatomy through inadvertent mathematics, the Smiths', and of course the Thayer Ranch.

There was an old lady who lived out near Jim Town and had an avenue of pampas grass which she sent to a great convention somewhere in America, and Rex interviewed her once, and there was a story about her in the *Saturday Evening Post*. The highway to Los Angeles was lined in those idyllic days with silvery olive trees on her big ranch, and when we drove past the avenue of thick tall grasses that curved away from it we slowed down to look at them, plumy and beautiful and even famous. But a brass vase filled with them? Where did I find this dream?

(And of course it seemed a shame to me, for several years, that we did not have hanging baskets of smilax ferns on our small front porch. Other people did. Nice people did, especially nice old ladies, which probably I thought my mother to be and took for granted that Grandmother was, at least socially. Mother was adamant. She hated, for one thing, to have to remember to water anything. For another, as she confessed to me many years later, she had always considered smilax middle-class and vulgar, especially in hanging baskets, because she had been told that the only way to keep them flourishing was to give them diluted human urine. This haunted her, perhaps with some titillation, for I remember her pointing out especially beautiful fountains of smilax on other people's porches and then laughing scornfully.)

South of the Fay house, one or two doors, lived a tiny ancient Kentucky colonel and first two devoted daughters and then one. Once there was an automobile parade past our house, on Memorial Day, and he rode in an open Pierce-Arrow in his Civil War uniform, not seeing anything, but fixed in a regal salute. Sometimes he sat on his front porch in a wheelchair, like Old Lady Ransome, but we knew enough not to bother him either. I think Mother liked the daughters, but they were still very unhappy about the Civil War and what it had done to them, and Mother was very busy.

Next to the Colonel, in a modest cottage compared to his faded yellow barn of a house, lived two little girls for a time, and they were friends of ours. Their mother had migraine headaches, which one of them later developed, and their father worked on the *News,* I think as a reporter. Helen and Alice the girls were, and Helen was almost too old for Anne and me, and already prone to biliousness and withdrawal. Although they moved away, they continued in the same school as we did, and that was fine, because Alice was a girl one wanted to see again.

Between them and us was a big ugly house where for a few years lived the Cutlers. There were several children. The oldest girl, Ethel, occasionally stayed in our living room at night when Mother and Father went out, which was increasingly rare as our family grew bigger and Rex grew busier and Edith grew heavier and more asocial. There was a sister about my age whose name I have conveniently forgotten. She was the first person I saw in Whittier.

All our furniture was being moved from a dray into the house. I stood far to the north of the small front lawn, against a spindly hedge which later fattened. On the other side, in the middle of her own scrap of Bermuda grass, stood a little girl sucking her thumb with one hand and fondling her private parts with the other. We looked at each other several times, for I was interested in what she was doing, but we never spoke, and the process of moving into the house was basically a better show. That night when I was lying in my bed in the new room, a wonderful big screened porch like a bird's nest high at the back of the house, my mother came to kiss me and welcome me there, and she asked me if I had noticed what the little neighbor was doing. I think I had almost forgotten, but I recalled it, and she said that she did not want me ever to bother myself that way, because it would make me nervous. I wondered what that might mean, but did not question it for many years.

The Cutlers took a Sunday paper, and so had funnies, which Grandmother did not allow in our house, and Anne and I became tricky at an early age in evading the Blue Laws. Ethel would bring them over in the afternoon, and we would meet at the far end of the long pergola of Cecil Brun-

ner roses which led to our garage, Anne and I and a few of
Ethel's siblings there, all of us loaded with heavy Bible picture books. We would lie down close together on our stom-
achs on the grass between the two car tracks of cement, with
our five or six heads pointed away from Grandmother's
room, and Ethel would read every delicious caption of every
page of the funnies as we kept our Sunday books open in
front of us. We knew, as if in a secret language, the Katzen-
jammer Kids, Mutt and Jeff, and another saga about a very
tall thin willowy character in a prison uniform whose name I
now forget. There was also Krazy Kat, which I did not really
enjoy for years, except for all those bricks that could close
any gap in his conversation.

It seems strange that the Katzenjammers did not suffer
from the War, when German Measles were called Liberty, as
also were Hamburger Steaks, and when somebody threw half
a brick through our side window near the piano.

This was because Mother was playing, and she and Rex
and Uncle Evans were singing, some German student songs
in variously bad accents, no doubt bolstered by either beer or
white wine and a common tenderness for one another. I
cannot remember that a curtain was ever pulled in our house
anywhere, so there in broad electric light were the editor of
the town daily, his wife who had once lived in Germany itself, and her uppity professor-brother from the East, laughing and singing in the enemy's own tongue! Somebody
lobbed the brick rather timidly into the subversive group: it
went through the glass, all right, but most of the shattered
stuff stayed in place, so that the next morning when Anne
and I came downstairs after our innocent slumbers, everything was fairly tidy, and by that night a new pane had been
installed. I feel certain that Edith cried, for she wept easily
and well, although hardly as often as she wished. The Ger-

man music was put away. Uncle Evans went back to his law classes and Rex to his desk, each mum for his own reasons.

For a while after we went to Whittier there was one bakery going, run by a German, and usually at Christmas our turkey would be stuffed and taken down to be roasted in his undying oven. I think this happened a few times with large pots of beans, too, which stayed there overnight. The baker left town in 1916, to fight at home, and his brother-in-law took over.

The day before his Grand Opening, he sent home with Rex a great platter of gleaming sweet cakes, called Butter Flies because they made the butter fly, his new ad would say in the paper. We had a special treat that afternoon, and sat around in the dining room and drank pitchers of milk and ate the delicious surprise.

Grandmother tasted one, pronounced it good, and then dismissed it scornfully as a bribe. Edith, who was a helpless gourmande as well as a mild cynic, could not resist eating several cakes, while she murmured coolly to her husband that they could not possibly keep to this standard and would soon be like all other bought stuff, not fit to have in the house. Anne and I devoted ourselves to keeping far enough within the bounds of courtesy not to be noticed, while we got away with more delicacies than we had ever eaten before. It was a fine occasion, on which I think my father drank a beer and sat watching us from behind a cloud of slowly exhaled Bull Durham smoke.

Not long after that, though, the second German baker left town, and this time it was because we had entered the War and it was being said that he had put ground glass in some of his excellent bread. It was a sad thing, and my mother held her hand over her brown eyes, and then withdrew to her darkened room.

There was one other commercial war casualty in our town: our butcher, who had lived there for many years but with a German name, disappeared after several weeks of harassment and gradual bankruptcy, because a little boy, locally famous for his disobedient and ornery ways, had stuck his finger in the sausage slicer. Rumor said that the butcher went right on making and selling sausages from that machine with the flesh of an AMERICAN CHILD!

There were, most of the time, two Jews who ran the town's variety store. They seemed to change, perhaps all in one family but spending a winter in turn, for their health, from some place like Chicago. They were always small, quiet, and kind, and I loved to go into the store for something like shoelaces or a paper of pins. I think that once a little daughter came to Penn Street School for a few months, but I do not remember seeing her in the store. Jews were simply not *there*, in Whittier. They did not really exist, except within themselves I hope. Their temple must have been long miles away. Nobody spoke to them. I cannot imagine what they did for proper food if they were Orthodox. I prefer not to think of their isolation.

Catholics were a step above Jews, socially, and one or two below the Episcopalians. This was largely because we were all white, while the Catholics had a few Mexican communicants. Rex had one very good friend, a Catholic who ran a garage in Whittier, who finally was frozen out of town (as my father was supposed to have been by 1913 or so). He moved to Santa Ana or Anaheim, or some place like that. He was never recognized as a friend by my mother, who took a consistently dim view of her husband's offbeat intimates.

After the Catholic left town, Rex bowed to pressure and became a Mason, which may or may not be important to this picture. By then he had learned what a small religious community can do to a human being, all in the name of the Lord, and it is probable that in Masonry as in Rotary and the Salvation Army he believed there was enough fairness left to counteract the bigotry all these institutions have been accused of. It is one of the many things we never discussed, later. I do not know if we would have been able to. We were a hot-tongued and articulate family, and by the time Time itself had cooled us, it was too late: we were dead, or physically deaf, or spiritually numb and wary.

There was a small Catholic community in and around Whittier, mostly Mexican and illiterate, and some of my friends in school, therefore, were Catholics, but we never bothered about rituals like going to Sunday school together, or comparing Friday menus. We learned to read and write, at school, and we played wildly and thoroughly, and then parted every twilight, content as calves going to their own barns from a common meadow.

My mother was not used to having people of different-colored skins near her, and was shy about it, but Rex had it heavily on his mind that the living conditions in Jim Town, out around Pio Pico's rotting house on the banks of the Rio Hondo, were not right for man nor beast. He found that the Catholic priest in Whittier was the townsman most in touch with the people there, and they began to work together. I am sorry that I cannot know what they got done, in that Mexican ghetto of so long ago. Certainly it was not the kind of action that would possibly result today from the friendship and concern of two good men, but at least it sufficed for a pair of renegades, and they continued a long life of golf, mild tippling, and zeal, both of them social mavericks but shrugged off, if not actively condoned, by the good Quakers.

Much later, and perhaps as a result of this suspicious activity of the priest and the editor, the Friends installed a small mission in Jim Town, and Rex asked its earnest heavy-breathing pastor to give all of us Spanish lessons. It was doomed to quick failure. Mother gave up at once, and retired to her genteel romance with everything John Galsworthy ever wrote but especially *The Forsyte Saga*. Anne and I were Wild Indians at that period, and could not long tolerate the endless afternoons with Señor Cobos and his fat little daughter Amparo, as we sat politely and drank lemonade and tried to understand the difference between Thee and You (if we had only been Quakers!). Finally Rex went alone to Jim Town and sweated over Spanish verbs, which were suddenly fun for him when he began escaping to Guadalajara, once a year or so. I have often felt sorry about being so stupid with Señor Cobos.

Later I studied Spanish hard and happily in school, and when I was much older I went to tedious night classes in Adult Education to recall some of it, and I can still read and hear it with pleasure. Of course I have never been hurt, except perhaps indirectly, because of another language I love besides my own. Nobody ever threw a piece of brick through a window because I was singing "La Cucaracha" or "Plaisirs d'Amour." But my mother never sang a German song again, after that night in about 1917—nor spoke a word of the language she had learned in several years in Germany, except when one of us would sneeze and wait happily for her *Gesundheit!*   —*Sag Harbor, 1973*

PALACES,
ETCETERA

Somewhere there must surely be a folk saying, not in *Poor Richard's Almanack* perhaps, but of equal logic and simplicity, about how every life has at least one fairy palace in its span. Usually these miracles happen when a person is young, but still wide-eyed enough to catch the magic that older people have forgotten or pushed away. For countless children, Disneyland has it, like Tivoli in Copenhagen. For both tourists and natives, the Changing of the Guard at Buckingham Palace does well ... prancing horses, flashing sabers, plumes and capes and trumpets in the fog ... the Palace is in safe hands, a solid dream.

Sometimes people can know two palaces before Lady Luck calls it quits, but of course they are never of equal enchantment. This happened to me, and all of it before I was about ten. It was an early proof of my good fortune.

The lesser of the two palaces was the Pig 'n' Whistle, a stylish ice-cream parlor in Los Angeles. Mother would take

Anne and me there for a treat, after we had bought long
black winter stockings or Easter hair ribbons at Robinson's,
and looked at yardage in Coulter's long aisles lined with ancient clerks who murmured to Mother about things like
prostate pangs and broken arches. The Pig 'n' Whistle was
on Broadway near the Orpheum Theatre, I think, and conve-
nient to the Pacific Electric Depot, where we would catch
the Red Car back to Whittier after refreshment and revival.
Anne and I understood that we must order only plain ice
creams, not expensive sundaes, since my little sister had in-
herited her grandmother's Nervous Stomach, and concoc-
tions at the Pig 'n' Whistle were notoriously exotic.

This scarlet den of sin and iniquity, as one of my later
friends who had been a Rough Rider with Teddy Roosevelt
used to call any place with wall-to-wall carpeting and soft
lights, had wide shiny windows out onto the street with the
insigne of a capering little pig playing a golden whistle as he
danced and smiled. He was lovable.

Inside, his palace was a wonderland of quiet elegance. The
paneled walls were a soft grey, after one passed the long
marble counters where people drank through straws from
tall silver goblets, and there was lots of gold on the carved
edgings and the magical little lights that glowed down onto
at least a hundred pictures that had been bought in a cultural frenzy after the Exposition held in 1915 in San Francisco. They were misty and vague, mostly of young women
gazing at butterflies or looking down at their Secret Diaries
or perhaps a love letter. They were discreet girls, almost piled
with filmy clothes, but there was a fine sunniness about
them.

Anne and I were permitted to walk silently over the thick
carpeting to peer up at these artifacts, except where people
might be sitting in the booths that lined three walls below

them. We whispered in the dim beauty, and she held my hand trustingly, being two years younger and very aware of the social amenities, as we moved languorously back to Mother's booth and our melting scoops of ice cream in their long silver boats.

Once a spendthrift kinsman took us on an Easter Sunday afternoon to the Pig 'n' Whistle, along with several of his own children. He must have been a nice man, because he plainly loved to look around the bulging boothful of omnivorous youngsters and say grandly, "Now, you order anything you want!"

We did, of course, almost stunned by such unaccustomed largesse. I can't remember what the four or five cousins wanted, but Anne and I asked for the Easter Special. It cost forty-five cents, right at the head of the menu, and on top of several kinds of ice cream and sauces and chopped nuts, there was a little yellow cotton chicken. We pulled these decorations out, licked their wire stems carefully, and stowed them in our coat pockets. Nobody paid any attention to the cultural assurance of all the pink-green-watery pictures on the glowing walls, but the air, even on that Easter debauch, stayed soft and supremely elegant. The Pig 'n' Whistle was a fairy palace, all right.

It could not compare, of course, with the Riverside Mission Inn. That magical place will always be for me a dream, awesome but built of pure delight.

When Father bought the Whittier *News* and we settled into our house on North Painter, in early 1912, he was something of a maverick, and a lot of other things the Quaker community was not. He wanted to know all about everything, and went far afield to learn it, and one of his goals was the Mission Inn. This was because of Frank Miller, who had founded the place. It was because Frank Miller had welcomed Booker T. Washington to his hostel when he could find no other lodgings open to him. It was because Frank Miller would house and feed broken-down circus performers and notorious ex-convicts and labor leaders and Indian chiefs as proudly as he would famous politicians and writers.

In other words, Father had a schoolboy crush on Old Mr. Miller, as he was called in family privacy, and we headed many times, on Sundays, toward the long stretches of hills and vineyards between Whittier and Riverside. The rows of eucalyptus trees near Cucamonga cooled us as the dusty air grew drier, toward the desert.

Once at the Inn, its magic spread over and into my little sister and me. We went up to Mrs. Miller's apartment, through halls unlike any others in our lives. We made our manners. Soon, we knew, Mrs. Miller would say, "Perhaps you two young ladies can have an hour together, if your mother agrees." This was all part of the ritual, and we could hardly wait for Mother's set speech: "Oh, how very nice! Stay together, children, and don't make any noise. Don't touch anything. Come back when you hear the bells ring twelve." And off we'd go, to step softly once again into the true, the real, the *only* palace.

We could go anywhere except the kitchens. We could climb any stairs, both narrow and twisting or wide and hung with dim old Mexican and Spanish portraits a million light-years from the ones in the Pig 'n' Whistle. We did not touch anything. We did not open any doors, especially ones with numbers on them. But the palace was *ours*.

Itself, it was a constant marvel, no matter how well we came to know its amazing structure, all quirky and unexpected. On the third and top floor, for instance, there would be a little courtyard, with a tinkling wall fountain and a beautiful stone cherub bathing in it and a thousand sweet-smelling plants. (Several decades later this hidden patio was made into a kind of memorial to dead pilots who had trained at March Field, I think. I went there often, no longer holding Anne's hand in mine.)

Or we would peek through a half-opened door and look up, or perhaps down, a narrow winding staircase made of roughly whitewashed adobe, perhaps with some crude paintings of the Sun and the Moon on the walls. We would take it, up or down, unafraid of the steps with their wide and narrow ends. (Is this why I have always loved circular staircases and longed to live with one?) Or we would go, almost dizzy with bliss and astonishment, down long cool corridors with huge dark wooden chests and armoires and pictures along the sides, and then armor standing as if real men breathed within, and at the end a grave golden Buddha with soft lights shining . . .

Once we went down a steep straight staircase and through a half-opened curtain, because we heard the sound of an organ playing and followed it to its right place. We were on the stage of a theatre, where "An Hour of Sabbath Meditation" was going on. The organ whuddered louder, and perhaps fifty people sat in front of us, some with heads in their hands, some upright with their eyes closed, or at least not seeing us on the stage.

No doubt the organist knew we were there, and no doubt he sent us some kind of message as his hands and feet made light sounds, and we squatted without fear on the floor, and listened until we heard one of the many bells in the Mission Inn ring twelve times. The soft music stopped, people rustled quietly to their feet, and we all went our chosen ways. Anne and I tiptoed up the stage stairs again, and did not report the concert until we were heading back to Whittier, after a delicious luncheon in Mrs. Miller's apartment. It always ended with orange sherbet from Mr. Miller's trees. . . .

He was, from the faint way I now remember him, tall and thin, with bushy white eyebrows and moustache, and keen bright eyes. He and Father would talk together, off in a corner. It was plain to us assorted females that the younger man was in love with every word he spoke. His wife, a short remote woman as I can now think of her, seemed to enjoy talking with Mother. Anne and I never said anything but "Yes, please" and "Thank you." We were in a kind of trance, from our secret wanderings through the fairy palace. We snoozed on the back seat of the topless Model T, all the way home.

The deep carpeting in the fabulous ice-cream parlor was like clouds to us, but there were glittering or softly glowing tiles everywhere in the Mission Inn, even on the steep steps of the circular staircases. The wide corridors had rugs laid over their tiles, all from Spain, Morocco, Mexico. They felt cool. We walked softly on them, as if they might chip or crack. (And that may be why I have chosen for much of my life to stay in houses with tiled floors. And of course many of the walls of the inn were of plastered adobe, whitewashed, so that even now I can look at paintings most easily when they hang against some such surface.)

When I grew up, Mrs. Miller was still alive, but although I went often to the Mission Inn, I did not present myself to her. I am not sure why there was this lapse in what seems common courtesy. She was very old. I felt shy and unwilling to intrude as an adult into the apartment I had quietly savored as a little girl. I had never gone back with Anne and my parents after old Mr. Miller died, although in several

later phases of my life I felt almost like an habituée in the
dim spy-ridden bar, the moonlit balconies looking down
from their bedrooms into unsuspected patios, all with their
fountains splashing.

It would be easy to verify a few things like dates: when
Old Man Miller started the Mission Inn; who were some of
his legendary guests. But this report is a private matter, and I
know what I know about magical places, both good and
evil. And what I know about this good one is more real than
any statistics can ever tell me.　　　　*—Glen Ellen, 1980*

YOUNG
HUNGER

It is very hard for people who have passed the age of, say, fifty to remember with any charity the hunger of their own puberty and adolescence when they are dealing with the young human animals who may be frolicking about them. Too often I have seen good people helpless with exasperation and real anger upon finding in the morning that cupboards and iceboxes have been stripped of their supplies by two or three youths—or even *one*—who apparently could have eaten four times their planned share at the dinner table the night before.

Such avidity is revolting, once past. But I can recall its intensity still; I am not yet too far from it to understand its ferocious demands when I see a fifteen-year-old boy wince and whiten at the prospect of waiting politely a few more hours for food, when his guts are howling for meat-bread-candy-fruit-cheese-milkmilkmilk—ANYTHING IN THE WORLD TO EAT.

I can still remember my almost insane desperation when I was about eighteen and was staying overnight with my comparatively aged godparents. I had come home alone from France in a bad continuous storm and was literally concave with solitude and hunger. The one night on the train seemed even rougher than those on board ship, and by the time I reached my godparents' home I was almost light-headed.

I got there just in time for lunch. It is clear as ice in my mind: a little cup of very weak chicken broth, one salted cracker, one-half piece of thinly sliced toast, and then, ah then, a whole waffle, crisp and brown and with a piece of beautiful butter melting in its middle—which the maid deftly cut into four sections! One section she put on my godmother's plate. The next *two,* after a nod of approval from her mistress, she put on mine. My godfather ate the fourth.

There was a tiny pot of honey, and I dutifully put a dab of it on my piggish portion, and we all nibbled away and drank one cup apiece of tea with lemon. Both my godparents left part of their waffles.

It was simply that they were old and sedentary and quite out of the habit of eating amply with younger people: a good thing for them, but pure hell for me. I did not have the sense to explain to them how starved I was—which I would not hesitate to do now. Instead I prowled around my bedroom while the house slumbered through its afternoon siesta, wondering if I dared sneak to the strange kitchen for something, anything, to eat, and knowing I would rather die than meet the silent, stern maid or my nice, gentle little hostess.

Later we walked slowly down to the village, and I was thinking sensuously of double malted ice-cream sodas at the corner drugstore, but there was no possibility of such heaven. When we got back to the quiet house, the maid brought my godfather a tall glass of exquisitely rich milk, with a handful of dried fruit on the saucer under it, because he had been ill; but as we sat and watched him unwillingly down it, his wife said softly that it was such a short time until dinner that she was sure I did not want to spoil my appetite, and I agreed with her because I was young and shy.

When I dressed, I noticed that the front of my pelvic basin jutted out like two bricks under my skirt: I looked like a scarecrow.

Dinner was very long, but all I can remember is that it had, as *pièce de résistance,* half of the tiny chicken previously boiled for broth at luncheon, which my godmother carved carefully so that we should each have a bit of the breast and I, as guest, should have the leg, after a snippet had been sliced from it for her husband, who liked dark meat too.

There were hot biscuits, yes, the smallest I have ever seen, two apiece under a napkin on a silver dish. Because of them we had no dessert: it would be too rich, my godmother said.

We drank little cups of decaffeinized coffee on the screened porch in the hot Midwestern night, and when I went up to my room I saw that the maid had left a large glass of rich malted milk beside my poor godfather's bed.

My train would leave before five in the morning, and I slept little and unhappily, dreaming of the breakfast I would order on it. Of course when I finally saw it all before me, twinkling on the Pullman silver dishes, I could eat very little, from too much hunger and a sense of outrage.

I felt that my hosts had been indescribably rude to me, and selfish and conceited and stupid. Now I know that they were none of these things. They had simply forgotten about

any but their own dwindling and cautious needs for nourishment. They had forgotten about being hungry, being young,
being . . .

In an essay by Max Beerbohm about hosts and guests, the
tyrants and the tyrannized, there is a story of what happened
to him once when he was a schoolboy and someone sent him
a hamper that held, not the usual collection of marmalade,
sardines, and potted tongue, but twelve whole sausage-rolls.
"Of sausage-rolls I was particularly fond," he says. He
could have dominated all his friends with them, of course,
but "I carried the box up to my cubicle, and, having eaten
two of the sausage-rolls, said nothing that day about the
other ten, nor anything about them when, three days later, I
had eaten them all—all, up there, alone."
What strange secret memories such a tale evokes! Is there
a grown-up person anywhere who cannot remember some
such shameful, almost insane act of greediness of his childhood? In recollection his scalp will prickle, and his palms
will sweat, at the thought of the murderous risk he may have
run from his outraged companions.
When I was about sixteen, and in boarding-school, we
were allowed one bar of chocolate a day, which we were
supposed to eat sometime between the sale of them at
the little school bookstore at four-thirty and the seven
o'clock dinner gong. I felt an almost unbearable hunger
for them—not for one, but for three or four or five at a
time, so that I should have *enough,* for once, in my yawning
stomach.
I hid my own purchases for several days, no mean trick in
a school where every drawer and cupboard was inspected,
openly and snoopingly too, at least twice a week. I cannot
remember now how I managed it, with such lack of privacy

and my own almost insurmountable hunger every afternoon, but by Saturday I had probably ten chocolate bars—my own and a few I had bribed my friends who were trying to lose weight to buy for me.

I did not sign up for any of the usual weekend debauchery such as a walk to the village drugstore for a well-chaperoned double butterscotch and pecan sundae. Instead I lay languidly on my bed, trying to look as if I had a headache and pretending to read a very fancy book called, I think, *Martin Pippin in the Apple Orchard,* until the halls quieted.

Then I arranged all my own and my roommate's pillows in a voluptuous pile, placed so that I could see whether a silent housemotherly foot stood outside the swaying monk's-cloth curtain that served as a door (to cut down our libidinous chitchat, the school board believed), and I put my hoard of Hersheys discreetly under a fold of the bedspread.

I unwrapped their rich brown covers and their tinfoil as silently as any prisoner chipping his way through a granite wall, and lay there breaking off the rather warm, rubbery, delicious pieces and feeling them melt down my gullet, and reading the lush symbolism of the book; and all the time I was hot and almost panting with the fear that people would suddenly walk in and see me there. And the strange thing is that nothing would have happened if they had!

It is true that I had more than my allotted share of candy, but that was not a crime. And my friends, full of their Saturday delights, would not have wanted ordinary chocolate. And anyway I had much more than I could eat, and was basically what Beerbohm calls, somewhat scornfully, "a host" and not "a guest": I loved to entertain people and dominate them with my generosity.

Then why was I breathless and nervous all during that solitary and not particularly enjoyable orgy? I suppose there is a Freudian explanation for it, or some other kind. Certainly the experience does not make me sound very attractive to myself. Even the certainty of being in good company is no real solace. —*Whittier, 1946*

I WAS
REALLY VERY
HUNGRY

I

Once I met a young servant in northern Burgundy who was almost frighteningly fanatical about food, like a medieval woman possessed by a devil. Her obsession engulfed even my appreciation of the dishes she served, until I grew uncomfortable.

It was the off season at the old mill which a Parisian chef had bought and turned into one of France's most famous restaurants, and my mad waitress was the only servant. In spite of that she was neatly uniformed, and showed no surprise at my unannounced arrival and my hot dusty walking clothes.

She smiled discreetly at me, said, "Oh, but certainly!" when I asked if I could lunch there, and led me without more words to a dark bedroom bulging with First Empire furniture, and a new white bathroom.

When I went into the dining room it was empty of humans—a cheerful ugly room still showing traces of the petit bourgeois parlor it had been. There were aspidistras on the mantel; several small white tables were laid with those imitation "peasant-ware" plates that one sees in Paris china stores, and very good crystal glasses; a cat folded under some ferns by the window ledge hardly looked at me; and the air was softly hurried with the sound of high waters from the stream outside.

I waited for the maid to come back. I knew I should eat well and slowly, and suddenly the idea of dry sherry, unknown in all the village bistros of the last few days, stung my throat smoothly. I tried not to think of it; it would be impossible to realize. Dubonnet would do. But not as well. I longed for sherry.

The little maid came into the silent room. I looked at her stocky young body, and her butter-colored hair, and noticed her odd pale voluptuous mouth before I said, "Mademoiselle, I shall drink an apéritif. Have you by any chance—"

"Let me suggest," she interrupted firmly, "our special dry sherry. It is chosen in Spain for Monsieur Paul."

And before I could agree she was gone, discreet and smooth.

She's a funny one, I thought, and waited in a pleasant warm tiredness for the wine.

It was good. I smiled approval at her, and she lowered her eyes, and then looked searchingly at me again. I realized suddenly that in this land of trained nonchalant waiters I was to be served by a small waitress who took her duties seriously. I felt much amused, and matched her solemn searching gaze.

"Today, Madame, you may eat shoulder of lamb in the

English style, with baked potatoes, green beans, and a sweet."

My heart sank. I felt dismal, and hot and weary, and still grateful for the sherry.

But she was almost grinning at me, her lips curved triumphantly, and her eyes less palely blue.

"Oh, in *that* case," she remarked as if I had spoken, "in *that* case a trout, of course—a *truite au bleu* as only Monsieur Paul can prepare it!"

She glanced hurriedly at my face, and hastened on. "With the trout, one or two young potatoes—oh, very delicately boiled," she added before I could protest, "very light."

I felt better. I agreed. "Perhaps a leaf or two of salad after the fish," I suggested. She almost snapped at me. "Of course, of course! And naturally our hors d'oeuvres to commence." She started away.

"No!" I called, feeling that I must assert myself now or be forever lost. "No!"

She turned back, and spoke to me very gently. "But Madame has never tasted our hors d'oeuvres. I am sure that Madame will be pleased. They are our specialty, made by Monsieur Paul himself. I am sure," and she looked reproachfully at me, her mouth tender and sad, "I am sure that Madame would be very much pleased."

I smiled weakly at her, and she left. A little cloud of hurt gentleness seemed to hang in the air where she had last stood.

I comforted myself with the sherry, feeling increasing irritation with my own feeble self. Hell! I loathed hors d'oeuvres! I conjured disgusting visions of square glass plates of oily fish, of soggy vegetables glued together with cheap mayonnaise, of rank radishes and tasteless butter. No, Mon-

sieur Paul or not, sad young pale-faced waitress or not, I
hated hors d'oeuvres.

I glanced victoriously across the room at the cat, whose
eyes seemed closed.

I I

Several minutes passed. I was really very hungry.

The door banged open, and my girl came in again, less
discreet this time. She hurried toward me.

"Madame, the wine! Before Monsieur Paul can go on—"
Her eyes watched my face, which I perversely kept rather
glum.

"I think," I said ponderously, daring her to interrupt me,
"I think that today, since I am in Burgundy and about to eat
a trout," and here I hoped she noticed that I did not mention hors d'oeuvres, "I think I shall drink a bottle of Chablis
1929."

For a second her whole face blazed with joy, and then
subsided into a trained mask. I knew that I had chosen well,
had somehow satisfied her in a secret and incomprehensible
way. She nodded politely and scuttled off, only for another
second glancing impatiently at me as I called after her,
"Well cooled, please, but not iced."

I'm a fool, I thought, to order a whole bottle. I'm a fool,
here all alone and with more miles to walk before I reach
Avallon and my fresh clothes and a bed. Then I smiled at
myself and leaned back in my solid wide-seated chair, looking obliquely at the prints of Gibson girls, English tavern
scenes, and hideous countrysides that hung on the papered
walls. The room was warm; I could hear my companion cat
purring under the ferns.

The girl rushed in, with flat baking dishes piled up her arms like the plates of a Japanese juggler. She slid them off neatly in two rows onto the table, where they lay steaming up at me, darkly and infinitely appetizing.

"Mon Dieu! All for me?" I peered at her. She nodded, her discretion quite gone now and a look of ecstatic worry on her pale face and eyes and lips.

There were at least eight dishes. I felt almost embarrassed, and sat for a minute looking weakly at the fork and spoon in my hand.

"Perhaps Madame would care to start with the pickled herring? It is not like any other. Monsieur Paul prepares it himself, in his own vinegar and wines. It is very good."

I dug out two or three brown filets from the dish, and tasted. They were truly unlike any others, truly the best I had ever eaten, mild, pungent, meaty as fresh nuts.

I realized the maid had stopped breathing, and looked up at her. She was watching me, or rather a gastronomic X ray of the herring inside me, with a hypnotized glaze in her eyes.

"Madame is pleased?" she whispered softly.

I said I was. She sighed, and pushed a sizzling plate of broiled endive toward me, and disappeared.

I had put a few dull green lentils on my plate, lentils scattered with minced fresh herbs and probably marinated in tarragon vinegar and walnut oil, when she came into the dining room again with the bottle of Chablis in a wine basket.

"Madame should be eating the little baked onions while they are hot," she remarked over her shoulder as she held the bottle in a napkin and uncorked it. I obeyed meekly, and while I watched her I ate several more than I had meant to. They were delicious, simmered first in strong meat broth, I think, and then drained and broiled with olive oil and new-ground pepper.

I was fascinated by her method of uncorking a vintage wine. Instead of the Burgundian procedure of infinite and often exaggerated precautions against touching or tipping or jarring the bottle, she handled it quite nonchalantly, and seemed to be careful only to keep her hands from the cool bottle itself, holding it sometimes by the basket and sometimes in a napkin. The cork was very tight, and I thought for a minute that she would break it. So did she: her face grew tight, and did not loosen until she had slowly worked out the cork and wiped the lip. Then she poured an inch of wine in a glass, turned her back to me like a priest taking Communion, and drank it down. Finally some was poured for me, and she stood with the bottle in her hand and her full lips drooping until I nodded a satisfied yes. Then she pushed another of the plates toward me, and almost rushed from the room.

I ate slowly, knowing that I should not be as hungry as I ought to be for the trout, but knowing too that I had never tasted such delicate savory morsels. Some were hot, some cold. The wine was light and cool. The room, warm and agreeably empty under the rushing sound of the stream, became smaller as I grew used to it.

My girl hurried in again, with another row of plates up one arm, and a large bucket dragging at the other. She slid the plates deftly onto the table, and drew a deep breath as she let the bucket down against the table leg.

"Your trout, Madame," she said excitedly. I looked down at the gleam of the fish curving through its limited water. "But first a good slice of Monsieur Paul's *pâté*. Oh yes, oh yes, you will be very sorry if you miss this. It is rich, but appetizing, and not at all too heavy. Just this one morsel!"

And willy-nilly I accepted the large gouge she dug from a terrine. I prayed for ten normal appetites and thought with amused nostalgia of my usual lunch of cold milk and fruit as I broke off a crust of bread and patted it smooth with the paste. Then I forgot everything but the exciting faint decadent flavor in my mouth.

I beamed up at the girl. She nodded, but from habit asked if I was satisfied. I beamed again, and asked, simply to please her, "Is there not a faint hint of *marc,* or perhaps cognac?"

"*Marc,* Madame!" And she awarded me the proud look of a teacher whose pupil has showed unexpected intelligence. "Monsieur Paul, after he has taken equal parts of goose breast and the finest pork, and broken a certain number of egg yolks into them, and ground them *very,* very fine, cooks all with seasoning for some three hours. *But,*" she pushed her face nearer, and looked with ferocious gloating at the *pâté* inside me, her eyes like X rays, "he never stops stirring it! Figure to yourself the work of it—stir, stir, never stopping!

"Then he grinds in a suspicion of nutmeg, and then adds, very thoroughly, a glass of *marc* for each hundred grams of *pâté.* And is Madame not pleased?"

Again I agreed, rather timidly, that Madame was much pleased, that Madame had never, indeed, tasted such an unctuous and exciting *pâté.* The girl wet her lips delicately, and then started as if she had been pin-stuck.

"But the trout! My God, the trout!" She grabbed the bucket, and her voice grew higher and more rushed.

"Here is the trout, Madame. You are to eat it *au bleu,* and you should never do so if you had not seen it alive. For if the trout were dead when it was plunged into the *court bouillon* it would not turn blue. So, naturally, it must be living."

I knew all this, more or less, but I was fascinated by her

absorption in the momentary problem. I felt quite ignorant, and asked her with sincerity, "What about the trout? Do you take out its guts before or after?"

"Oh, the trout!" She sounded scornful. "Any trout is glad, truly glad, to be prepared by Monsieur Paul. His little gills are pinched, with one flash of the knife he is empty, and then he curls in agony in the *bouillon* and all is over. And it is the curl you must judge, Madame. A false *truite au bleu* cannot curl."

She panted triumph at me, and hurried out with the bucket.

I I I

She *is* a funny one, I thought, and for not more than two or three minutes I drank wine and mused over her. Then she darted in, with the trout correctly blue and agonizingly curled on a platter, and on her crooked arm a plate of tiny boiled potatoes and a bowl.

When I had been served and had cut off her anxious breathings with an assurance that the fish was the best I had ever tasted, she peered again at me and at the sauce in the bowl. I obediently put some of it on the potatoes: no fool I, to ruin *truite au bleu* with a hot concoction! There was more silence.

"Ah!" she sighed at last. "I knew Madame would feel thus! Is it not the most beautiful sauce in the world with the flesh of a trout?"

I nodded incredulous agreement.

"Would you like to know how it is done?"

I remembered all the legends of chefs who guarded favorite recipes with their very lives, and murmured yes.

She wore the exalted look of a believer describing a miracle at Lourdes as she told me, in a rush, how Monsieur Paul threw chopped chives into hot sweet butter and then poured the butter off, how he added another nut of butter and a tablespoonful of thick cream for each person, stirred the mixture for a few minutes over a slow fire, and then rushed it to the table.

"So simple?" I asked softly, watching her lighted eyes and the tender lustful lines of her strange mouth.

"So simple, Madame! But," she shrugged, "you know, with a master—"

I was relieved to see her go: such avid interest in my eating wore on me. I felt released when the door closed behind her, free for a minute or so from her victimization. What would she have done, I wondered, if I had been ignorant or unconscious of any fine flavors?

She was right, though, about Monsieur Paul. Only a master could live in this isolated mill and preserve his gastronomic dignity through loneliness and the sure financial loss of unused butter and addled eggs. Of course there was the stream for his fish, and I knew his *pâtés* would grow even more edible with age; but how could he manage to have a thing like roasted lamb ready for any chance patron? Was the consuming interest of his one maid enough fuel for his flame?

I tasted the last sweet nugget of trout, the one nearest the blued tail, and poked somnolently at the minute white billiard balls that had been eyes. Fate could not harm me, I remembered winily, for I had indeed dined today, and dined well. Now for a leaf of crisp salad, and I'd be on my way.

The girl slid into the room. She asked me again, in a respectful but gossipy manner, how I had liked this and that

and the other things, and then talked on as she mixed dress-
ing for the endive.

"And now," she announced, after I had eaten one green
sprig and dutifully pronounced it excellent, "now Madame
is going to taste Monsieur Paul's special terrine, one that is
not even on the summer menu, when a hundred covers are
laid here daily and we have a headwaiter and a wine waiter,
and cabinet ministers telegraph for tables! Madame will be
pleased."

And heedless of my low moans of the walk still before me,
of my appreciation and my unhappily human and limited ca-
pacity, she cut a thick heady slice from the terrine of meat
and stood over me while I ate it, telling me with almost
hysterical pleasure of the wild ducks, the spices, the wines
that went into it. Even surfeit could not make me deny that
it was a rare dish. I ate it all, knowing my luck, and wishing
only that I had red wine to drink with it.

I was beginning, though, to feel almost frightened, realizing myself an accidental victim of these stranded gourmets,
Monsieur Paul and his handmaiden. I began to feel that they
were using me for a safety valve, much as a thwarted woman
relieves herself with tantrums or a fit of weeping. I was serving a purpose, and perhaps a noble one, but I resented it in a
way approaching panic.

I protested only to myself when one of Monsieur Paul's
special cheeses was cut for me, and ate it doggedly, like a
slave. When the girl said that Monsieur Paul himself was
preparing a special filter of coffee for me, I smiled servile acceptance: wine and the weight of food and my own character
could not force me to argue with maniacs. When, before the
coffee came, Monsieur Paul presented me, through his idola-
ter, with the most beautiful apple tart I had ever seen, I al-

lowed it to be cut and served to me. Not a wince or a murmur showed the waitress my distressed fearfulness. With a stuffed careful smile on my face, and a clear nightmare in my head of trussed wanderers prepared for his altar by this hermit-priest of gastronomy, I listened to the girl's passionate plea for fresh pastry dough.

"You cannot, you *can*not, Madame, serve old pastry!" She seemed ready to beat her breast as she leaned across the table. "Look at that delicate crust! You may feel that you have eaten too much." (I nodded idiotic agreement.) "But this pastry is like feathers—it is like snow. It is in fact good for you, a digestive! And why?" She glared sternly at me. "Because Monsieur Paul did not even open the flour bin until he saw you coming! He could not, he *could* not have baked you one of his special apple tarts with old dough!"

She laughed, tossing back her head and curling her mouth voluptuously.

I V

Somehow I managed to refuse a second slice, but I trembled under her surmise that I was ready for my special filter.

The wine and its fortitude had fled me, and I drank the hot coffee as a suffering man gulps ether, deeply and gratefully.

I remember, then, chatting with surprising glibness, and sending to Monsieur Paul flowery compliments, all of them sincere and well won, and I remember feeling only amusement when a vast glass of *marc* appeared before me and then gradually disappeared, like the light in the warm room full of water-sounds. I felt surprise to be alive still, and suddenly very grateful to the wild-lipped waitress, as if her presence had sustained me through duress. We discussed food and wine. I wondered bemusedly why I had been frightened.

The *marc* was gone. I went into the crowded bedroom for my jacket. She met me in the darkening hall when I came out, and I paid my bill, a large one. I started to thank her, but she took my hand, drew me into the dining room, and without words poured more spirits into my glass. I drank to Monsieur Paul while she watched me intently, her pale eyes bulging in the dimness and her lips pressed inward as if she too tasted the hot, aged *marc*.

The cat rose from his ferny bed, and walked contemptuously out of the room.

Suddenly the girl began to laugh, in a soft shy breathless way, and came close to me.

"Permit me!" she said, and I thought she was going to kiss me. But instead she pinned a tiny bunch of snowdrops and dark bruised cyclamens against my stiff jacket, very quickly and deftly, and then ran from the room with her head down.

I waited for a minute. No sounds came from anywhere in the old mill, but the endless rushing of the full stream seemed to strengthen, like the timed blare of an orchestra under a falling curtain.

She's a *funny* one, I thought. I touched the cool blossoms on my coat and went out, like a ghost from ruins, across the courtyard toward the dim road to Avallon.

—Vevey, 1937

THREE
SWISS INNS

I remember three restaurants in Switzerland with a special clearness: one on the lake near Lausanne, another behind it in the high hills toward Berne, and the last on the road to Lucerne, in German-speaking country.

When we went back, in June of 1939, to pack our furniture and bolt the shutters, we could not believe our friends were right to make us do it. All of Europe stretched and sang under a warm sun; the crops were good; people walked about and ate and drank and smiled dreamily, like drugged cancer sufferers. Everyone was kind to us, not consciously thinking that we might never meet again, but actually knowing that it was so.

We drove toward Lucerne one day. Children were selling the first early Alpine roses along the roads—tight ugly posies, the same color as the mottled purple that the little girls' cheeks had.

At Malters, one of the few villages of that part of the

country not almost overpoweringly quaint and pretty, we stopped at the Gasthaus zum Kreuz. We wondered if Frau Weber would remember us, and if her neurasthenic daughter Anneli would be yearning still to be a chambermaid in London, and if—most important—if there would still be trout swimming in the little tank of icy water that stood in the dining room.

Frau Weber, looking more than ever like a virile Queen Victoria, did indeed remember us, discreetly, at first, and then with floods of questions and handshakings and general delight. Anneli was there, fat, pale, still yearning, but this time for Croydon, where she hoped to exchange her Cockney accent for a more refined one. And the trout still darted behind glass in the bubbling water.

We stayed there for many hours, eating and drinking and remembering incredulously that once we had almost driven past the Kreuz without stopping.

That incident was several years ago, when my husband and I had been roaming about the country with my parents. The chauffeur was sleepy after a night spent in a hotel filled with unusually pretty kitchen maids, and he lost the way. We went along roads, mazily, that led where we did not want to go at all; and we all got very hungry and perhaps a little too polite.

Finally we said to stop at the first *Gasthaus,* no matter what it looked like. We could certainly count on beer and cheese, at the least.

Pierre stifled a yawn, and his neck got a little pinker; and in perhaps a minute we had come to an impressive stop in front of one of the least attractive buildings of German Switzerland, in the tight village of Malters.

The place had a sharp peaked roof and many little windows; but there were no flowers on the wooden ledges, and a smell of blood came from the sausage shop on the ground floor. Dark stairs led up from the street through a forbidding hallway.

We wanted to go on. It was late, though; and we were hungry and cramped and full of latent snarls. I told Pierre to see what the place looked like.

He yawned again, painfully, and went with false briskness up the dour, dark stairs. Soon he was back, beaming, no longer sleepy. We crawled out, not caring how many pretty girls he had found if there was something in their kitchen for us, too.

Soon life looked better. Frau Weber herself had led us solicitously to ancient but sparkling toilets, and we had washed in a porcelain bowl enameled with swans and lavender chrysanthemums, and were all met again in a little piney honey-colored room full of family photographs. There was a long table with chairs primly about it, and cupboards and a beautiful rococo couch. We felt happy, and toasted one another with small glasses of a strange, potent bitters.

"Whatever you have," we said to Frau Weber, and sat back complacently waiting for some sausage from her shop and maybe a salad. We watched the trout swimming in a tank by one of the windows, and thought them an odd, enormous decoration.

Anneli came in. She was pretty, in a discontented way; and we knew Pierre would have a pleasant lunch. We talked to her about England, which she apparently loved as some women love men or some men the bottle. She set the table, and then came back with a net and a platter. She swooped up a trout, held it by the tail, and before we could close our ears or even wince, had cracked its skull smartly on the sideboard.

My mother lay back farther on the couch and gulped wanly at her bitters; and Father muttered with a kind of sick

admiration, "That's the way! By George, that's the way!" as
Anneli whacked the brains loose in some ten trout.

She smiled and said, "You 'aven't long to wite naow," and
hurried from the room.

By then we were eating slices of various strange sausages,
surprisingly delicate, and drinking cold, thin white wine of
the country. Nothing else much mattered.

Frau Weber and her daughter came in carrying a long
shallow copper pan between them. They set it down carefully; and Anneli stood back puffing while the older woman
lifted the lid, her white hair bristling upward in a regal
pompadour, and her face flushed and dewy.

The trout lay staring up at us, their eyes hard and yet
somehow benevolent. Our heads drew nearer to the pan,
willy-nilly, pulled by one of the finest smells we had ever
met. We sniffed and murmured. Frau Weber beamed. Then
she scolded at the girl, who ran from the room for little
white potatoes and a great bowl of hot buttered peas from
the garden. The mother served the fish herself, and then disappeared proudly.

It was, of course, the most delicious dish that we had ever
eaten. We knew that we were hungry, and that even if it had
been bad it would have been good ... but we knew, too,
that nevertheless it was one of the subtlest, rarest things that
had ever come our way. It was incredibly delicate, as fresh as
clover.

We talked about it later, and Frau Weber told us willingly
about it, but in such a vague way that all I can remember
now is hot unsalted butter, herbs left in for a few seconds,
cream, a shallot flicked over, the fish laid in, the cover put
on. I can almost see it, smell it, taste it now; but I know that
I could never copy it, nor could anyone alive, probably.

Finally we were eating large, fragrant strawberries and

drinking quite a lot more wine. It amused Anneli that we wanted our coffee in the tall porcelain goblets we saw in the cupboard. But it was the trout that really mattered. They were more important than getting to Lucerne, or than the pride of Frau Weber, or than the girl Anneli, frustrated and yearning. They were, we felt, important like a *grisaille* window or the coming of spring.

And we went back many times to the Kreuz, and the trout were always that way ... important.

The second restaurant I remember now was near our old home, in Châtel St. Denis, where the army used to send its ski-learners to use the fine, easy slopes all around. It was called the Hotel des XIII Cantons.

We knew Mademoiselle Berthe there. Tall, she had a thin, spirited face; and her dark hair was rolled in odd corkscrews behind each ear, in the disappearing fashion of her village. She had hips that were wide and firm, hung low on her legs; and her feet, on which she always wore exotic beach sandals, were very long and flat. She flapped about on them, and was the best waitress that I have ever known, in Europe or America.

The upstairs room held perhaps fifty people on market days and times like Easter; yet Berthe was always alone and always unruffled. Sometimes in winter, when army officers were there, teasing and flirting and barking, she got more taciturn than usual. But no matter what kind of people she served, she was always skillful and the most impersonal woman I have ever watched.

She never made mistakes; and no matter how many people were tapping their empty glasses and calling, she would always see that plates were hot and platters properly bubbling above her innumerable alcohol lamps before she left one table for another. She sped about, flat-footed, heavy-hipped,

unruffled, waiting for the day when her mother would die
and she could renounce the dining room for the glories of
the kitchen.

In the meantime, Madame reigned on the other side of the
wide stairs which led to the square pine dining room with its
mirrors and white linen curtains and window ledges heavy
with hideous, meaty begonias.

Madame Mossu was famous for her trout, her frogs' legs,
and her shrimps. I have eaten them all many times. Some
sticklers for gastronomic etiquette have criticized what she
called *truites meunières* because the fish were always curled like
truites au bleu. Once I asked Berthe why that was. She
shrugged and said, "What of it? A trout dead not a minute
curls with agony in hot butter. One can flatten him: I admit
it. But Maman prefers to let him be as comfortable as possible." There was nothing more that one could say.

The season for shrimps is short, and Madame Mossu paid
well for all the boys and old men could find in their hundred
icy streams. But there were never enough; so diplomats from
Geneva and Bernese politicians and horny shepherds on
their annual gastronomic bender in Châtel would make ap-
pointments in advance for cold shrimps in their shells, or in
a *court bouillon*.

There was a general who always had to unbutton his
tunic, and at the bottom of the table a lieutenant with a
gleam in his eye that meant, by God, someday he, too,
would be a general. Once, on All Saints' Day, there were
three peasants in full black linen smocks, and two sat smiling quietly while the third stood up and sang a little mountain song. None of us listened, and yet we all heard; and
probably we all remember his serious, still face flushed with
feast day drinking, and the way he sat down after the song,
and wiped his lips and put a piece of trout between them

with complete unselfconsciousness. Then, besides all the diplomats and such, there were *pensionnaires;* a tall, beautiful girl
dressed like a Paris mannequin, who played cards every night
with the butcher and young Mossu, and then went away
without a word; the lame pharmacist, who had widowed
himself four times by his own vitality; a dried, mean, sad old
woman who might have been the librarian if there had been
a library.

One night a little woman with a black wig came in. She
went straight to the long table usually reserved for the military and seated herself. Then a strange party of domestics sat
down facing her. One was a woman who looked as though
she took dictation daily from ten until two. Her hair was
like mud, and she was probably a "companion." One was a
flirtatious man with a mouth too terribly sensitive; two
others were poor, beaten-down maids with mean eyes and
stringy skins; and last was a young, healthy, arrogant chauffeur. Berthe scuttled with her usual dexterity around this
motley table. First of all, as if she well knew what to do, she
brought one glass and a large dusty bottle of the finest cognac to the old woman, who poured it out hastily for herself, all her dirty diamonds a-tremble. Then Berthe brought
cheap wine for the others, who did not speak, but drank
thirstily without looking at their mistress.

An enormous platter of twisted trout Berthe carried in
next and put down before the old woman, who drained her
glass for the fifth or sixth time and started shoveling fish
onto the plates the others held out to her. While we all tried
not to watch, the poor souls slashed and poked at the fish
until each plate held its neat pile, with bones tidily put on a
side dish. The clatter stopped.

Old Wig lifted her glass again, and tossed the brandy
down. The servants stood up; and she looked at each plate

with its heap of the best trout in Switzerland, boneless and delicate. She nodded finally; and the companion, the weak-mouthed secretary, the two maids, the chauffeur picked up their plates obediently and went out the door and down the stone stairs.

Berthe's long face was expressionless, but her little ear curls vibrated gently.

"Curiosity grips my bowels . . . excuse me," my husband said. In a few minutes he was back, full of news: the five servants, solemnly, as though they were serving some obscene Mass, had filed out into the little square before the Soldiers' Monument, and had stopped by three immense and anti-quated limousines. In each car were three or four tiny feeble Mexican dogs, the shuddering hairless kind, yapping almost silently at the windows. The humans fed them, and then stood in the cold thin air for a minute, silent.

They came back to the dining room and ate well. The secretary flirted dispassionately with the companion and the less dreary of the maids, and the chauffeur stared arrogantly about. Old Wig ate little; but as the evening went on and the brandy warmed her, she smiled occasionally, and spoke to Berthe once about how cold she had been for the thirty years since she left Guatemala.

She makes me think of Fritz Kuhn's sister, in the last of the three Swiss restaurants I remember so well.

Monsieur Kuhn ran the Hotel de Ville et du Raisin at Cully, near Lausanne on the lake. He was quiet, with sad eyes and a long face. The only things in the world he cared about were fishing for perch and cooking his haul.

The inn itself was strange and secretive, like its keeper, with cold, high halls, dank air, and an enormous kitchen which never showed anything like a live fire or a sign of bustle. There was a gaunt dining room, always empty, and the café where we sat, a long, queer room with a big stove in the middle, local wine advertisements on the murky walls, and a paper rose in the vase that topped the elaborate coffee machine.

From that dead kitchen into that bleak, smoky room Monsieur Kuhn would send his wonderful filets. He ripped them from the live, stunned fish, as they were ordered. The filets were perhaps three inches long, always with a little crisp point of the tail left on.

Monsieur Kuhn would creep shyly into the dining room, after we had come to his café for a year or more, and bow and shake hands and smile painfully when we thanked him. His long, lined face was always sad and remote and we felt that we were wrong to distract him.

His sister and his wife were different, and grew to like us almost too much. At first we thought they were blood sisters: they both looked so virginal that we could not believe that one of them was married to Fritz Kuhn. He himself looked quite beyond such bothers as cohabitation. It took us some time to learn that the taller of the two women was his wife.

She was very thin, and something about her was out of a drawing, out of an El Greco. Her eyes were bigger than human eyes, and slipped upwards and sideways; and her mouth was pale and beautiful. She was shadowy—a bad liver probably—but mysterious-looking. She wore black always, and her long hands picked up sizzling platters as if they were distasteful leaves from a tree. She had a light voice; and there was something good and fine about her, so that I always warmed to her.

Her husband's sister was quite different. She was short; and although she had a thin face, she looked puffy, with a white, thick skin, the kind that would bend a hypodermic needle. She wore her mole-colored hair in an elaborate girlish mass of curls, and her hands were small and pretty. She, too, dressed in black; but her sweaters had gold threads in them, and her skirts were broadcloth.

Madame Kuhn adored her more plainly than is often seen, and saved all the easy work for her, and did all the ugly jobs herself.

One time we took Michel to the Raisin. He was the kind of short, virile, fox-like Frenchman who seems to have been born in a beret, the kind who is equally ready to shoot a wild boar, make love, or say something which seems witty until you think about it. He was unconscious of Mademoiselle Kuhn.

She, on the other hand, was completely upset by him. She sidled and cooed, and put down our plate of bread as such a thing had never been put down before, and smiled again.

We finished our celestial filets, and drank more wine. Madame Kuhn hovered in the cold darkness near the kitchen, agonizing with her great dark eyes for the poor tortured sister. We paid the bill, cruel and wrapped in our own lives.

As we got into the car, Mademoiselle ran out with a knot of the first wild narcissuses, and thrust them loosely into Michel's hand.

"Some are for you, Madame," she cried, but she looked only at him, and his neat aristocratic bones and the power in his flesh. Then she ran back into the cold glare of the doorway and stood close against the stone, saying, "Oh, you are adorable, adorable . . ." in her bad Swiss-French.

Michel suddenly broke into a sweat, and wiped the flowers across his forehead. *"Mon Dieu!"* he cried.

We drove away as fast as we could, leaving the poor soul there against the stone, with Madame watching her through the colored glass door, and the smell of the little filets all around.

But when we went back, that June of 1939, things were changed. Madame stood with a plate of bread in her long hands, and tears ran down her face. Mitzi was in a clinic. "Ah, she is not the same. My little dear will never be so sweet, so innocent again," the woman said. And her eyes, as dead and haunted as something from a Spanish portrait, stared at the wine posters on the murky walls. "Nothing is the same. Nothing will ever be the same."

She walked toward the cold, dank kitchen, truly grief-stricken; and we, sitting there in the café, felt lonely and afraid. The filets, though, were the same as always; and when Monsieur Kuhn came from the kitchen and smiled proudly at us, we forgot his foolish sister and why we were there at all, and remembered only that some dishes and some humans live forever—remembered it thankfully as we do now.   —*Hemet, 1941*

PACIFIC
VILLAGE

 Preface

This is the first thing I ever wrote that I was paid for. I did it because I wanted to, and was amazed when I got a check for it from *Westways,* where I had sent it without introduction because that was the only magazine I knew that might be interested in a piece about Southern California. Timidity is obvious in more ways than my giving a false name to Laguna Beach, of course. When I casually sent off this story, Phil Townsend Hanna was running his crazy shop for the Auto Club, as it was then called.

Nobody ever notified me that the article had been accepted, but I got a check: $25 for three drawings and $10 for accompanying text. This was a puzzlement to me, because I knew by then that I must either draw or write, to justify taking up space, and I had a puritanical feeling that because writing was easier and more fun, it could not be the worthier choice. The magazine cuts of my sketches were almost unrecognizable; still, I saw that I would never be much better as an artist, but that I might possibly improve my use of words.

Since this piece was the first and last one I ever tried to illustrate, my decision was obvious, and meanwhile I have never had as sweet and untroubled a time in my whole life with something I earned by myself. I spent the money, all of it, on riotous living. Not a penny of it went for taxes, or agents, or anything like that in those full Depression days. It was simply *money,* a mysterious bonus from somewhere, and never again has it felt so silky and exciting.

I bought a bottle of VSOP Hennessy cognac for my husband, which took about $10, and several Modern Library books, which then sold for from 95 cents to an outrageous $1.25 for the Giants, for my siblings and other friends. I gave my mother a tiny bottle, perhaps an eighth of an ounce, of sandalwood oil to rub inside her handkerchief drawer. I found a necktie hand-painted in iridescent colors for my father (my sense of humor was as simplistic as my prose!).

Long after this innocent spree, Father told me that one day at lunch with his friend Phil Hanna, he had felt somewhat embarrassed when he was asked if perhaps Fisher was his daughter using an ambiguous pseudonym. He wondered distastefully if I had mentioned his name to Mr. Hanna when I submitted the article to the magazine. I told him that it had not occurred to me, and he seemed pleased, and reread it.

So here is the first thing I wrote about a place as it was, at least for public view. It is no great shakes in a literary sense, but may amuse people who know "Olas" as it is now. And it made up my mind for me, in a basically brutal way: it said, Do what you most want to do, whether or not it is of any value to anyone else.

Olas is a coast village, beautifully located. Artists and pseudo-artists flock to it, and people in hurrying autos go more slowly along the smooth state highway past its hills sloped up behind and the coves and curving beaches along its edge. And Olas itself, the village, is far from ugly—if you know where to look. It has many most desirable qualities, social, political, commercial—if you know how to choose.

And Olas is on the spot, for those who have long known it as a quiet, lovely place and want it to remain so, and those who feel in its present restless state a promise of prosperity and prominence as a booming beach resort, are lined up grim and hateful on either side of a wall of bitter prejudice.

Santa Catalina lies west from Olas on the sea-line, with San Clemente its shadow southward. A hard, broad road, as neat and empty of character as a dairy lunchroom, strings the village. Out of Olas to the north it hurries toward Los Angeles, and south, down the coast, curves less straightly to San Diego and the dimming pleasures of Mexican border freedom. Inland, roads lead from Olas through the endless tawny rollings of round hills, through orange-valleys to the mountains.

Near Olas, the coastline is erratically lovely. It is the kind that inspires nine out of ten visitors interviewed by the weekly news sheet to reminisce of the Riviera, Italian or French. They usually speak of the blue sky, the yellow sand, and the foam-sprayed cliffs of any correct postcard, comparing them more or less hazily with the sky, the sand, and the cliffs of Olas. And they are more or less right.

There are people, though, who feel that if a place is a place, with a personality strong and clear, comparisons are as unnecessary as they are annoying. There are people, many of them, who feel that Olas is such a place.

Some of them, artists, old settlers, young enthusiasts for life in the raw with no hate and no golf clubs, want to keep it just as it is—or, even more desirable, as it used to be: quiet, so unknown that Saturday and Sunday were like Tuesday, beaches empty, rocks and cliffs free for uninterrupted sketching of any kind.

Olas' other lovers, just as sincerely, want to exploit to the bursting point its strong and attractive character. They want to develop it, to lure more people to it, so that all the houses may be full. Then more roads will be built into the silent hills, more houses sown on more lots, and more businesses will flourish on the bustling streets of what will soon change from village to town.

Olas itself is very sensitive to this inner struggle. There is restlessness in the air, and a kind of bewilderment. Change bubbles and fumes like yeast in a warm beer crock. Overnight the face of the village changes.

Streets are being smoothed and straightened. Old eucalyptus trees are uprooted to make way for curbings. "Desecration!" the artists shriek. "Necessity," soothe the progressives, and they plant more trees in much more orderly rows.

Hills are chopped and scarred into level roads, and the old guard moans in pain. "Ah, but we must take out dangerous curves," the developers explain, and as a palliative, "See how we are planting groups of ornamental shrubs, and neat rows of ice plant on the banks."

In the meantime, the outlines of the village are intact. Hills behind and around, sea before, it lies small and pleasant in a little hollow, with houses clustered north and south along the coast. The streets are not quite straight. Fine trees shade some of them. The buildings are small and for the most part extremely ugly, possessing the one architectural virtue of unadornment.

The upper end of the village proper, with the housing and amusement of impecunious weekenders its main excuse, is plainly hideous. It is Olas' more interesting half. A tent city, many umbrella and hot-dog concessions, a movie house, and a squat dance hall make patterns vivid and noisy.

Strange here are the two municipal halls to Beauty and Science, the art gallery and a California college's marine laboratory. One, knowingly built like an electric power plant, houses monthly collections of bilge and occasional greatness. The other, strangely suggestive of a ratty old Louisiana mansion, fills every summer with earnest biology majors and peculiar smells.

Toward the south, the other half of the village pulls discreetly away. Its tent city is a bulky hotel or two. Its hash houses become restaurants whose food, if no better, is served with less clatter and more pomp. Its shops of abalone shell souvenirs and leather pillows stamped *X the Beach Beautiful* suddenly change to "antique" shops. They are equally cluttered, but here the prices are higher, the variety is infinite, and the wares range from raffia beach sandals to jade—real jade—opium pipes. There are Chinese, Mexican, Florentine, and Persian stores. And there are a myriad "Gifte Shoppes." Most of them, like their humbler competitors at the other end of Olas, are promisingly crowded on weekends, and quite deserted in between.

The weekly visitors are, of course, divided like the village topography into two main camps. To the first belongs the usual army of clerks from banks and stores, college professors, movie extras, and various types of professional weekenders. They are in Olas to get away from noise and business, or to make noise, or to do business. They live inexpensively in a part of the village that makes enough money from their two days' occupancy to send its proprietors to Palm Springs or Lake Arrowhead for the other five.

The other army that swarms into Olas on Fridays and Saturdays heads straight for the synthetic luxury of the hotels and restaurants to the south. It comes in bigger cars. It has fatter paunches and purses. It is made up of bank presidents and college trustees, movie magnates of the first and second rank in white turtleneck sweaters, fussy old ladies in conservative town cars. And, as in the other army, there are many professional weekenders. And business flourishes.

For two days the beaches teem with people. Back roads have their full share of puffing bicyclists, and the dusty bridle paths more than theirs of riders trying to make tired rented nags prance like polo ponies. The dance hall sags and shudders and every hole-in-the-wall sends up a cheery reek of popcorn and hamburger. Drugstores outdo their own versatility. Motorcycle officers herd people handsomely across the car-lined streets.

Monday morning is like dawn on another planet. The hordes have fled. Six or seven cars are parked sheepishly in the quiet streets. A few people walk about. At eleven, after the morning mail is distributed at the post office, the villagers do their marketing. There is a mild stir. A few go to the sand in the afternoon. At five, mail again collects small gossiping crowds. At night, a quiet shuffling about sends various groups to rehearsals, the movie, the chamber of commerce, the bridge clubs. Olas is normal again, living that life so completely unsuspected by the people who come and go each weekend.

Socially this seven-days-a-week Olas is very complex. Two main divisions separate it roughly into the artistic and the progressive elements, but that is a crude simplification. Each element has its interweaving intricacies, with all the bad and most of the good qualities of a small-town society long and firmly established.

Old settlers, in Olas since its cow-pathian days, take quite for granted their positions as social and political arbiters. They would be politely incredulous if by some shock they were made conscious of the affectionate mockery which surrounds them. They live smugly, simply. Reminiscence flows in mild flood from them, monotonously interesting.

They speak of the old road, the true Camino Real, that wound like snail-silver along the cliffs. Indians once camped by it, and gave fish to the ambling padres. There are gardens now whose grey soil prickles with the thin bones of their bass and corbina—gardens and gas stations.

Then there were the old ranches, five or six of them back in the hills. The cowboys would sweep down the canyons in the fall of the year, and gather on the beach at Olas for three-day drunks. They sang wildly. Their children still race seaward, still sing, but oftener.

Then the days of the old post office with its high steps easy for sitting—ah me!—and the little newspaper! Didn't that old Dutchman write it, set it up, print it, sell it all himself? And the artists! Real ones they were, not pretty boys who just love color! Well, those were the days, the good days.

And the old settlers shake their heads, lonesomely. All about them is bustle and confusion. They hear nothing but wind in the groves of tall trees long leveled to the earth.

Theatre groups breed plays like maggots. They inter-hate ferociously. Two and three shows open on one night, ethics and economics are swept aside, clandestine throat-cutting springs gleefully into the light. Whole casts are shanghaied.

The result is amusing and valuable. Directors of unusual ability, in their burning hope and hate, drag powers of beautiful, almost great acting from local lifeguards and waitresses and unemployed professors. Butchers and service-station flunkys design fine sets and do most artful lightings.

There are writers in Olas—too many to count. Some have made a steady sum for years from pulp magazines; a few have sold to publishers novels that people wouldn't buy, or have seen lone stories starred in minor anthologies. One or two have written best-sellers. But most of Olas' "authors" rank among the permanently unpublished. Their publics are small: wives, friends, awed offspring. They write for the chosen few, quite happy. They gossip glibly among themselves of agents and markets and pulps and slickies. And sometimes they discuss Letters.

Somewhere between this group and the theatre enthusiasts lies a strange band of stragglers from both: the Talkers. Where do they sleep, where eat? With an uncanny knowledge of when to appear, they crop up from nowhere at picnics and parties and informal meetings. At the first lull in sound, they pounce. And the evening is theirs. Art, politics, abalone fishing, sex, Tahiti, California wines: information fills the air, like a rushing of winds. The Talkers are pests. Oddly enough, they are for the most part charming pests.

And it is these muse-fed villagers and these old settlers who lead the artist faction in Olas. It is they who cry "Down with billboards! Away with publicity! Out with subdividers and go-getters!" And they are very bitter. "Olas has been ruined, prostituted," they howl. "Her trees are felled, her hills pitted—give us back our old Olas!" And they stay in Olas and bring their friends, who usually stay too.

And all, artists and old settlers and the indeterminate

stragglers of many professions, are equally unaware of the
amused tolerance with which they are treated by the other
half of the village. Misunderstanding is mutual, perhaps, but
where the artists dismiss with scornful ravings the dull
bourgeois of Olas, the latter view with a kind of embarrassed
enjoyment the incomprehensible antics of their enemies.

They live the ordered existence of good citizens of any
small town on the earth. Their pleasures are cautiously li-
centious, their business dealings honestly corrupt. They sup-
port, with some prodding, a Red Cross branch and a municipal church.

Clubs thrive in their circles. There are several different
varieties of women's organizations: junior, senior, garden,
parent-teacher, sewing. The men have rival luncheon clubs
with all the usual backslappings and buttons and good os-
tentatious charities. The children of the club-goers go to
clubs: puppy clubs, doll clubs. And bridge clubs knit the
whole faction into a nightly knot of systems and four-sided
animosities.

Frequent elections exercise all the political muscles of the
various groups, and real estate salesmen, garagists, and
chain-store managers stalk past each other on the street with
an axes-at-twenty-paces look which changes at the next pri-
maries and then shifts again.

And all these people, these reactionary progressives, these
bank employees and owners of drugstores and gifte shoppes
and eating places—why do they want Olas to thrive and
grow fat? It is very natural. They want to grow fat with her,
to thrive that their children may thrive.

Real estate dealers need water in distant subdivisions.
They cut holes in the hills for pipes. Then they sell lots and
make money and build more houses to rent to more people.
And those people buy food and bathing caps and Chinese

lanterns. And billboards bring people, and so does publicity in the city papers and on the air.

To the progressives it is a natural, a logical thing to want Olas to be bigger and noisier and more popular. They are patient enough with the grumbling, sneering artists, and, most ironically, use them as part of their publicity program. *Olas, Famous Artists' Colony,* the billboards blurb, and *Visit Olas, Artist Haunt.* At the New Year's parade in a near neighbor, a great palette of roses represents the village, with hired Hollywood beauties dressed in transparent smocks and berets to represent Art. And at the annual fiesta, the aesthetic high note is reached when all the storekeepers and mechanics and beer-drawers don orange-and-green tam-o'-shanters and flowing ties. They too represent Art.

So the two sides live together in the little village. One could not well exist without the other. Each fights with the tactics of righteous sincerity: each fights dirty.

And while shouts and sneers and low groans gather like warring birds in the air, Olas lies still in the creases of the ocean-slipping hills, one bead strung with many like it on the long coast road. It is rather uncomfortable. It aches at times. Rheumatism or growing pains?

P.S. Meanwhile—meanwhile the real artists, those men and women whose pictures of Olas will perhaps still be looked at in a hundred years, continue to paint. They are few—as always. They are unconscious of any village strife. All the high talk of Art, all the politics and scandal, all the hullabaloo of growth and change, is to them as unimportant and as natural as a sea gull's dropping on a clean canvas. They paint as they did those years gone, trees and rocks and an old mission in a garden. And three hundred years from now—   *—Laguna Beach, 1934*

THE FLAME
AND THE ASH
THEREOF

 Preface

In 1931, when my young American husband and I went to
Gérardmer, it was an old settlement on a little lake in the
Vosges Mountains in Lorraine. It was between a village
and a small town, with between four and five thousand res-
idents, and between two wars, although nobody there
knew that.

A few of the oldsters remembered the Franco-Prussian
trouble, of course, and most of the townspeople knew all
too well the times after 1914. But life seemed blissfully
tranquil again in the early thirties, and during the summer
months small shops did a fine business with the "summer
people." Quiet middle-class Alsatians and Germans liked
the gentle mountain climbing; city cheeks grew safely rosy
in the mild altitude of less than 1,500 feet; the streams

were generous with trout, and swimming in the lake was nice for the children and grandchildren, and there was even a small casino for cautious whirls at the tables, between Pentecost and the beginning of September. One fairly large hotel, the Beau Rivage, and a dozen or so smaller inns and boardinghouses took care of the visitors, and since the new vogue of skiing seemed to attract some dauntless sportsmen in the winter, there was talk of keeping a few places open and warm for them.

Flax grew well in the meadows around the lake, and the linens of Gérardmer made sturdy trousseaux for many brides in Lorraine and even Lyon and Paris. Summer people liked the small frosted buns of gingerbread called *nonnettes,* and a cheese called *Géromé,* and they would often buy loose pieces of amethyst that lay alongside the goodies, to take home for better polishing and setting, or losing in dusty drawers.

It was as placid as a postcard, in 1931.

In 1945, when I was alone and older than my years, I read about what the Invaders had done—some obscure lesson in retribution, perhaps. Gérardmer was left numbed, with about 2,000 old people there, and even a decade later there were not more than 3,500 people in the whole little valley. The few men were often too maimed to act as guides, and there were not many summer people and almost no winter people to guide, anyway. Most of the hotels had been burned, but the Beau Rivage had been kept for an officers' rest spot, and even enlarged, and the Casino still stood, in a dismal way peculiar to such abandoned "dens of scarlet sin and iniquity." Nobody bothered to make *nonnettes,* or stretch lengths of thick white linen over the meadows.

By the middle of the seventies, though, Gérardmer was almost a boom town, at least compared with its last few hundred years. More than 10,000 prosperous doctors, law-

yers, shopkeepers lived there. The summer people were
a thing of the past, and the region had become popular
and almost fashionable for winter sports, with ski lifts
and yodelers in the pubs and sleek clinics for the broken
bones.

There were two luxurious hotels: the good old Beau Rivage, much enlarged and more elegant, and an even bigger
swankier palace called something like the Grand Bragard.
There were half a dozen slightly smaller hotels, and then
countless inns, boardinghouses, *relais,* and hostels. Needless to say, they all had bars (except for a couple of Tem-
perance places necessary to the national streak of puri-
tanism), and they either closed in the summer or stayed
open all year, with an occasional shutdown for new paint
and a change of staff.

Nobody recalled the local cheese once called *Géromé,* but
quiches Lorraine and *truites au bleu* became standard dishes
in every dining room and bistro, along with the Beatles on
hi-fi.

The famous linens of Gérardmer no longer flapped
in the open meadows, which were cut up in subdivisions
filled with fake chalets. The little shops that once
sold pieces of amethyst alongside their *nonnettes* were Parisian boutiques. And the people who used to come for a
week in the summer, to take easy walks and perhaps row
on the little lake, retired to warmer climates like Nice
when it came time to shut up shop in Strasbourg or
Besançon or Münster. The Casino ran all year, and its
rock 'n' roll drowned out any lappings of the little lake at
night.

By now it is likely that the two young Americans who
drifted in their own bemusement to Gérardmer in 1931
were part of a whole Age of Innocence. Certainly nobody
was actually aware of our being there, except fleetingly the
Silenus who shared our hotel now and then. But neither

were we aware of anyone at all. We were like the people of the town, between wars, between worlds, breathing the golden autumn air as if it would be there forever.

In a flash things are in focus. Sometimes it is hard to keep them there. It is as in a dream, when with a shifting of the elbow in sleep under the body, or a twitching of the toe, the whole light changes, and what was pleasure turns to horror, or its opposite.

On the night of January 28, 1945, a woman about thirty-five named Elsa was sitting before a small intense fire of manzanita wood. It burned on a hearth of flat Western stones. Her feet were up, naked under a black long dress. The room was warm and good, a kind of bulwark against loneliness. She ate from a nicely prepared tray, and drank a glass of mountain Zinfandel. She read a magazine as she ate, avoiding such things as the weekly description of corpse-strewn strategy or stock-market slaughter.

It seemed to her that always with her supper, her one time for reading in peace, she ran into such tellings, and then had to put aside the pages and the food. She must eat, she knew, and she must have some idea of what was happening in the war. It was unfortunate that blood and hunger had to mix. Lately, she had taken to reading non-news journals as she fed herself dutifully before the tightly blazing fire. Tonight it was, column by column, the January 15 edition of *The New Yorker*.

She read through "The Talk of the Town," a few phrases of which she envied, and then she looked casually at all the ads about whiskey and star-sapphire clips, and then she started an article by Janet Flanner, whom she had always admired and to whom she still had a letter of introduction given her in 1937 and never presented.

The article was all right for a while. Then it said, speaking of German atrocities in a way she admired because it was the cold stifled way she would have had to employ herself:

In the Vosges, the Nazis ordered the medieval spa of Gérardmer and its fifteen hundred Alsatian houses burned. When the anguished mayor protested, the Germans agreed to spare a hundred and fifty houses in the center of the city, and all the city's inhabitants were driven into them. Then, during three infernal nights, the rest of the dwellings were burned in a neat and controlled ring around them. . . .

The people of Gérardmer! May God rot and blast the souls of those who hurt them, Elsa said silently, pushing aside her supper tray and finally swallowing the bite that had stayed in her throat since the word "Gérardmer."

And what of me? she asked. What of all of us, rotted, blasted?

She took the tray away, and then stood like a solid forlorn tree beside the hearth, listening to the manzanita wood burn hotly, neat and controlled . . . "neat and controlled . . ."

Fourteen years before, she was in Gérardmer, so bright, so thinly sparkling. "Oh, you *must* go to Gérardmer," said her landlady and friend, who was Alsatian and very loving. So Elsa and her husband, to celebrate their second year in integrality as it then seemed to them, took one train after another to get to that medieval spa.

People corrected their pronunciation pleasantly in every

station, but the word as Elsa remembered it so long later was "Géramé," in spite of Parisian professors and ordinary citizens who spoke of the little lake town as if it were on *la mer de Gérard*.

In some such place as Besançon, Elsa got separated from her husband, and sat in the station café clutching a coffee glass, in agony because she was young and tender and in love. When she found herself again with him in the train, they laughed helplessly, until they realized that they were with four stiff French people in a second-class compartment.

There was no sound for a while except the chuffing of the little engine up the grades. It came clearly through the two open windows, along with a great many cinders and one bee who soon left. Elsa slid her hand into her husband's; she was still weak with relief at being with him, at being alive with him. . . .

She saw that two of the four people were watching her, and gradually she dared look at them and at last smile shyly. They were the kind of daughters so often seen then in France with their parents: beginning to grow plump from too much food; dressed greyly in half-mourning for uncles or brothers or even fiancés dead more than a decade before, in the War not yet called First; dutifully, slyly bitter or very sentimental, but leashed to their parents' purse strings, paying with filial devotion for the comfort of Papa's last years, and their own.

Elsa, who numbered several of these withering girls among her friends, recognized as such the two who peeped at her, and felt through her glow of love for her husband a mild amazement at their advances. It must be the altitude, she thought, that so successfully broke down their careful *bourgeoisisme*. Her own cheeks were hot, like apricots. (Later, sitting by the manzanita, she smiled without envy, knowing

that only her own innocence kept her then from seeing that
it was the man they breathed toward, not her. . . .)

Finally, as the little train pulled itself up through meadows and pine groves so foreign to the sweet viny slopes of its
home station, even the parents of the two girls melted. It
was surely the altitude that let them dare venture the com-
mencement of what became a long good conversation.

The wife shed a black knitted pullover, and one of her
daughters hid her eyes behind her fingers like a child at the
sight of a wedge of grey cotton slip above the skirt band.
The husband casually laid his used copy of *Le Temps* down
on the seat opposite him, pretending at first not to notice
L'Intran and *L'Ami du Peuple* which Elsa handed from her
husband to the empty seat beside her. And suddenly they
were all talking and smiling at once, with bright eyes.

It turned out that according to the French family her accent was not exactly Dutch, but probably Swedish. What,
not *Swedish?* But surely, *surely* not American! Impossible, incredible!

Elsa tried, with the acquired wisdom of almost twenty-two
years, not to be annoyed. She reminded herself of what her
husband had told her, that such a remark was meant sincerely as a compliment. She smiled coldly, and then softened
again before the happy shyness of the sisters, who unfolded
like night-blooming cereus buds before the warm moon of
their parents' approval of these two socially inoffensive
foreigners.

Chitchat, chitchat. The eyes grew less hostile, the smiles
came out petal by petal. Americans? Then what about the
gangsters, hah-hah-hah? And how does one pronounce
knockout, O.K., whiskey sour? The papa had very pink cheeks,
and was slapping *L'Intran* against his knee, and Elsa felt that
soon the girls and their mama would ask her why she had

been married two years and had no little gangster, hah-hah-
hah.

Then the train began to pull more slowly. Inside and out
it was as if wind were dying from an accordion dropped from
faint hands: the tone lagged, sagged, flatted, groaned. . . .
The trees came to a stop and stood still so that each window
was a postcard: "Scene from the Vosges Mountains near
Gérardmer Station, Portrait of French Family Preparing to
Descend from Second-Class Compartment."

They did descend, with such a lack of any farewell, even
dutiful, that Elsa felt cold and lonely suddenly, after the shy
warmth of their questionings. (Later, she knew that the two
sisters and the mother, even the fat stiff father, might still remember her as one of their great adventures, but it took a
long time for her to feel like anything but a lopped-off berry
on a currant bush when she thought of their harsh leaving.)
She did not want to exchange addresses, as on a docking
ship, but she felt unfinished.

The train seemed to be relaxing, with much noise but
only a mild muscular stretch, as if it meant to rest for the
night. The young foreigners got off into the lemon-colored
autumn dusk. A plump old newsboy with a bush of white
hair came up as they watched the only porter leave with the
sternly mute French family. There was some bartering. Elsa
stood watching dreamily, listening to bells in her head in a
daze of love and weariness, and then trotted behind her husband and the old man.

The hotel they went to was second-class, not the big one
on the lake. They were in the Annex, a forbidding house
with purple wallpaper and good plumbing; special rates, end
of season, Elsa heard. They would eat in the hotel dining
room. The lake was but a stone's throw from the bedroom of
Madame. Madame would enjoy all modern comforts . . .

The ancient newsboy, wicked Silenus of Alsace, pocketed his tip and was gone.

That night Elsa was sure she heard the lake lap lapping. She dreamed she was a tree. She dreamed her husband was the father of two girls in a second-class compartment, and she was the mother and her slip showed where . . . no, *their* slips . . . *no*. . . .

The next day, all day, was like a dream too. There were meadows around the village, with long rough strips of linen bleaching in the thin sun of the mountains. In the few shops still open, the linen, by the meter, cost too much to buy, but it was good to touch. There were shelves of uncut jewels, mostly amethysts. They were sharp, intense, flawed as if by lightning or white fire. In a rowboat on the lake, with the shore jumping to her husband's strokes, Elsa saw the black shadows of the pines, and dreamed of their odor, their shape, their cool impregnability.

In the Annex later there had never been such a dream state between the two people who loved and knew each other. Their cheeks were bright, and bright were the blue eyes/green eyes, and their lips were full and red, for they were high in the world although not as high as they would later be, and they had come in from a trippers' trip to a mountainside left from the War, horrible but less so than they would later know horror to be.

It was a hill facing another hill, bleak as a Goya etching, with the pines blown off to their rotting stumps and the soil rancid with old poisons. All colors were there, it could be said, but they made *black*. The air should by rights be as clean as any mountain air, but in the nostrils it held a faint far stink to it, as of phosphorescence. The guide—yes, there was a proper guide to this interesting site, this point of historical importance—told how for four years the French sat

firing across the little valley. The French sat here, on this
unkempt miserable rathole of mud and excrement, and the
filthy Boches sat over there across the stream bed and fired
back from their concrete reinforcements with plumbing,
grand pianos, Parisian opera stars, caviar. Oh God, Elsa
thought, I am too old and too tired to be only twenty-two.
All the colors are black. No grass can ever grow here again.
It is not the altitude. . . .

But back in the Annex bedroom that night the dream was
sweeter. She pulled a scarlet shirt over her shoulders, and in
the mirror of the armoire she enjoyed her husband's eyes, intolerably blue, watching her.

In the hotel dining room they felt heat slap against their
faces after the September air and the run from their purple
chamber. They stamped to the farthest table, across a floor as
echoing and shiny as any at Versailles, and there a special
dinner had been ordered by the thoughtful loving husband,
in honor of the day: a little roasted pullet from Bresse,
braised endive, hothouse peaches, champagne. But the regular dinner was served to them along with it all, and they
could not seem to stop it, so that in a kind of mirthful help-
lessness they ate enormously, and the servants beamed: thick
peasant soup, sweetbreads in white wine, a galantine of veal,
caramel custard, and then with a great flourish *crêpes flambées*
in honor of the anniversary . . . and then the peaches lying in
their fine cotton nests . . . and the champagne after all the
white wine and the red wine. . . .

Elsa in a gentle stupor fixed her eyes on her one true lover.
She would never enslave *her* daughters, she decided fiercely.
Her petticoat would never show, never be grey, and in trains
she would always always smile at the end of the journey. . . .

The dining room was empty when they left. As they
walked carefully past the office door the clerk called to them,

and said with a knowing cackle that it might please them to
learn that the Annex that night would be theirs, theirs
alone. The end of the season, he shrugged . . . but not for
'Sieur-'dame! Hah-hah, Elsa thought. Gangsters, hah-hah!
What is that joke about?

Later she awoke. Her heart was pounding thickly. At first
she thought it was the lapping of the lake waters, or the
sounds from the great black pine trees, and then she knew a
shadow hung over her, as from some dream already forgotten. It was a minute, perhaps, before she heard clearly the
noises from the next room. They were muffled and yet
sniffly, small and yet full of all the ugly suggestion of a nasty
secret joke. They turned the small sweet cries, the willing-
ness of her own immediate remembrance, into a death's-
head. She lay frozen with disgust, and then fear, for it became plain to her as she lay in the purple room, now black as
a blasted hillside, that there was a plot against her and her
love.

The seemingly naïve family on the train who smiled and
probed and then repulsed her; the white-haired newsboy, a
grotesque in the lemon-colored twilight, leading them here
. . . and the waitress and the man who rented boats and the
guide who told how many Frenchmen had died in '15-'16-
'17-'18 to no apparent avail; they all worked together to
bring two American lovers to their end. Yes, that waitress,
the one who had smiled so knowingly as she placed the
peaches in their cotton bed upon the stained tablecloth! And
the clerk . . . ah, what had he said about being alone?

Alone? On the other side of the door into the next room
there was a faint horrid giggle, as if some cretin watched an
eyelid being tweaked from a dead body. Elsa shuddered. Her
skin rippled, and she was amazed, in an intensely dramatic
way quite unfamiliar to her, to find herself still lying behind

her husband instead of being propelled silently out past the plaster and the glass, over the black pines, and she burning brightly, but without ash, and the trees likewise.

There was a clicking, a snipping, a snarking. Counterfeit key! Yes, soon now . . .

She prepared herself to fall between her love and the dagger or the bullet, whichever it would be, for it was most plainly a dreadful plot: the two befuddled strangers, the hurriedly emptied Annex, the *bourgeois* family to calm suspicion, the conniving smiling servants. Elsa was flat with horror, incapable even of sweating. She wanted to cry out to her dear husband, to warn him of his nearing end, for such she recognized it to be. And all she could do was to ready herself stoutly to save him the first agony. She could see the path of the bullet, a straight line through the air from the keyhole to his strongly beating heart. She would have time to place herself across that line, neat and controlled, mathematically, precisely. He would never know.

It was sad, so sad. They were young. He would live on, even more a poet after grief, and never know the reason for her foolhardiness. Her heart beat like a brick thrown against granite, with fear and regret and indigestion, and her mind was on fire. From the next room, through the thin door, the heavings and whisperings died down, though, and outside whatever small autumnal breeze had stirred the water and the branches died dead away among the farthest treetops, and in the purple room Elsa's outraged organs, heart and all, composed themselves as only those of a young healthy animal can do.

She softened in her straightness, all unknown to her lover, and dreamed that he was a black pine tree and she in some indescribable way his lover too, like a meadow, like the sky, like a dagger or a bullet.

The next morning when they left Gérardmer, already dozing like a bear cub before the coming of the cold, the fat old
white-haired newsboy grinned at them and carried their bag
and thrust yesterday's newspaper through the train window
for them as they left. Elsa's husband grinned a little too, for
several miles. Then grudgingly, as one man will who even
slightly betrays another, he told how Silenus had been able
to bring their waitress up to an empty room in the Annex
because of their good tips and exemplary behavior.

Elsa shrugged, a frightening portent of herself in twenty
years if she turned wry instead of straight, sour instead of
sweet. Men, she thought impatiently. Silenus and a greasy
strumpet! They had sniffed and snorted and giggled, and
there I lay, ready to die before assassins reached my love! She
felt foolish, certainly, and quite bilious.

Her husband read the refolded paper, and there was no
French family to woo. The black pine trees thinned, and finally turned to open fields, and she was in a station café (was
it Besançon?) and not so afraid as she had been before, three
days ago or whenever it was.

Her love was gone, yes, and she knew where. He would
come back ... or he would not. If he did not, she would
surely live. And at that knowledge, sharp as a dagger thrust,
hard as the plowing impact of a bullet, the impervious well-
bred Elsa put her face in her gloves and wept. The high air
and then the low, the family so eager and suspicious, the
champagne and the cotton-wrapped peaches and the whisperings, the burning cheeks, the black black pines ... no, she
could not bear it!

Her husband, who was also well-bred, was much embarrassed, certainly, when he found her thus undone in the
public station café, and he left a large tip.

And that was in 1931 in Gérardmer, Géramé. Elsa, willy-nilly, thought back upon it. The horror of the girl, so full of love and food and wine, was real again to her. She respected and admired that sincere shadowy fool, who without plan prepared to throw herself before a flashing knife or an invisible flying bullet. Hail, young love, she thought.

The manzanita burned pungently, sweetly, not like a pine but with the same intense hot light. "All the city's inhabitants," Elsa read by it ... all those people, and the white-haired newsboy and the clerk and the waitress, were driven into the center of the town, while for three nights the rest was burned in a "neat and controlled ring around them."

She put her head down the way she had in the station (Besançon?), but this time no one came out to comfort her and lead her away, and there was no surcease to her old anguish. Everything was in focus, for once, and she fought not to keep it there, as in a dream, in sleep.   —*Hemet, 1945*

THE
FIRST CAFÉ

The first time I ever went to a restaurant, the waiter, I have been told, thought me delightful and my little sister even more so, in spite of the sad truth that children to waiters are professionally hell.

She was four, and I was six. We behaved nicely; we spoke neither too high nor too low, we sat up straight, we spilled almost not at all, and at the end of the meal she said to our man, "Oh, I am so sorry to leave all these dishes for you to wash, and a nearly clean napkin too!" He, who already loved us, or so it appears in Apocrypha, grew dewy-eyed.

Whatever his feelings then, he took care of us for some thirty years more in one or another of the respectable restaurants in Southern California, and when I strolled, a little while ago, into a beach chop house, there he was, celebrating his last night in the profession, and we embraced and touched several glasses together before he left for his chicken farm. If he wanted to take time from his capons and his poults to write a book, I cannot help believing that he would speak kindly of the two little girls who got such a fine start under his snowy, flickering napkin.

That was in Los Angeles, at Marcel's, in 1914 or a little later. There were a few good small restaurants there at that time, a kind of backwater from San Francisco, undoubtedly. Marcel's was, according to my parents and a great many other hungry provincials, very good indeed. And *Pinafore* was playing a matinee at the Mason Opera House. So my mother took us twenty-five miles each way on the trolley to see it and have our first meal in public, which she and my father decided—with no dispute—should be as fine as possible. I can remember nothing about it until we were sitting in the small room lighted with candles behind pink silk lampshades, with incredible expanses of snow-white linen, and a forest of glasses sparkling everywhere at our eye level, and with a fine, thin-nosed man dressed in black to take care of us—only us.

I do not know if Mother ordered in advance. I do know that she threw any dietetic patterns overboard. It seemed almost unbearable that a little fire should burn there at our table so dangerously, under a silver pan, and that the man could lean over it without going up in flames, and put the plates so tenderly before us with a napkin over his fingers, while candles flared in the middle of the day and people we had never seen before ate in the same room, as if we were invisible.

There was no mention of milk to drink, but instead we lifted the tall goblets of forbidden ice water waveringly to our lips, and looked up over them at the pink rose nodding in a silver vase between us and the world. There may have been other things to eat, but the chafing-dish chicken is all my sister and I can remember now, and of course the won-

derful waiter who kept on remembering us too, after that
first hushed luncheon.

It was a good start for us, that is if, in a world of shifting
values, it is good to start two humans off with such firm
high ones. I often think of it, almost as strongly as I did one
day in Paris when I was lunching in the back part of the Café
de Paris and saw that the table next to mine was being
dressed with particular care. Finally people came to sit at it: a
handsome, famous actor, his beautiful British wife who was
divorced from him, and their two children. The little girl
was very English and of course lived with her mother, and
the little boy was completely Parisian, as any reader of the
gossip columns could have told you. But they all spoke easily together and were charming and happy. It was obviously
a rendezvous that had been kept often by the four separated
people, there in that opulent, gracious eating house.

The father and mother drank a cocktail and talked pleasurably, while the children sipped with courtesy at a very
good sherry, enough to cover the bottoms of their proper
little glasses. I forget the rest of the meal, but I sat long after
I should have gone to keep an appointment, watching the
cautious delight of the children at the rather elaborate dishes
the waiters brought for them, and the quiet enjoyment of
the parents. I was watching myself and my little sister, and
feeling within me the way my mother and the English
mother must have felt before the wide eyes, the hushed
voices, and the trembling polite hands of their children.

Now I have Anneli, almost ready for it: in a year she will
be a little past five, halfway between the ages of my sister and
me when we first sat ecstatically under the ministrations of a
well-trained restaurant staff. In spite of the world-sickness
that her father and I feel, we still want her first restaurant
meal to be good. We have discussed it pleasurably, recogniz-

ing without shame the same eagerness in us that makes some parents buy elaborate electric trains and five-foot sailboats for their uninterested offspring. There must be chicken à la king in a chafing dish, and perhaps a baked Alaska because the heat and the cold of it are so exciting to a person like Anneli, and a gentle white wine for us and, if possible, cooled water in a little French bottle for her.

Meanwhile Anneli is being prepared with infinitesimal bites of whatever we find most subtle, slipped to her—without benefit of pediatrician—between her daily rounds of chopped green beans and pears and such. When she behaves unusually nicely, we think with complacency of what it will be like—that first lunch.

We will arrive about one-thirty at the very best, most formal restaurant we know in our city, having sustained ourselves with a short nap and two whole-wheat crackers spread with sweet butter. She will wear some sort of smocked short dress made of wine-colored linen, white cotton gloves, white sandals on her thin little very brown feet. I suppose she should have a hat, though she doesn't often wear one. Her eyes are as big and purple-brown with excitement as well-cooked prunes and she stands up like a minuscule princess to the salute of the *maître d'hôtel*.

We go to a table perfect for three, half facing the door to the kitchens so that she can watch the waiters and learn from them, half turned from the bar where a great many people are drinking—as she has often seen us do—but without as much enjoyment as we have. There is a drowsy diminuendo of chatter, and the human beings who have given themselves the time to be leisurely seem much more human than they may have earlier that noon.

Anneli looks at the strangest of the women, and the men most like her father, and then watches solemnly, tremblingly, as a split of Perrier water is poured for her, for her alone into a stemmed glass, and a waiter—we know the very one, past sixty, with the sly monkey-face of a college professor (but will he be there then?)—her own waiter, prepares on a wheeled table the silver bowl and the flame. Yes, we see her, my husband and I, as much this minute in our minds as we ever will at Voisin or the Café de Paris or dead Marcel's; and she is those other children; she is us; she is whatever tender creature can thus begin the long nibbling through the invisible tunnel of the world.   —*Hemet, 1955*

TWO
KITCHENS
IN PROVENCE

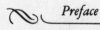 *Preface*

Anything can be a lodestar in a person's life, I suppose, and for some fortunates like me, the Kitchen serves well. Often the real influence of a lodestar is half understood, or partly unsuspected, but with a little reflection it grows clear to me that kitchens have always played a mysterious part in my shaping.

Since I wrote about two of them I knew when I stayed several years in Provence, I have known two more in that fair country, in Aix and Marseille. Like the first ones, they are vivid in my recollections, each with its own smells, its own views onto the world and into myself.

The one in Marseille, in 1973 I think, was perhaps the least dignified of any of a long lifetime of them. It was part of a miserable little bathroom: a two-burner gas plate beside the washbowl, a saucepan and a soup pot on the shelf for toothpaste and combs. To pretend to bathe in the small scarred tub, which never ran anything but tepid water whether it came from the hot spigot or the cold, my sister and I had to duck under the sagging string that held our dish and face towels. Above the spigots there was a high window perhaps ten inches square, which we had to stand in the tub to open or close. It opened onto a dim air well, so that we knew intimate things about our unseen neighbors.

But past this dreadful cell were two big airy rooms with good red tiles on the floor, with a big window in each room looking far down on one of the most exciting places in the world, the Old Port of Marseille, and then far out to sea, far up into the blanched cruel hills. For part of the months we lived there, rapt by all we saw, we could watch the sun both rise and set, so high and wide were the windows. We never stopped looking, except when we slept lightly through the night-sounds of police sirens, small ships, bugles blowing in the barracks across the street, now and then a band rehearsing on the empty sidewalks for some celebration.

We ate as close as possible to one of the windows, shut against the mistral, open to the warm sun. The foul little bath-kitchen produced miracles of good plain food from its two pans, and we bought some plates and bowls of Provençal pottery, and two sturdy wineglasses, so that everything tasted even better. Salads were easy. So was good *café au lait,* and we soon learned where to find the most commendable croissants, the most pungent mountain honey. We could get local cheeses, and homemade *pâtés* sent to our shopkeepers by cousins in Normandy or Alsace. Now and then we bought a little roasted chicken from an elegant catering shop on the Rue de Rome. And the *vins rosés* were ever-flowing. . . .

The kitchen in Aix-en-Provence, a couple of years later, was nothing but a counter in the single room, with a shoddy little "frigidaire" at one end and a small dauntless water heater at the other, and a typical hideous sink in the middle, like the first two I had known in that part of the country: scooped from a slab of gritty brown marble and completely inadequate for anything at all that one has to do in a kitchen sink. Like the others, it was probably at least two hundred years old, made in the days of pitchers and pails and open drains, not meant to have water splashing into it from a tap. . . .

Again I was with my sister, and again we found a big airy room to live in, twice the size of the two in Marseille, and on the second storey instead of the ninth. There was no view this time, but the sky and its wheeling whistling swallows was close to us. The floor was of red tiles, of course, and we could keep a few pots of geraniums in the windows, since we were on a narrow street out of the mistral's way.

The fruits and vegetables of Aix were, as always, picked at dawn and meant to be eaten by nightfall. It was exciting once more to find myself racing decay, as I had learned to do at Le Tholonet and then L'Harmas. A peach bought cool and unblemished from the greengrocer on the Cours Sextius at nine in the morning looked sulky by noon, and by suppertime was bruised and voluptuously dying. The bright yellow blossoms on zucchini from the Marché aux Herbes had wilted by noon, and the first waxy glow of the slender squashes was gone by the time they made our supper. But eggs and unsalted butter stayed fresh in the miserable little icebox, and the wine was always cool.

That time in Aix, there was a rebirth of local pride, and along with the clean restoration of beautiful old façades and courtyards there was a new interest in regional cooking, so that we could buy excellent breads and cheeses and *pâtés* from a dozen somewhat artsy "caves" and "boutiques."

In Marseille, not long before, we had eaten well but in a limited way in our flat, and had satisfied more than our basic hungers in many restaurants both great and small. In Aix we ate better food in our one-room flat than we could find in the town. We had perhaps four pans and kettles instead of two, and could braise little quails for a treat, or make a lusty ratatouille, or even a dainty omelet . . . and of course it was pleasant not to have to push aside the toothpaste to find the forks and spoons.

In Marseille we had ushered in the Free Market vegetables and fruits being shipped enthusiastically, if without experience, from Israel and Portugal, which in their dried-out, half-ripe, half-frozen state were almost nostalgically like the California supermarket produce my sister and I had hoped to escape. Every time we went by bus from Marseille to Aix, which happened more often as we bowed to our helpless devotion to the town, we brought back *good* things to eat. We felt disloyal, because we loved the city too. But it was better than ever to sit by one of the big windows above the Old Port and eat *real* green beans instead of the ersatz half-dead things for sale in Marseille.

And in the flat in Aix it was good to sit by one of the big windows and pretend we were looking down at the Old Port instead of across at a line of dripping red and pink laundry hung from a neighbor's kitchen out over the street. Perhaps the fish of Aix was eighteen miles older than in Marseille, we agreed, but its radishes were as fresh and delicate as dewdrops . . . the cherries were as crisp as new almonds. . . .

It is fortunate to recognize lodestars as such. They light our paths, and shape us mysteriously, and in the process can teach true humility. How and why, I now ask myself, have I known not one or two but four kinds of kitchens of Provence?

I

I have had two kitchens in Provence. The first was above the empty stables at the Château du Tholonet, about five miles easterly from Aix, near the village of Le Tholonet. My two young girls and I were living there for a few months in 1956, before we had to leave, after a long stay, for America and home.

The kitchen was about nine by nine feet, with a ceiling fourteen feet high and a window looking west toward Aix, over two rolling meadows bright with scarlet poppies and sweet grasses and then to the slopes of the Châteaunoir, covered with humming pine woods. It was one of the best kitchens I ever worked in, although it was inefficient, inadequate, and often filled with flies.

The walls were plastered stone. There was a hood built into the east wall over a low platform with three grates in it. A long time ago, this had served as a stove for the grooms and stableboys who slept and ate there above the carriages and horses of the château, and now a small white enamel butane stove sat with an air of embarrassed practicality upon its red tiles. Behind it was a black iron plaque about three feet square, of a wild-haired hero whipping a giant lizard— St. Michael, no doubt, worsting his dragon. I forget the anti-

quarian name for these iron chimney guards; they were used
to protect the soft chimney stones against the steady blaze
on such hearths, which all kitchens once kept hot and
bright.

To the right of the hearth, by the window, which looked
down on a fast brooklet and a rocky path where the shepherd
led his flock each night and morning, was a marble sink with
a tap that now ran water, now did not, depending on what
the farmer was doing in his garden. It was a shallow oval
hollow in a slab of the local stone quarried up behind us in
Bibémus, where Cézanne used to roam and struggle with his
vision of what light is made of. When there was water and I
used it, I always kept it as clean as I could, for it splashed out
directly from the hole in the wall onto the shepherd's path
twenty feet below. The sink was faced with the same red tiles
as the old stove and the floor—the rough glazed squares of
red and pink and ochre clay that comes from the soil of Provence, the clay that makes the roofs there glow and burn
even in the moonlight. They were cool in summer, warm
and comforting in winter, and easy to clean, and altogether
so pleasing that the prospect of ever having to walk about on
another surface was painful to me. Except for the tiles, the
kitchen was whitewashed. There were three shelves above
the drab little sink, which was reinstated several times a day
in my favor because it had, if I wished to go into the bathroom and light a heater, hot as well as cold water. Or perhaps I esteemed it merely because it had water at all.

There was a worn pine table, on which I kept a clay water
pitcher, and the wine bottles, and a wicker tray for the vegetables, and a reed satchel filled with rapidly staling bread.
Then there was a shallow high cupboard with screen doors,
where I kept everything that was not on the table and the
sink shelves—food, plates, the rare leftovers, tubes of mus-

tard and concentrates. I had very little equipment. I had borrowed two pans and a skillet, and I made a pleasurable investment in Provençal pottery casseroles, plates, and bowls. The Monoprix solved in a fortunately temporary way the problem of decent knives and forks and spoons, except for one viciously beautiful all-purpose blade.

Downstairs, in the enormous, echoing stone carriage room through which we passed to our ironwork stairway, was a little wire-screen box in which I was supposed to safeguard things. But in Provence food spoils very quickly, and except for a few hard-rock sausages and green bananas, which I left down there, I found it simpler to buy the minimum of butter and so on and keep it upstairs in the kitchen cupboard.

I took a while to get into what is basically an easy rhythm of marketing, and a couple of times I found myself facing one withered lemon, a boiled potato, and a bowl of subtly rotten green beans for supper. Alone, I would have gone to bed with the latest edition of a Georges Simenon, but with my little girls Anne and Mary there, it seemed providential that the Restaurant Thomé was only a quarter mile away. We would walk down past the château and its tranquil ponds of water, teeming in the late spring with still speechless froglets, and under the rows of trimmed and untrimmed giant plane trees, and across the bridge above the lively little river, and there would be the welcome, as it had been for almost a hundred and fifty years—the smiling owner, his nice wife, all her sisters and brothers, and always a new baby somewhere under an impeccable mosquito net. Perhaps the fancy electric spit would be turning a few pullets for a big country wedding tomorrow, tablecloths would be fluttering in the garden, and not a sound now from the discreet little viny pergolas where Prince Edward and his less noble but equally gallant imitators used to entertain their traveling companions.

There was a bus that zoomed through the village three mornings a week, on market days in Aix, and at least once weekly my girls and I hopped it, at five minutes after nine. At the markets, we would fill the two string bags we carried with us, and the two or three woven baskets, all bulging with hard vegetables at the bottom and things like wood strawberries on top, and head for our favorite taxi at the top of the Cours Mirabeau, picking up packages along the way—a square of Dijon gingerbread and a pot of Alpine honey at the little "health-food store" on the Place Forbin, an onion tart for a treat at the pastry shop on the Rue Thiers, a bottle of vermouth at the Caves Phocéennes. We would be loaded to the gunwales, full of hope that we had purchased enough for another week.

In a short time, I learned that I was lugging things home from Aix that I could get in the village, and then only occasionally did I find myself with either too much, all withering and spoiling, or nothing at all and no bus for two days and the store in the Relai de Cézanne (the store is the other half of the old café-inn where Cézanne often stopped when he was painting along the Route du Tholonet) in Le Tholonet, across from the Restaurant Thomé, closed because of a wedding-funeral-christening—or just closed. (I soon found that on Mondays it always was.) I knew that the good bread from Palette, which leaned like fat and thin bean poles in a big basket in the corner, was fresh on Tuesdays and Saturdays, and that on those days I could usually buy some milk and butter. Saturday mornings, there would always be a few crates of fresh vegetables. I could buy, for instance, little artichokes, new potatoes, carrots, zucchini, tomatoes, bananas;

bread and butter and milk, of course, and some Gruyère cheese; a couple of soup sausages; and a copy of the weekly Mickey comics for the children. In the middle of the week, though, the stock at the store might consist of some dusty packages of noodles, a few big cubes of yellow laundry soap, and penny caramels for the twenty-eight children of the school district.

In addition to the store, there were several little trucks that came regularly up the narrow roads from the national highway at Palette. On Wednesdays, the butcher drove right up to the front of the château, blowing his horn long and merry, and the shepherdess would come from the beautiful stone barns, where she lived with her husband and two hundred sheep, several rams, two goats, three astonishing sheep dogs, and forty chickens and four pigs; the farmer's wife would come from the wing of the beautiful hollow stone château, where she lived with her husband and a little abandoned child they had saved; the gardener's wife would come up from the beautiful gate cottage; the miller's wife and mother would come down from the beautiful stone house in the mill beside the waterfall behind the château; and I would come from the beautiful stone stables. We would watch one another's purchases and spendings casually, and talk in a somewhat artificial overcordial but friendly way about whose children had whooping cough and whose had chicken pox and whether it would rain, while the suave young butcher, with the remote, weary face of a night clerk in a cheap hotel, cut deftly into his slabs of meat, and weighed out black and green olives, cheese, and marbled lard. Gradually, we would go back under the chestnut trees and the plane trees to our kitchens, and he would drive away, to return Sunday at noon, when he would stop in front of the water pump in the

village and blare his horn commandingly to the people returning from Mass and sitting in front of the Relai with
their milky *pastis* in front of them on the little tables.

Fridays at Le Tholonet, a small fish jeep tooted in, with an
old cornet cracking out its jaunty message, past the tranquil
straight ponds in the front of the château. By the time it got
there, only a few fish would be left, but they were still fresh,
and usually good. All Mediterranean fish seem much
stronger in their smells and flavors than those of colder waters. Once, I remember, I bought the tail end of a large silvery one with a tough skin and a big backbone, and it sent
off quite a fume from the beginning, although not at all a
tired or suspicious one. I rubbed it with olive oil, put some
thin slices of lemon on it, and poured about a cupful of
white wine over it in a shallow casserole. Then, instead of
allowing fifteen minutes as the fisherman had advised, I
baked it for about a half hour in a gentle oven, which was
the only kind I had—the two burners on top of the little
stove on the hearth were almost too lively, but the oven
never worked up much enthusiasm.

That was the night we tried a package of dried mushroom
soup that the Aix grocer had given me to prove that such
innovations could be good, and we enjoyed the smooth,
well-seasoned creamy mixture so much that we decided to
eat the fish cold the next day, with a mayonnaise I would
make with an egg from the shepherdess and a plastic gadget
I had bought some time before from a very fat man in a
chef's bonnet, who was showing at a little table in the market how it could be done in twenty seconds with never a failure. I put the fish back in the cool oven, and the next morning took it out to skin and bone, when I heard the
postman's whistle at the château. Quickly, I covered the casserole with the breadboard and a towel, to protect the fish

from flies, and went over to talk with him about if and how I could register a letter without going in to Aix.

On the way back, Whisky, our guest poodle, who came three miles by himself every day or so from the Château-noir to amuse us and sample our cuisine before he puffed up the hill again to his real home, dashed away from me, through the stables and up our long flight of stone stairs in the dim coach house. Just as I got to the bottom of them, the biggest black cat I ever saw, and one I had certainly never seen before, whipped down past me and then out the enormous door, with Whisky yapping nobly at a safe distance.

Of course, the kitchen was a shambles. That stranger cat had caught, perhaps from miles away, the pungent invitation of my baked fishtail. He had come to it as unerringly as one rare insect in a jungle finds his only possible mate. He had snatched open the cupboard door, which was too warped to latch shut, and had fiercely tossed to the floor everything unfishy. Then he had slapped his way through the wastebasket. Finally, he had clawed off the heavy bread-board and towel from the casserole and he had dragged and flapped the whole oily, dripping mess down onto the red tile floor, where, from the look of things, he had not only torn the meat to small bits but rolled in it. So we did not have to try out the mayonnaise gadget for a while longer.

Saturday afternoons, there was always the visit of the rolling *épicerie,* with things like shoelaces, aspirin, custard powders, and boxes of cookies with bright-pink frosting on them and names like Bébés Délices or Nounous de Titi. The man who jolted it around that rocky country had a good face, like a tired village doctor or lawyer. Usually I would need almost nothing, but I would buy two lemons, perhaps, or a piece of good soft-firm reblochon cheese from the Savoy—the kind that the houseman I had when I was living in Switzerland used to smuggle dramatically across the Lake of Geneva in a rowboat on dark nights and sell at a high sum to me and other dupes in Vevey. It tasted just as good from the back of a beat-up old grocery truck in Provence.

We always added the lemons to the artichokes and the tomatoes and the other vegetables I kept on the wicker tray, in vague memory of a still life seen somewhere with the same whitewashed walls for background, and we would eat most of the cheese for supper after big bowls of the broth from the soup—the sausage soup, which seemed to be standard in that part of the country and which I soon grew to make almost automatically, like the other housewives. The sausages were lean, dry things, and were boiled whole with whatever vegetables were at hand and then either sliced into the broth or fished out and eaten cold the next day with bread.

I could agree with all the women living in that wild, beautiful country only five miles from Aix and less than two from the screaming Nice–Marseille highway and with three buses to the market a week: it was good to hear the brave, bright, insistent horn-blowing and know that there would be food for our families. And it was good, in a way hard to explain even to myself, after years of deep-freeze and run-of-the-mill marketing in California, to know that, willy-nilly, the fish would spoil by tomorrow, the chops would be practically incandescent in thirty-six hours, and the tomatoes would rot in twelve. It was a kind of race between my gluttony for the fine freshness and my knowledge of its fleeting nature.

To cope with this inescapable rapidity of decay in a warm, bacteria-rich, fly-infested ancient land without any means of cooling except the stone cellars and wells, I kept a small supply of canned vegetables and fruits, and the omnipresent and very handy tubes of everything from salmon butter to various good mustards to concentrated milk and tomato sauce. Then I had on hand several packages of those ugly but valuable soup powders (potato-and-leek, chicken-consommé, fish), which I found made good sauces, too, in a pinch. I had wonderful olive oil, ladled into my bottle from an unctuous vat in Aix that I would not mind being shipped home in, instead of malmsey, and good gutty red-wine vinegar, and I could go up to the farmer's garden whenever I wanted to for tough but delicious salads. Salt is a lot saltier in Provence than at home, and less refined; the pepper is called "grey" and has an overtaste of turpentine, somewhat like the berries I used to chew when they dropped from the feathery pepper trees when I was a little girl in California. And then, of course, there were things that most tin-can cooks have in any modern country: sardines, anchovies, Alsatian sauerkraut for a moment of gastronomical debauchery for my children, one little can of lark *pâté* for me—complete with the first French can opener I had ever been able to work, which I paid rather a lot for in the cutlery shop across from the Palais de Justice.

With the mistral surging and leaning against the windows and the chestnut trees and the red poppies in the meadows, and the spiritual food a part of the whole, we would eat at breakfast canned grapefruit juice, large bowls of *café au lait* with brown sugar, slices of Dijon gingerbread with sweet butter and Alpine honey; at noontime whole new potatoes boiled in their jackets in a big pot of carrots-onions-sausage, which we'd eat later, sweet butter, mild cheese, and a bowl of green olives and little radishes; then for supper the vegetable broth, with the sausage cut in thin rings, the whole new carrots and onions drained and tossed with a little butter and chopped parsley and celery tops from the farmer's garden, and a bowl of three cans mixed together of peaches-pears-pineapple, all with hot, delicious, somewhat charcoalish toast made on one of those flat grill things our parents used at least forty years ago. The next day, there would still be some clear broth, and I would make a jelly from the fruit juices. And I would start over again—probably a big salad, which I would soak in the fountain to rid it of most of the innumerable critters that are considered correct for country produce in Provence, and then a pot of hot small artichokes to eat with melted butter and lemon juice, and sliced tomatoes that had lasted two days after marketing instead of only one because the mistral was blowing, and then maybe soft-boiled eggs from the shepherdess for supper.

There was always that little rich decadent tin of lark *pâté* in the cupboard if I grew bored, or we could stroll down past the great ponds under the plane trees to the deft, friendly welcome of the Restaurant Thomé and eat a grilled pullet or a trout *meunière,* and an orange baked *à la norvégienne.* Or we could stay home and I would try at last the mayonnaise maker I had bought from the fat man in the market.

I I

The second kitchen I had in Provence, when we lived in a part of an old farmhouse at L'Harmas, about three miles from Aix on the Route du Tholonet, was somewhat different from the one at the château a few years before. There was much more luxury. There was a small noisy electric refrigerator called, as everywhere in the world—except, perhaps, America—a "frigidaire." There was an imitation-modern white enamel stove with an oven and four burners. Two of the burners always blew out at once, so, except for the oven, which could not be adjusted to anything but a blasting roar and which I never used, I was just as before, in the older kitchen at the château, with the portable two-burner butane stove. There was the same slab of hollowed marble for a sink, with a round instead of oval basin scooped in it, but it had two taps, which usually had water in them, and quite often there was hot water without my having to light anything, unless someone had taken a bath in the past twelve hours, or there was a drought, or the farm pump was out of order. And there were several more shelves, for dishes and pots.

Two windows, not so high from the ground as in the kitchen over the stables, gave upon a terrace shaded by the tall trees of that country, which must bend to the mistral and shed their branches almost to their tops—a little like the wild pines in Monterey in California, but higher and thinner. The terrace was half wild, too, and could be deep in voluptuous sweet grasses and flowers in the spring, or dry and stinging with pointy weeds, or almost bare until the snow brought soft rains again. It heartened me to watch it and to smell its changing wildness as I stood in the kitchen, using it for its destined purpose—to feed people near me.

The food was the same in both kitchens; it dared me daily. But I must go to Aix for everything this time, for the jeeps and trucks that had come to the château did not seem to come this near the big town. I must get to the open markets and to a few little shops, and then on home, *fast,* before things spoiled. I went on foot. I did not want to have a car; it was too rare a thing to miss, that walking along the little Route du Tholonet—Cézanne's road—in all weathers, against all tides, between the farm and Aix. I rose very early to head for town, carrying a nest of the light straw baskets

that the Gypsies still wove, and then bringing them back
full and heavy in a taxi. (There were few paper sacks in that
country, and baskets and string bags were uniform.)

The Big Market is held three times a week—on Tuesday,
Thursday, and Saturday—but every day, behind the post office, there is the Little Market. Both of them are beautiful
and exciting and soothing, a tonic to the senses, but I think
I loved the little one more.

The Place Richelme et aux Herbes is small, and shaded by
very tall and noble plane trees, which in summer sift down
such a green light as I have seldom seen. Perhaps some fortunate fish have known it, but for human beings it is rare to
float at the bottom of the deeps and yet breathe with rapture
the smells of all the living things spread out to sell in the
pure, filtered moving air. There are snails in cages, ducklings
bright-eyed in their crates, trembling rabbits. There are baskets of fresh herbs, and little piles of edibles gathered at
dawn in a hundred gardens: peas and strawberries in the
spring, small cabbages, apples, new potatoes, and onions and
garlic, following inexorably the farmers' almanac, so that
one soon accustoms the purchases and their uses to the crops
that have been sowed and harvested thus for two thousand
years at least.

Sometimes there was a man with a tiny donkey, selling
baskets of fresh lavender, or crude mint drops from the
Pyrenees, or cough lozenges made from Alpine herbs and
saps. He always put a ringlet of what he was selling that day
over the patient head of his little beast—in hot weather, on
her hat. On one corner, behind the beautiful old grain market that now housed harried postal clerks, there was a quiet
man with a folding table, making metal nameplates for people's doorways, in every kind of painstaking elaborate letter-
ing. Once, he gave me a tiny ring, cut from a peach stone. It

was for *me,* he said without irony, but it would not have fit a newborn babe.

At either end of the little square are small cafés and shops, and opposite the post office is a bleak, busy annex lined with fish markets and shops selling poultry, butter, and all kinds of smoked sausages and hams. Underneath this annex is a well-run and modern public toilet, new since our first stay in Aix and built by the city.

The other market, the big one, is comparatively gigantic, and always very crowded and amusing, but not dream-like, not deep golden green, even in its generous summer shade. I came to know it well, and soon. It is in a long square that is not square at all, with the Palais de Justice on one side, and many small shops and cafés and pharmacies and honorable bookstores and even the Girls' High School fringing it, dominated by the somber, vaguely sinister Church of the Madeleine and—at the time I was there—by two monuments. One of these, the statue of Mirabeau down by the Palais, is now gone. It is said to have been the most ridiculous public monument ever erected in France. This is a broad and daring statement, given the evidence against it, but certainly the small furious figure of Mirabeau, his wig askew and no pockmarks showing, with a knee-high lion cowering against him like a fat poodle, the two shooting up from a stony froth of great-breasted Muses, was very funny, even to the respectful. The monument that remains, the obelisk at the opposite end of the square, is fine indeed, and it rises pure and classical from the fountain at its base, where people dip water for their stalls and the flower women douse their posies.

At the low end of the unsquare square, on the regular Tuesdays, Thursdays, and—especially—Saturdays, is the Flea Market, a reputable debauch of canny snoopers for the great

antique dealers of Paris and London and New York, and
housewives looking for old wineglasses or copper pans, and
happy drifters. Next come the merchants of nails and screws,
junk jewelry, clothes, and kitchen stuff—and very few of
them are fly-by-nights; most have their regular patrons
among people like the farmers and the Algerians, who prefer
to shop under open skies. Then there are always a few bark-
ers under umbrellas, selling the kind of paring knife that for
them alone will cut everything but the Greek alphabet with
a flip of the wrist, or patterns for chic dresses that can be
made from four dish towels. Even Bibles.

And then come the real market stalls, the ones where people buy to live. First of all, next to the café where we had
long liked to eat couscous occasionally, there was (and probably still is) a woman who sold fresh peanuts in their shells.
She was Algerian, I think, or half so, and she had such a de-
lectable texture and color to her skin that I was glad she sold
something I could buy from her, in order to talk a little and
look at her. She was like a ripe, washed apricot, with the
same glowing deep color coming through, as if from far underneath her smooth, tight skin. I have seen such tones in a
few faces and in some stained glass in churches. Most of her
customers were the thin and thick Algerian women who
drifted by twos in their floating flowered dresses along the
aisles of the market, and sometimes I listened to her speaking with them in their breathy language. She thought I was
very funny, to be so plainly Anglo-Saxon and to be buying
peanuts from her.

All the stands were alike and violently different, of course,
and the prices were much the same, and the high quality
was, too. It seemed to be a question of growing used to one
vendor instead of another, and I soon confessed to myself
that it was part of the pleasure to be recognized by some of

the quick, tough people who carried on that never-ending business. They looked so fresh and strong, three times a week, and I felt flabby and exhausted to think that every day—not just three—they must buy, or grow, and load their wares, and drive to this town or that, and set up their stalls, and then at the end start home again. They were cheerful, and as watchful as cats and as impersonal, and yet they knew most of the people who traded with them, and smiled and joked as if I, or she, or that old woman with no teeth, or the smart young matron in white gloves, were a special pet. "Ah, how did they remember *me?*" one would ask delightedly, piling the brass weighing bowls higher with the new potatoes round and hard as plums, the stiff buds of artichokes purple and succulent.

Each time I went in to the markets from L'Harmas, I had quite firmly in my mind what we needed for at least two days ahead, what we might need in case of company, and what I would undoubtedly fall heir to or in love with at the last minute—that minute of decision between a good clean rabbit hanging with his own dignity, albeit naked, or some plucked, blackish pigeons I had just spied in the poultry woman's stand. I would start out with three or four empty baskets, and a coin purse full of the small change essential to such hectic purchasing. I would end with heavy baskets and the purse much lighter, of course; money goes fast for food, and even faster for good food, and although I knew better, I always thought in terms of pounds and ounces and I bought in kilos, so that often when I thought I had two pounds of new peas I was toting two kilograms, or more than double what my mind stupidly kept reckoning. Then I would add two kilos of soft, sweet Valencia oranges from Spain, and a half kilo of lemons; two kilos of beans as long as hairpins and not much thicker; two kilos of country tomatoes, smaller and more pungent than the big handsome ones from up near Avignon; a smoked sausage, the kind still packed into clean, uneven gut skin instead of smooth plastic; some cheese; a last generous basket of dead-ripe gooseberries; a kilo of fresh spaghetti from the fat woman by the fountain; and a clumsy bunch of pale-pink carnations: "Five dozen for two francs today—take advantage, my pretty ladies."

I would be hot, harried, and overladen. Down on the wide shady Cours Mirabeau, which, perhaps rightly, has been called the most beautiful Main Street in the world, there are taxis. I would push toward them. The peanut woman smiled always at me with gaiety and some mockery—she so solid and ripe and apricot brown, I so tottery and foreign—and I would feel stronger for her casual warmth. And under the trees of the Cours, Fernand or Michel would take all my baskets and then me into his taxi for the drive out along Cézanne's road, toward home.

Sometimes I would want him to go faster, for I could almost feel the food in the baskets swelling with juice, growing soft, splitting open in an explosive rush toward ripeness and disintegration. The fruits and vegetables of Provence are dying as they grow—literally leaping from the ancient soil, so filled with natural richnesses and bacilli and fungi that they seem a kind of summing up of whatever they *are*. A tomato there, for instance, is the essence of all tomatoes, of tomato-ness, the way a fragment from a Greek frieze is not a horse but *horse* itself.

As soon as I got back from the markets, I always reorganized everything I had gleaned, as fast as I could, against the onslaughts of time (especially summer time) and insects. First of all, there were the flies. The flies of Provence are said to be the most audacious in the world. People have remarked on this for at least twenty-five hundred years, and I have read that slaves being led in chains from the north to man the galleys anchored at Toulon marched fastest on this last lap of their death trip because of the flies that goaded them. Flourishing descendants of those foul, hungry insects still zigzag in a year-round dance there, especially in spring and summer, or perhaps autumn, and the grim acceptance of them is one of the requirements of life, especially on farms, where the soil itself is an age-old amalgam of droppings from beast and man. They were much worse at the château, of course, for there we lived close to the barns, where the shepherd kept all his sheep-goats-chickens-rabbits, and at least three or four pigs, in a timeless, fruity muck that must surely have glowed in the dark. At L'Harmas, there were only pigeons and two peacocks, but there was fine shade in the summer for the flies of that hillside, and warmth in the winter, and the general interest to be found in four families of two-legged creatures.

The ants are almost as powerful in Provence as the flies, surging relentlessly from the red earth, seeming to walk through wood and stone and metal and glass toward whatever they want. And there are other pests that like the cool tiled floors, or the dark of cupboards, or the moist dimness under old drains: scorpions, centipedes, bees, and wasps, earwigs, crickets, several kinds of gnats, now and then a snail or a tick. It was the flies and the ants I tilted with first and constantly, and I do not think I disliked them the most because they *were* the most but because I hated and still hate the sound and feel of flies, and the smell of ants. We are at odds always. Sometimes I can acknowledge their complacency—they will be here long after I have made my final stand against them.

In the part of the farmhouse where we lived at L'Harmas, there was a dim room that had once been a buttery, or even the farmer's office, I think. It had an uneven tiled floor, two

windows with the shutters left bowed to form a kind of airy
cooler, an old piano with no wires in it, and several hooks let
into the plastered stone walls. From these hooks I hung
whatever I need not cook the minute I got home from Aix:
white onions in a crocheted bag, two kilos of long purple
eggplants that not even a bee could sting, a basket of small,
satin-skinned potatoes. On the old piano I would put a tray
of red tomatoes, which I had placed gently, bottoms up,
with some soft ones, already doomed for tomorrow, to be
eaten tonight, even though they had all been firm and
greenish a few hours before. I would do the same with a tray
of peaches and apricots, and then cover them against the
midges.

Baskets of green peas and one of beans I put upon the
table in the dining room, with pans to catch them when
they were shelled and de-strung by whoever passed by. It was
a house rule, and since everybody talked and sat and drank
and worked in that big white room, as well as eating there
when we were not out under the pine trees on the terrace, it
seemed a pleasant and nearly automatic thing to prepare for
cooking whatever was set out for that.

In the little kitchen, I put things away as fast as I could. If
I had bought meat, it must be prepared for cooking at once,
or at best kept in the minute frigidaire overnight. (In winter, of course, things could be thoroughly wrapped and put
on a window ledge or into a wire cooler, but winter is not
long in that country, and the rats and half-wild farm cats are
very clever about getting around such casual arrangements.)

Then I would pack the sweet fresh butter into a crock and
put it on the old piano in a bowl of water. I washed the
strawberries and cherries tenderly and put them, too, in
heavy bowls in the buttery, to be eaten that day. Salads I
stripped of their bad leaves and soaked for a few minutes in a

dishpan, and then shook out and wrapped in a towel, to be eaten within twenty-four hours. Sometimes I could store clean curly endive or chicory and the coarser lettuces in cellophane bags for a little longer, but not in summer. It was fine, in winter, to have plenty of good Belgian endive—so easy to clean, to store, to serve in many ways.

It takes little time to learn the tricks of any new kitchen if it is a question of survival, and after only a few days at L'Harmas I knew which pans had bad handles, which skillets heated unevenly, which burners on the stove were not worth bothering to light. I knew where I was going to put bottle caps and broken corks and empty anchovy tins, all separate, and what I was going to do about garbage, and where I would hang the dish towels. I also knew where not to trip on a loose tile, and how to keep ants out of the honey jar forever. I remembered a lot of tricks from the last time in Provence, at Le Tholonet.

I remembered that in summer it is dangerous to make any kind of soup and hope to keep some of it for the next day; it will send off the sweet, sickly death smell in only a few hours, even from a jar in the frigidaire. And I remembered how to stew fruits lightly, to keep them overnight for a cool bowl for breakfast or lunch instead of having to eat them all and immediately. Once more I was washing everything fast in pure water from the well instead of the tap, to keep my people from the queasy gripes and grumbles that can plague countryfolk and that used to frighten pioneer American mothers with names like "summer complaint" and "fruit fever."

Soon I would go without thinking to the little icebox and that cool dark buttery, about twice a day, to sniff with my curious nose and to discard ruthlessly what it always hurt me to waste: a bowl of berries delicately veiled with a fine grey

fuzz that was not there an hour ago, three more rotten tomatoes that were firm and fine last night. I would lift the lid
from a pot of leftover ratatouille—was it really all right, or
did I catch a whiff, a hint, of death and decay in it? A deep
sniff might make me decide that it would be safe to bring it
again to the boil, beat it well with some more olive oil, and
chill it to be eaten cold with fresh bread for supper, before an
omelet. There might be one lamb chop left. It would not be
good by noon. I would eat it cold for a secret breakfast, with
a glass of red wine, after the family had scattered. Tomorrow
would be market again.

In winter, when alone, I ate by the fire on the hearth of
the living-dining room. In spring, I carried my plate and
glass into the new warmth of sunlight on the terrace, ankle-
deep in wild flowers and a hundred tender grasses. In summer, I sat by the bowed shutters in the dining room, dim to
baffle the flies, cool already against the blaze of white dusty
heat, vibrating with the love call of the *cigales*. In the autumn, I walked a little away from roof and room to the
meadows turning sere, to the pine woods past the wheat
field, and I put my back against a tree and looked north toward the Mont Ste. Victoire, rising so arrogant and harsh
above the curling foreground. I would think of what I must
buy the next day, and load into the baskets, and then sort
and store and serve forth in the order of Nature itself: first
freshness, then flavor and ripeness, and then decay. And always there were the needs of the people who must live from
Nature, and learn to do so to the best of all their powers and
not die from the traps that she can lay for them, especially in
this ancient teeming land.

It was a good way to live.   —*St. Helena, 1966*

WARTWORT

The first time my two little girls and I lived in Provence, we seemed to fit almost too easily into a pattern that, of course, held rough moments, especially for them as strangers in a land and a language where I had been before. I knew that sooner or later we must leave, and get back into our California skins before we shed them too far. I began to ponder the calendar. We had four-plus months left.

I made a brutal rude switch in all our orderly lives, and we moved abruptly to Le Tholonet, a hamlet about five miles out of Aix that we knew well, as weekend walkers.

Mère Tassy, Mother Superior of the children's school, was disappointed in my bad manners, and regretful at losing two loving receptive young students. Our almost equally dignified landlady, Madame Lanes, was disapproving, and perhaps regretful too. But my daemon was in command, and I had waited and listened and then obeyed, and we decamped.

First we house-sat for a fortnight in a beautiful little *mas* in Châteaunoir, where I had to gather eggs from under

angry hens every day, and Anne and Mary hated to go out
at night to the privy down the path.

But that was where Cézanne had lived and worked, and
they were his intimates, in a strange way I never ques-
tioned. The first day we walked out from Aix along the
Route du Tholonet and sat under a big pine to wait
through a passing autumn rain, and they pointed out
seriously to me that the cracks in the bark of the old tree
were packed with pigments, where someone had scraped a
palette, and then told me that HE had left them there. I
never argued their acceptance of the painter's presence.
(How could anyone, living under the Mont Ste. Victoire?)

The Château du Tholonet had been left in bad shape by
the Invaders after World War II, and was on the rocks financially, people said. The rooms in the old stablehouse,
above the huge dim cave where the coaches and carriages
and hay-wagons had been kept, were being cleaned for possible summer rental. Our friends the Léo Marschutzes were
coming back from their trip to Italy to gather their own
eggs at the *mas* in Châteaunoir, so we moved into the
newly whitewashed dormitory of the old grange.

The first time I went in to the village, over the bridge, I
thought I should try to put my girls in the local one-room
schoolhouse for the rest of the year, but friends said No,
that they would get a bad Provençal accent within a week
or so and learn country playground slang (as if they had
not already done so with the good Dominicans!), and the
schoolma'am was far from welcoming the thought of two
small foreign wanderers tangling up her duties. She had
four grades to teach, and was a skinny old girl, to boot. . . .
And as I watched my daughters turn sweeter and rosier in
the pure air, and heard them gossiping happily with the
old shepherd as they started out for a day with the dogs
and sheep, and listened complacently to their increasingly
Provençal accents, I knew I was right to let them have four

months of freedom, after more than ten of stern discipline, no matter how compassionate, in a new world and another tongue.

My daemon was worth listening to, that time.

That was the summer John and David came to stay with us for a while. In *A Cordiall Water* I did not mention David in this report about John's adventure, because I wanted to keep that small book as short as possible, but he was indeed there! He was a dark-eyed boy of about seven who liked to play kickball outside the stables, under the linden-trees. . . . He and John did not speak French then, but they knew they were with their cousins and went along trustingly with Anne and Mary and the old shepherd and his flock and his dogs, and waded with courage down to a secret pool in the tricky stream under the Tholonet bridge, and smiled correctly if we took them to tea in Aix with old ladies. And that was when Peter Grattan, a true descendant of the Pied Piper on the Irish side, cured John's cruel wart.

How and even why he did it makes a much shorter story than why we were all there at that right time. The conjunction of places and people and of course Time and Space was magical, or perhaps merely miraculous.

I

I have never seen a man recover from a mad dog's bite, even when dosed with powdered liverwort. But I have seen a wart push itself out and away from a boy's hand because of a wort called, plainly enough, wartwort.

This was interesting to watch. It happened a few summers ago, when a little boy called John came from California to

stay on a farm in Provence with me. He arrived with several
bottles which I could see had been very costly, and a habit of
keeping one hand always in his pocket. He did indeed have
the ugliest-looking wart I had ever seen, on the back of his
right hand where it seemed to get hit with things, and to
bang into them and rub against them. John said that he had
used a dozen different medicines, and that if he had not had
his ticket to Provence his mother would have arranged for
an operation to remove this angry lump. Instead, he was
supposed to dab on various things from the bottles, but they
hurt and he kept forgetting. Meanwhile it grew worse, and I
could see that he was humiliated as well as in some discomfort.

I told all this to a friend named Peter who lived in Aix
and who knew so many strange things about other strange
things—a kind of male Lolly Willowes really—that I
thought he might well suggest something about John's bur-
den.

"Of course," Peter said briskly. "Wartwort. Plain everyday
old wartwort. We are walking right on it this minute."

And sure enough, the soft green carpet of June weeds, so
soon to turn dry under the sun of the Provençal summer,
was at least a third made up of this husky little plant. I do
not know any other name for it, but I remember it from the
hills of my childhood in the spring: of a tender green, fairly
low to the ground but straggly, and with fragile juicy stems
which when broken give out a drop or two of sticky white
milk.

How I would have loved to know its impossibly silly
name when I was little! Now, even despairing John bright-
ened at it, and when Peter told him the treatment he
laughed with a mixture of doubt and delight and started it,
right there on the path.

To Get Rid of a Wart in the Spring

Squeeze from the broken end of a wartwort stem the drop of milk, and dab it gently on the wart. Cover the whole wart, using as many stems of this limitless supply as you wish, but do not spread the milk past the edges of the wart. Do this three or four times a day for about two weeks. When the wart begins to push out of the healthy skin, take care not to joggle it and to push the wort milk gently under its loose edges. It will come off of itself, and then for a day or two put the wort milk on the place where it was, in case it left even a trace of its old tissue.

It was fine weather in Provence for the next two weeks, which meant that we ate outdoors and sat or walked or lay within arm's reach of John's remedy.

"Are you joking?" we had asked, and Peter had answered firmly, "You'll see," and we did, for the wart became almost a part of the family, not disgusting or humiliating at all, as we all picked the pretty weed and took turns touching its milk gently onto the intruder.

It changed every day, and once or twice at first it looked rather inflamed and rebellious and I got Peter to reassure me that I was doing no possible harm to indulge in this absorbing game. It began to grow out of the little crater it had made. In about ten days it was gone, one morning when John got up. He looked everywhere in his bed for it, because he wanted to keep it in a little matchbox he had found, to take back to California, but it never showed up.

I emptied the expensive bottles into the compost pit, feeling that plant decay would offset their noxious chemicals. It is possible that they contained exactly what hid in the pearly milk of the wartwort: I shall never know.

But when I look at John's smooth hand now, I remember

what fun it was to rummage in the green weeds for the one
we wanted, and then touch it so daintily to the ugly vanish-
ing lump. Since that summer we have told a few people
about it, but unless they are either from Provence or from
very simple farm stock they do not really believe us.

I I

I know firsthand of a few other cures that use weeds, like the
one for John's wart and the cure for burns from the leaves of
the rabbit ear plant soaked in olive oil. Both these remedies
came from Provence, where I think that everything that
springs from its earth, here rust-red where the vanquished
Saracens dyed it with their infidel blood, there grey with
powdered marble and granite or bright white with salt, every
single tough odorous leaf and stem is known intimately by
the people of the country.

There is not a flower in the wild hills or the tamest gardens there without some quality of cure in it, whether dried,
powdered, steeped, inhaled, pounded. Usually men and
beasts eat the same plants, and for much the same reasons,
but occasionally there is one like the autumn crocus, which
cattle shun, but which is an active remedy in folk medicine
against the gout.

Another cure I learned firsthand on the farm near Aix was
for bad insect bites. It was a kind of rune in the dialect that
Gaby the farmer's wife used, part Provençal and part Pied-
montese, but I cannot rhyme it in my own language.

She sang it out in a rough shout when her husband came
running into the courtyard from the olive orchard, rolling
up his trouser leg as he stumbled along. He yelled something
at her, and "A scorpion bite . . . he's been bitten!" she cried

out. She yelled, then, the rhyme at us, and when we did not understand she ran off herself and came straight back with a handful of leaves, which she scrubbed hard against the part of the farmer's foot where we could see a white blotch already formed from the bite, with pinkening skin around it. The crushed leaves made a greenish stain.

He grinned at us and his cursing died off, and we all drank a cool beer.

Once he had gone back to the orchard, Gaby taught me the remedy in her bad French, which still sang as she repeated it. Here is the only way I can write it, but it is good anyway, a perfect combination of superstition, instinct, and primitive knowledge which may well be part of our own pharmacopoeia, for all I know:

Sure Cure for a Scorpion Bite

Run fast and find three kinds of leaves, one jagged (like the dandelion), one round, and one long. Crush them in your hand and rub them hard over the bitten place. Rub rub *rub*.

"Or if you can't find any leaves," Gaby said, "rub rub *rub* with plenty of good wine vinegar. Same for wasp stings, bee stings. Or any plain brandy.... But the three leaves work the best." —*Aix-en-Provence, 1961*

A
MISSION
ACCOMPLISHED

It seems odd, now when on the turn of a button we can hear and look at fiscal and moral derring-do in capital places, that before things like Watergate, many otherwise preoccupied Americans felt worried by a mere rumor of some peculiar plumbing in central France.

Of course, it is common knowledge that various kinds of emotional excitement, such as anger or even incredulity, can cause startlingly obvious reactions: pallor, faintness, tremblings, and so on. A fine example of this was the audible rumble of an outraged digestive system in our body corporate of Gastronomy in the fifties, when it was reported in metropolitan dailies that a hotel in Dijon, the capital of Burgundy, had red and white wines piped into its bedrooms for the unlimited and free consumption of its guests.

Top-drawer members of eating clubs and wine-and-food

societies from Boston to San Francisco clipped this outrageous bit of information, and passed it around with a basically frightened combination of anger and scornful amusement. What next, what next, in this world of pre-prandial alcoholism—cigarettes with the roast?

It was coincidental that gastronomers of Boston and equally devout colleagues in San Francisco sent me, almost on the same day, the horrid clipping. There was an air of tremulous and almost nauseated disbelief in their accompanying notes. In effect they said, half weeping, half accusing, "You used to live in Dijon. Find out for us. This cannot, must not be. What will people think, if in the wine-capital-itself, ignorant tourists guzzle from taps and fall sodden on their beds? How could any respectable Frenchman have permitted such display of cheap sensationalism? *It cannot be!*"

However, it *was* and it *is* true. I have drunk, myself, from the neat tiny taps in Dijon, and more than once.

First I wrote to my friend Georges, who in the past had been university dean, mayor, and practically every other kind of Dijonnais official except a bishop. I sent him the fullest of the several clippings forwarded to me by outraged American wine-lovers. And then, there I was again, in Dijon where I had learned so much, and so much less than I should have, so many years before. I felt fluttery as once more I walked into the café-restaurant of the Hotel Terminus. I was with Georges, my revered teacher.

The place was trimmer and smarter than it had been years before, more modishly designed for leisurely dining and drinking and card playing and the things Burgundians do in a public room when they like it. Georges told me that it had been badly shattered when the Germans blew up the big station across the square as the last military measure on retreat-

ing in 1944. Certainly the modern translucent glass panels
down the middle of the room were much worthier than the
old *art moderne* imitation Lalique things I remembered, and
the two big dim paintings of student life in Paris in the
eighties had been cleaned and better hung. There was still a
flourishing movie behind the restaurant, with the hotel
above it, and my friend told me that it too remained plain
and good, in spite of the bacchanalian aura of its notorious
Burgundian Rooms. We were to see them as soon as we had
finished our *coq au Chambertin* and I had met Monsieur
Maillard, the proprietor, or one of his hotelkeeper sons.

We went up the wide pleasant stairs to the first floor, and
into one of the four *chambres bourguignonnes,* in the tumbled
process of being turned out between guests. A young Maillard, an attractive solid-looking man who had spent several
years in prison camps and confessed that he still ate green
salads with a barely repressed gluttony, told us that the
rooms were no more in demand than any others in their
price range, but that when travelers found that one was
available, they would take it with an understandable mixture
of amusement and curiosity, in spite of the noise from the
street and the station.

We went through a large simple bedroom hung with soft
green, past two beds which were low and "modern" and the
two shuttered windows which looked out into trees along
the Rue de la Liberté, and into the bathroom. I felt a kind of
quiet nervousness in both myself and my companions: was I
going to be annoyed, scoffing, repelled, shocked, by this
really ridiculous idea of piping good wine through the walls
like water?

"And there it is," Georges said without expression. "You
will notice that Monsieur Maillard has very prudently placed

it near the washbasin, in case some tipsy guest forgets to turn it off properly, and it dribbles."

"More teasing," Maillard said mildly. "Go right ahead, old fellow. You know such a thing has never occurred."

On the wall to the side of the basin, and about breast-high, was what looked like the front half of a fat little wooden wine cask, with two toy spigots sticking out and two pretty little silver *tastevins,* typically Burgundian, hanging beside them. It was the sort of fakey amusing toy an assistant director in Hollywood might order built into his bar, filled with scotch for his housewarming party and then a dust catcher until he became a producer and ordered a bigger and better one. . . .

Monsieur Maillard rather solemnly took down one of the *tastevins* and half filled it with a couple of tablespoons of red wine. "The reservoir is almost empty," he said as he handed it to me. "It is filled every morning, on the top floor, and of course checked at night. In the summer we keep the white wine chilled, but we leave the red alone."

The wine was a good firm *grand ordinaire,* the same Georges and I had drunk downstairs for lunch. It was, the proprietor's son told us, one of the *passe-tous-grains,* a yield from the noble Pinot Noir grape, stretched with Gamay, which some vintners lied about but he felt proud to serve as what it was. Certainly it was pleasant to drink, and he said smilingly that he had never had any complaints about it, either in his restaurant or up in the bedrooms.

I did not taste the white wine, but recognized it from the day before, when I had drunk it at my friend's house with some cold ham and a mild cheese. It had been correctly labeled as an Aligoté, and like the red was a *grand ordinaire* from the southern edge of the Côte d'Or, near Mâcon. By now, in spite of the basically ridiculous position I was in, crowded with two gentlemen in a small bathroom with a fake silver winetaster in my hand, it was plain that I was not at all annoyed, repelled, shocked, or even faintly scoffing. The discreet unvoiced tension vanished. I drained the last sip of the *passe-tous-grains* and as we went out through the shadowy peaceful bedroom I said, "I'm truly glad I saw that, you know."

Georges laughed, and said to Monsieur Maillard, "I showed you the clippings Madame sent. It seems that the venerable wine-and-food boys in the States were really upset at the thought of your vulgar publicity stunt. They envisioned crowds of drunken American tourists, roaring and hiccoughing out of the hotel, spreading scandal and general ill-will."

The young Frenchman grinned comfortably. "I have a pile of clippings a foot high, mostly from America and England! It was indeed a kind of stunt, but I never considered it vulgar. And it has never contributed to the alcoholic problems of the world. The average consumption for two guests in twenty-four hours is much less than a quart, and of course it is mainly white in hot weather and red in the cooler months."

When I asked him which nationality drank the most, he looked thoughtful and said he had not noticed, but would devote himself to some sort of census during the next winter.

"It never occurred to me to raise the price of the rooms," he went on. "With me it was simply a sort of advertising for Dijon, and not for our hotel."

"But how did you ever *think* of piping wine through the walls?" I asked half teasingly as we stood by the clerk's desk in the small entry hall downstairs.

He looked with an air of pretended surprise at Georges. "But listen, old man! Didn't you explain that it is basically an American trick I stole?" They both grinned at me, and Maillard went on, "It happened a couple of years ago during a very dry summer. We had two charming schoolteachers from New York in the room you just saw, and they needed an astonishing amount of ice, or so it seemed to us provincials. One night the maid was ill or something, and I myself ran upstairs with a bowlful from the café. And somewhat to my surprise"—and here Monsieur exchanged a poker-faced look with Georges—"these elderly but charming travelers were drinking floods, literally floods, of plain chilled water!

"I asked them respectfully if this could not be a dangerous habit, digestively speaking, and they assured me that they had drunk nothing but ice water, both night and day, since their arrival in New York from the Midwest some thirty years before. New York, they said, is the ice-water capital of the world, with thousands of miles of pipe carrying nothing but this glacial flood throughout the whole metropolis!

"I put two and two together then, like any businessman, and decided that as a citizen of the wine capital of the world"—and here he and Georges bowed slightly to each other and to me—"it was my clearly indicated duty to pipe wine at the proper temperature into as many of my rooms as possible."

We all sighed and smiled. Maillard held up his hand apologetically. "So far," he added, "that is only four." He sighed again, and we parted with even more than the usual spate of amenities.

"One more proof that water can indeed be changed into wine," Georges murmured as we walked slowly under the trees toward the station. "And now perhaps you can reassure some of those Doubting Thomases, and ease their blood pressure. Tell them that you came, you saw, you *drank*. Even gastronomical publicity is not as indigestible as it sounds in the newspapers. . . ."

Several times over several years I went back to the little bathrooms. It still irked me to tap a cool decent white wine (best before breakfast!) from between the toilet and the washbasin, but I surmounted this aesthetic quibble bravely. And late at night, when traffic thinned below the windows and mysterious bleeps and hummings came from the station, I slipped unsodden into Burgundian dreams with a *tastevin* of "the red" beside my bed.

I had done my earnest best by letter to reassure Yankee doubters that this was no more a trick than any other. It was as logical as the American pipe dream of constant ice water, once as prerequisite to elegant hotel life as air conditioning seems to be in the seventies. There were other things to worry about, perhaps more politic ... but not then, in Dijon.   —*St. Helena, 1970*

A COMMON
DANGER

The Rue Brueys in Aix-en-Provence was named for a venerated Abbé who was born at No. 3, and who lived almost the full span of the seventeenth century. Once, when he was very old, Louis XIV asked about his failing eyesight, and he said enigmatically, "My nephew, sire, who has supplied me with spectacles, says that it is much better."

That is the only anecdote I know about the street where I lived in 1976 at No. 16, so while I was there I decided to talk about the noise, rather than the view through my own eyeglasses, and about the apparent acceptance of it. The street looks much as it did to the old Abbé Brueys, no matter how foggily he may have seen it, but the noise is something even his attentive nephew could not have done much about, much less foretold.

It may be that I was the only resident who was aware of it at all. The one time I saw heads at the windows was when a man gave his first of a series of tremendous sneezes, but as

soon as his strange bellowing yelp was identified, there was
no further interest in him, as far as I know. One night an old
woman on the third floor of No. 16 dumped a pail of water
on some noisy young people who were arguing in the street
about whether to go to a dance hall or listen to Algerian
drumming at a friend's, and I thought things sounded tense
for a few minutes, racially anyway, until the old woman
yelled down that she would call the police and the little
gang dissolved. But not a shutter had opened, not a light
gone on.

(A contradiction: there was one thing that brought heads
out every time, and left small children with their jaws
dropped, the occasional passing from the Place des Tanneurs
to the other end of Brueys of a young man, perhaps seventeen, on the most pitiable motorbike that ever gasped and
clattered. It seemed impossible, each time it happened, that
it *could*. The bike had been tinkered with for so many years
that it resembled nothing ever produced under its own
name. It was small, perhaps once a Honda or Toyota, but
not as big as a Harley 500, nor as puny as a Solex. It seemed
held together with odd bulges of cotton waste, a ragged
scarf, ropes cut out of abandoned tires. There were no real
colors anywhere, like a red fender or a chromium pedal: it
was muckle dun, my mother would have said, which I assume means drab. But its noise, once it started haltingly
down Brueys, was noble. It spluttered and coughed, but in a
lordly, insistent, and somehow very admirable way. It
sounded like an oil drum filled with scraps of glass and iron,
being kicked erratically along the pavement. It *needed* to be
kicked. Every few yards it would stutter and slow down and
then recover itself. And the rider was proud, as he kicked it
along. He did not look at the awed children on the sidewalks, or their parents peering at him from upper windows.

He snorted his way down the street as if he rode a mighty charger. He could never guess that when he finally turned left at the end of Brueys, a kind of sigh went up, a real wave of compassion for such dogged pride.)

Most of the almost constant noise I liked, or at least accepted, but I am constitutionally, ethnically, and perhaps morally averse to noise as such, and am exasperated by it when it is unnecessary or plain ugly. Then it becomes an indefinable invasion of human privacy.

It can also drive some people mad, and I believe the theory that it gradually wears down the subconscious abilities to hear, think, feel. Sometimes, on Brueys, I wondered almost idly . . . impotently anyway . . . how this noise would affect me years from then, in the silence of the ranch in California. Would I lie waiting for the brutality of the Garbage Beast, chewing its horrid cud six days a week? Would I listen in the birdy half-silence of noon in my Far-West valley for the Whistler, and feel strange if a flute did not tootle before suppertime on my hill, where all I could expect would be the deliberate passage of the cows toward their cool troughs?

No. None of this happened, and the noises of Brueys, sometimes almost intolerable and occasionally nightmarish or equally exquisite, were at once as far away as Aix is from Glen Ellen, measured in my private meters.

Brueys is the kind of street that always has clean laundry hanging out of some of the windows, on ingenious plastic and wire gimmicks that housewives attach to their kitchen sills. That is to say, it is a street lived in mostly by working people. If the washing hangs out only on Sundays, it means that both wife and husband have jobs all week. If it is out any-old-day, the woman stays at home to cook and market as well as clean.

There are plenty of children, who trot down toward the

Cours Sextius to the nursery school or, when they are older, play kickball after supper or, when they are still older, speed about on their little Vespas or Toyotas. There are also some retired people: the wives have time to dress up and window-shop as well as market, and the men are not ashamed to carry small baskets of laundry and large boxes of detergent up to the laundromat on the Place des Tanneurs and sit in a café while the suds take over. There are some young couples, mostly night owls, who sometimes talk loudly as they come back from the Hi-Fi Club but usually murmur through their close entwinings. (In 1976 most girls of their age wore stylish wooden clogs, which made footsteps on the street between one o'clock and five in the morning sound as sharp as a newly-shod pony's.)

A lot of the tenants on Brueys are masons, with Italian names of course, who live by choice in their own enclave and often own their buildings. They are more affluent than for some two hundred years, thanks to the boom in renewing old façades and interiors in Le Centre, and their kids ride the snappiest motorbikes, and they give long, noisy dinner parties, and keep on working like demons or angels through heat and hangovers.

The street is one long block of houses on the north side, where I lived, and is intersected halfway along the south side by the Rue de la Fontaine, where the only sign of a fountain is a big dripping hydrant used by the early morning gutter-sweepers. There is a fine fountain at the northeast end, in the Place des Tanneurs, but Brueys is too narrow and bare for its own splashings, or even for a tree.

It is some three hundred years old, and therefore built outside the former city walls. That is why it is straight, instead of being like the crooked lanes-alleys-impasses inside: it was designed deliberately to house wagoners delivering goods to the town, and the few fountains that are left in that whole quarter are obviously made for horses as well as men. The street is perhaps twenty feet wide, with a narrow uneven sidewalk on either side that was probably not there at the beginning, and the dull buildings, much like those in industrial suburbs built in England or America in the past century and today, look scarily alike. Now and then one of the doorways will sport a faintly elegant bit of carving in the stone lintel.

The houses are three or three and a half storeys tall, above the ground floor, and with two or three windows on each storey. On the sidewalk level, there is the front door, one window if the house is three windows wide, and then a garage door of wood or corrugated roll-up metal, into a long, dark, narrow room, often with a dirt floor, where wagons used to be kept among their barrels of oil and wine and their piles of hemp and suchlike. Now almost everybody on Brueys except infants and perhaps a few of the young lovers has his own car, and these can with infinite care be parked three to a cave, with two at the back where the room widens under the staircase, and one in the narrow neck in front.

All Frenchmen are reputed, at least by Anglo-Saxons and Italians, to be unpredictable, erratic, explosive behind the wheel, but they are the most expert backers I have ever watched. In a town like Aix, the street parking is a major problem, and it is as exciting to sit in a café and watch two drivers compete for a curb space not more than six inches longer than one of their cars as it is to look at West Germany beat France in football on television.

One man must and will win. The other laughs, waves, and drives on for another luckier try. All this involves not only perfect balance, but a basically philosophical approach to equally basic proposals like safety, insurance, even sanity.

How can a harried young bank clerk, much less a rising barrister, stay cool and courteous in the face of such decibelic and logistical happenings, several times a day? France is a nation of daredevils, on the tightrope called *le parking*.

This, on a side street like Brueys, is even noisier and more dramatic than on the Cours Mirabeau, because there are no café-sitters to admire and gasp at the maneuverings, no cops to watch for and smile at. Here the action is compressed, and as if seen through the wrong end of an operaglass, but the sound of it has ten times the volume of a looser, wider place. The high walls, facing each other perhaps twenty feet apart; the lack of any trees or vines to absorb some of the noise; the implacable straightness to hold everything knife-sharp in a long, narrow box instead of letting it twist and fade and die as it would farther inside the Old Town: all this makes noise, and what best to do with it is a constant defiance to one's toleration point.

Brueys is marked as a one-way street, but cars can and often do enter from both ends at once, size each other up, and then agree without excitement or visible signals that one or the other will go up onto its nearest sidewalk while the other inches by. Seldom are there horn blasts or screeching brakes. The only sign of frustration is that both cars, purring along until they have passed, will suddenly spurt ahead with a roar worthy of the Grand Prix at Monaco. This unusual license (or tolerance) in Aix, where traffic problems are an increasing trouble for one hundred such reasons, makes for an especial lot of backing and filling on Brueys, already so narrow that it takes a good ten minutes to maneuver even a small car out of the deep garages.

The two wooden doors will be swung open, blocking the sidewalk as well as the view in either direction, or the heavy metal door will be shoved up with a violent crash, and the game will begin: little puffs of pressure on the accelerator, then short violent brakings, a ten-inch dart sideways, a four-inch dart forward, and then eighteen back at a new angle, on and on. Suddenly, the snappy fat new Citroën is *in* . . . or *out* . . . for a few hours, the garage doors slammed down or crashed shut, and the driver roars to the nearest end of the street, whichever way he is pointed.

The essential need to park three cars into every old wagon-room must perforce involve an intimate relationship between the tenants, for mutual agreement as to which one uses his car the most and the most urgently, or does not work on Wednesdays, or is a Sunday driver and can park in the farthest worst corner six days a week. Once, on my way over to the Cours Sextius for vegetables, I watched an old man in felt slippers and the kind of soft brown sweater some Frenchmen seem to grow into like a used skin as soon as they have been retired and start sitting around the house a lot. He looked frail, as if he had been ill during the past winter, but he was an excellent driver, and I felt almost invisible as I admired the way he got a big black sedan onto the street from his garage, in about eight minutes of precise backings and finaglings.

He parked it up on the sidewalk with deft ease, and I went on. When I came back, though, in about a half hour, with my two heavy baskets of vegetables, he was still at work. His elderly wife stood near the garage door, holding his sweater. He slowly wangled a third car up onto the sidewalk behind the black, and then a blue. She opened the trunk of the last car, threw in the sweater, and went into the house. He stretched himself carefully, and began to back the black car deep into the cave. She came down with a small suitcase and a wicker picnic basket. Neither of them seemed to see me, so I stayed to watch, as without a frown or a curse he maneu-

vered the blue car back into the long narrow room lit by one
feeble dangling light bulb, and closed the wooden doors
gently, locked his own car doors because of the stuff inside,
and went into the house with his old lady. I suppose he had
to change into shoes for the weekend ... get a jacket ...
perhaps take a short snooze. I too felt tired. I wondered
about their return. Would he soberly, as today, move out
the two other cars and put his in the far corner and then
move them back, as probably he promised their owners to
do, if ever he and his wife went away for the weekend? Perhaps he would never come back.... But while I still stood
leaning against the wall across the street, dreading to pick up
my two heavy baskets, the people hurried out their door,
with a little fat white dog on a leash, and hopped into their
car like teenagers and roared off down the street. They were
smiling contentedly, and I was still invisible.

Except on Sundays, big trucks turn ponderously into
Brueys from about three o'clock in the morning until six at
night, and if they obviously will meet head on, the one
nearer his end-goal has the right-of-way and the other must
back out. This of course makes for great growls from the
frustrated engines, a lot of amiable shouting from the drivers
and interested onlookers, and clouds of fouled air. And, from
about 4:30 a.m., workers along the street are picked up by
friends, and it seems part of the game to wait in one's flat
until the car roars up and blasts three to six signals, and then
lean out and shout down some pre-dawn badinage like: "Is
that you, you old son-of-a-gun?" "Step on it, Marius!" the
friend will yell back. "We're late already. Give her a kiss for
me, and get on down here," etc., etc. The motors drone in
and out of the windows, and up past the rooftops, impatient,
loud, soft, loud. Every Marius slams shut his door, slams
shut the car door; his friend slams down the street.... They

all try to sound belligerent and mean, *muy macho,* dragging off to work while their pampered Little Women snooze between the sheets. But really they are vigorous, enthusiastic men eager to get out, get away, and then get home again.

A little while after the last of the workmen has driven off with a friend, or has revved up his ancient *"deux chevaux"* and got it jerkily onto the street and banged shut the garage doors and shot off as loudly as possible toward one end or the other of Brueys, the Garbage Monster comes. It really comes twice, once halfway down the street and then backing out; next, about twenty minutes later, up the street from the other direction, after it has apparently gone to some spot and purged itself of the haul so far.

It is an enormous machine, as high as three men, a Juggernaut with a cab up in front and at the back a great revolving mouth. Two small people toss trash into it, everything that has been left out for it the night before, in cartons, plastic bags, old wooden crates. When there looks like a good mouthful, one of the men whistles, or occasionally yells a signal, which apparently can be heard in the cab over the noise of the machinery, and a dreadful crunching starts, with bottles and cans and even old bedsprings being ground and crushed and chewed into a stinking pulp of paper-plastic-metal-glass-rags-chips-of-plaster-and-stone, all held together by rotted food. There are a few more cabalistic whistles, and finally the gigantic Thing moves on toward the Place des Tanneurs and then toward wherever it will spew out what we have fed it.

Once or twice I have neatly and resolutely *not* heard all this pre-dawn rite, by hanging on to a perhaps hypnotic state of near-sleep, of awareness but not consciousness. The Monster has come partway, backed out, disappeared to disgorge itself into some municipal bowel where it will be treated, digested, turned into "fill" for a new subdivision. I have gone into a deep, deliberate trance, perhaps. . . . But then there it was, right under the window, its engine working double-time to turn over the great glut, the two men chirping their signals before they all rumbled and crashed on down the street. I felt sleepily triumphant, in a very fleeting way. Mind over matter, I said, as the Juggernaut trundled along, rolling over past, over present. . . .

Once it almost got ahead of me. I heard it start along the street and then turn back. Something said very distinctly in my over-awakened consciousness, in a too-clear voice, "You are going to be afraid, this time." "Afraid of what?" "Afraid that on the top floor an old woman will toss her fat dog down into the great chewing mouth, or a young woman her baby, or herself, or you. . . . You might lean out, fall out, tumble, get sucked into it with such a crunch soft snap-ping. . . ." I said, "This is not a valid argument about any-thing at all." The voice yelled something about noise. We argued angrily, and my guts shook, and then the Monster had gone past 16 Rue Brueys without my really hearing it, and I took a peaceful post-dawn nap, with gentle dreams. It had been a bad moment, surely, but all was calm on the street for a few minutes after it, and there was a sweet air of survival inside me.

I have long held that everything, inside and out of one's self, is more intense in Provence than anyplace else I know or know about. Salt is almost dangerously saltier. Foods that grow from the earth taste stronger, or subtler, or stranger. If a person feels unwell, he is usually more miserable there than he would be in Sussex or Mendocino County, and if he is exhilarated and happy, it is immeasurably better than it could be anyplace else. In the same way, sound . . . *noise* . . . goes deeper into one's head-mind-innards. It is sharper, or rounder, or more cruel or beautiful. A very few times I felt a flash of panic and near-despair, on Brueys, because of a fear that I could not really tolerate its noise.

Almost everywhere in Aix and, I was told, in every population center in France, or perhaps the world, the constant scream and mutter of too many cars-motorbikes-people-sirens-TV-sets is something to cope with doggedly but not passively (i.e., "It *need not* be this dreadful, Mr. Mayor!"). Conversation is difficult and even impossible in a sidewalk café, and often was in my own flat. Thinking about a laundry list or perhaps a new pair of sandals, or why Pentecost is a national holiday, can for a few minutes or seconds become impossible, a smoke of sound, whirling and rising, a dizzy ride otherwise, before one is back at the desk again, noting and pondering. Sleep, if one permits even a slight tinge of exasperation to color the necessity of being acceptive, can be impossible. And a normal human being who cannot sleep, because he is protesting the constant harsh interruptions of his dark dream-world, can soon fall ill in any of a dozen ways.

So, early in my life on Brueys, I decided to do what I could to make myself a part of the occasionally mad sounds. Otherwise, I still believe, I might well grow wrathy and confused, and thus endanger the whole *élan vital* that I always feel in Aix. After much practice, I think that, except for a few flashes of irrational irritation at people's thoughtlessness or panic at my own craven subconscious, I stayed philosophical and on sane ground. I never ran a fever, and seldom felt dizzy. . . .

Of course the center of any town, the core of existence, now called in Aix *Le Centre,* must have a high decibel level. (There were half a million people there in 1976, instead of less than forty thousand when I first lived there some thirty years ago. And they have cars, motorbikes, power tools, TVs. . . .) But I think, perhaps egocentrically or in self-protection, that 16 Rue Brueys was the *whole* decibel-center, the core of the *core,* of impure as well as innocent pure sound, sound never-ending, always changing, but with a recognizable if erratic rhythm.

With time I felt familiar with much of the hourly and weekly beat of the street's heart. Saturday nights are noisy until dawn, in a generally pleasant, robust way, with long, unmuffled conversations between two men and two girls, or three young men. They are rarely angry, and only once have I heard a drunk: a kid being rescued from an ignominious night by two kindly and comparatively sober peers. A nice thing about Saturdays is that the Juggernaut will not trundle by before dawn on Sundays. Another, at least in the summer, is that some people have gone off for the weekend and the rest will feel like snoozing next morning, not turning on their radios, not banging around their kitchens. Of course there are the women who do the week's wash on Sunday, while the men sleep, and it is a day to walk wisely down the middle of the peaceful street, because of the dripping water from the windows above.

The other days of the week are wilder, sonically. One or two alarm clocks ring, after the Garbage Monster and the car-pool honkings. A few canaries start flirting from their cages with the sleepy swallows. Somebody turns on a radio full blast to catch early broadcasts that are always a lot of senseless commercials cut with snatches of banal folk-loric brayings or accordion wheezings. Doors bang, TVs go on, children eat and yell and then run to school. Somebody tunes in an Algerian station and then perhaps goes out to market with it wailing on alone. Masons and carpenters start on the eternal repairs of an old city; sandblasters saw electrically through half-petrified timbers, chip-chip-chip at stone, plaster, nibble on the strong walls of the Quarter. Countless motorbikes scud or thunder down the street or up. A few teenagers head for school or their apprentice jobs on outrageously overstimulated motorbikes, all insecure and thankful for the lethal power between their legs, unconsciously aware that in a few more years or months they will be happy with a small cheap car and a little wife.

Then women, the housewives untrained or too old for paying jobs, emerge like square solid *forces* from their flats, often with a grandchild or two in tow, and head for the markets. Their voices are robustly, resolutely cheerful, and when one calls, "And how about your old man, Marie-Celeste?" the other yells, "Oh, it's not for long! No pain now . . . numb from the hips down . . . and does he watch me like a hawk!"

I call these hard, gallant female voices "Marseille-fishwife," although they are really plain Mediterranean, and I am always held by the latent sex under all the tough old stridency. Such women turn into burdened animals almost as soon as their breasts bud, but they live a long time and never stop being loved in many ways.

Morning and late afternoons are a good time for practicing music, and within earshot, there can be a flute (sometimes beautiful); a couple of recorders (poor) and a dreadful saxophone; two pianos running a short gamut of abysmal non-promise (one player doing a boogie-woogie left hand with the pedal down, the whole time). Then there are several TV programs of music and talk, all on high volume so that they can be heard by their owners in small flats, and two or three Algerian stations: endless chanted stories of unrequited love, I assume, with a drum or a flute or two.

A lot of dogs bark whimsically but in a frustrated way at all hours.

And this went on above the steady backing and filling of cars and trucks trying to pass, to park, and of roaring, swerving motorbikes. And above it, then, there was and might still be the subtly changing cry of a baby who sounded angrily newborn when I came, wailing day and night, but soon with a stubborn authority in his rage. I worried about his parents: would he succeed in driving them crazy, or neurotic, or plain furious? Mostly I worried about him-her-it; what could weeks of such helpless protest do to his spirit? But in a couple of months there was a calculated cadence in his caterwauling, and I could hear him decide to sleep a little, to pretend to eat. I still worried subliminally. Could I simply not say to him, one person to another, "Let's be *reasonable!*"? Would he not hear my calm voice and give his rage some thought, plan things differently?

There is another noise that is intrinsic to the summer air in Aix: the high whistling of swallows. They swoop in bands over the buildings, in classic formation, and their wings move too fast for the average human eye to follow. They are looking for tiny insects that rise in the early morning and then settle toward the warm earth again at twilight, it is said, or perhaps the insects come down in the cool mornings and then rise at night. . . . But why do the birds sound so shrill, as if they were not live creatures but whistles on long sticks that a thousand little boys whip above their heads? It is a Chinese sound, almost too high to hear, and sometimes it is also almost intolerable, rising and falling as the swift black bodies weave themselves faultlessly into a net of sound in the air.

In 1961, just before the Mutiny in Algeria, people in Aix shook their heads over the early and gigantic waves of swallows from the far troubled south. The last time so many had come so soon was just before the Occupation, they said somberly. Some old people recalled great flocks of them whirling up from Africa before this or that catastrophe in 1914, even by hearsay in 1870. Of course, in 1961 the Mutiny was squelched, and newspapers were printed again in Marseille, and the radios played music once more. But the whirling, shrieking swallows kept on their rehearsal for the next invasion, whenever it might be. Their mad voices, like the angry baby's, still carry over any other roar in the streets, sharp as needles to the merely human ear.

There are other noises on Brueys that make more for pleasure than for pain. There are the voices of Provençal men, for instance. Even when they talk for half an hour under my windows at about four in the morning, or yell pleasantries to one another above the zooming of the waiting car, they sound the way men's voices want to. They are resonant, fairly deep, very flexible, as if their users sing a lot, or perhaps think all speech is indeed song.

The sound of children was always good, except perhaps for the new ones born in protest. I listened without listening, smiled without smiling. Sometimes one little boy spoke Midi-French to a friend answering in what I thought without thinking was Corsican. Once three girls about ten years old were squabbling in Algerian, and finally one of them broke away, saying fiercely in what could as well have been impeccable American or perhaps even Dutch, "Blah, blah, *BLAH*!" The other little girls were struck dumb, and I had learned another international password like "O.K." . . . or "blumjens" for faded denim pants.

Two or three mornings a week a young man with the

brightest red hair I have ever seen came to play water-games along the gutters of Brueys and the Rue de la Fontaine. He crouched over the hydrant across the street from my windows, and shot great tumbling streams this way and that. He looked joyful, and there seemed no real method in his blessed cleansing of our sidewalks, any more than there was in what mornings he might be there. Mondays were always cluttered, because the Juggernaut had two days' garbage to digest, so that animals had found time to drag out bones and rags that the whistling slaves could not pick up. The Redhead would guide a massive flood at them, and look gleeful as they rushed and tumbled along to the nearest drain, and surely Monday was more fun than Tuesday or Wednesday, so why did he sometimes stay away? What was he doing, where? He always made a fine rushing noise in the air, and the street was cool and sweet for a while, but I never heard him make any sound of his own. Once I saw him wave in a serious way to a young mason working on No. 22, down Brueys, but he did not look involved in anything but the big stream of water he could shoot this way and that.

The canaries that old women had in cages in their windows sang a lot, especially while the swallows whistled wildly overhead, but such bird-talk has never interested me. I found it far less disturbing, certainly, than the ridiculous ugly roar of Vespas mounted by adolescents, and perhaps it could be called pretty anywhere but on Brueys, or simply silly. At least it could be unheeded. . . .

A lot of the records people played grew familiar very soon. The best were when the person with the flute practiced by playing counterpoint to chamber music, mostly 'cello. That was something to hope and wait for, and I came to know when things were going well, when the unknown flute player was tired-sad-happy. The worst, probably, was a popular recording of "Donne-Moi," which for a few weeks echoed from one end of Brueys to the other, always loudly, always stupidly. It was sung by a massively "male" baritone, with orchestra, organ, chorus, girl quartet, probably sequinned shirts. . . . I thought of having lived once on a small square in a poor part of Dijon, and the constant sound from two cafés, of Josephine Baker singing *"J'ai deux amours."* I thought of living once above a bar in Chapala, and its nonstop jukebox playing "Amor, Amor, Amor." I liked Baker's bird-like whiney plaint the best. "Donne-Moi" asked for body, kisses, trust, faith, all with much urgent thumping of drums and perhaps chest, but there was no *amor* at all . . . perhaps I mean that there was no real music: no bird voice, no flute. And all three songs had the gift of turning themselves off even while they whirled on insistently for one's outer ear. . . .

For about a week while I lived on Brueys, I fell in love with a whistler, at least enough to wait for his sweet true music and then to miss it when he went away. At first I was struck by the way he carried a long tune with such sureness of pitch and rhythm, and with such obvious enjoyment. He came up the Rue de la Fontaine every day about twelve-thirty when there were few cars and motorbikes, and turned down past my flat, walking briskly in the middle of the street, and not changing one note of his melody. He whistled firmly and clearly. Once he went through three Sousa marches, with all the flourishes. Another day he did "Birth of the Blues," with variations I felt sure were in the recording he had listened to. I decided he was a homesick American student. I had a little fantasy about calling down to him, "That's beautiful." Instead I looked; the fourth day he sounded nearby so sweetly, and sure enough, there was a slender young man in a black velvet suit. . . . But his step was languid, and his face looked loose and peevish, not tight for whistling.

Then around the corner came a short plump man about seventy, swinging along with his bald head a little back, and a look of rapt pleasure at the pure true fluidity of the sound that flowed out of him. He wore the soft, ugly, knitted sweater of a retired clerk or shopkeeper, buttoned over his little round stomach, and his moustache was more white than grey. He walked briskly, with his eyes squinted into light, and that day, he was whistling smoothly knitted excerpts from *My Fair Lady*.

He came three more days, at exactly the same time, and at first I thought his wife did not like him to whistle in the apartment, so that he took the long way home before noon dinner to exercise his lovely companion, the secret music. But after he stopped coming, I decided that his wife was up at the Thermes Sextius for treatments, and that he was whistling either to feel brave or, likelier, to express his relief about her, or fate, or something else.

Once there was the Sneezer, not so joyful, but basically engaging. He walked up the Rue de la Fontaine and past 16 Brueys for about ten days. He had an almost cataclysmic sneeze, with three or four of them during the few minutes it took him to come and then be silently gone. It was almost surely a voluptuous experience for him, occurring between twelve and two when people were at their noon meals and the narrow echoing street was empty, and at first heads showed in several windows, as did my own, for it sounded as if the man was either dying or about to begin a Gargantuan vomit. I have a bad reflex to the sounds of throwing up, and I would press a little secret button in my system and not quite hear the horrible retching sounds coming toward the windows and then growing dimmer. It was soon plain, though, that the big shambling man was not sick, but simply enjoying or at least relaxing himself, perhaps like the Whistler going through a Sousa march in noontime privacy. He made truly mystic uninhibited yelps of preparation for his final paroxysm, and each time he reached the peak of a sneeze, I would wonder, willy-nilly, if he might then fall dead, with satisfaction on his face. But he always went roaring down toward the Cours Sextius, and nobody bothered, after the first few astounding seizures, to do more than half-listen. I still wonder about it, vaguely: such obvious enjoyment . . . perhaps an added pleasure in the narrowed intensity of sound on Brueys, surely more dramatic and more rewarding than on the wide, shady Cours Mirabeau, where few would notice. . . .

At times, from about five-thirty to seven-thirty on weeknights, there was the feeling that I listened to a whole carnival, blurred, just off a cosmic Midway. It was almost tangible, above the racket of the Vespas and trucks hurrying from work, the cars backing into their impossible old garages for the night. It was a kind of pulp, a huge sponge dripping with sound, drops splashing against the walls of the straight, tight street, falling into the sogged air. It was a dozen radios or TVs, a flute tweeting, someone practicing slow clumsy riffs on a one-man percussion set, two pianos with one heavy pedal adding to the blur; it was dozens of families banging pots and clinking forks against their plates; it was the new baby and an Algerian record wailing, and the quick clop of wooden shoes keeping unconscious time to them.

Then, suddenly, a kind of quiet came, on weeknights and even more on Sundays: everyone home, supper finished, the air cooling and sweet. There was no need for extra noise, and even the TVs were turned off. A rare car moved down the street, but slowly, with no need to betray its horsepower. Voices murmured; no need to shout. Brueys sounded much the way it must have in 1650 at the same hour of such a day. Mechanization, for a few fine minutes, had lost command. There was no need to fight noise and its erosion. The respite was balm to frayed jangled inner ears, ears within ears. What would come next, known or unknown, held less danger after such surcease, and not even I, the eavesdropper, felt more puzzled than usual.   —*Aix-en-Provence, 1977*

ABOUT
LOOKING ALONE
AT A PLACE
Arles

 Preface

In December of 1970, after several fine months in Provence
with my sister Norah, I went alone to Arles and Avignon
and then Marseille. We had been in all these familiar places
lately, and I thought that after she left to catch a slow
freighter from Le Havre to San Francisco, it would be an
interesting idea to see how well I could return by myself to
towns where I had always been with loved and trusted
people.

The experience was indeed interesting. I found Arles
bound into the first days of what was to be a national disaster of cold and wind, involving much more than the tradi-
tional mistral. Avignon was even colder. Marseille, later,
was in a state of near-siege, and indeed most of France was
half paralyzed, although the outside world stayed almost

unaware: Army helicopters rescued stranded motorists and
farmers; Red Cross workers fed them in village stations and
churches; passenger trains and planes stopped running. I
got the last train from Avignon to Marseille, and after
some days there I told the concierge at the Good Old
Beauvau that I might stay for another week or more, without a penny, until planes and trains ran again, and he
laughed for one of the few times in his professional life and
said, "Don't worry." So I did not.

There was time to think about Arles, among other
things, as I looked down on the Old Port heaving heavily
under a strong mistral. I decided that it had been a good
stern adventure, mostly for reasons I have clipped from my
discursive report, the rambling kind written by solitary
people. What remained was of others' vitality rather than
my own doggedness. Why write about walking alone
along the Rhône in bitter wind when there is still the
sound of superb Gypsy music in one's head?

I think the winter view of this fascinating town in Provence is not a familiar one, even to people who love the
place as I do. Myself, I do not want to see it again that way,
although I know that it would be easier with a partner.

I The Calendar

In Arles there were no porters. I asked a lot of the people delivering mail and cartons if somebody might come to help
me. They were very busy, but kept telling me not to move.
It was cold on Quai 2, and the trains that tore through the
station made a terrible wind of blowing sand. In about a half
hour an electric wagon loaded on my three bags, and I went

through the underground passage and met it at the baggage office, and a taxi took me to the Hotel Nord-Pinus. I had always liked it because a part of the Roman Forum is carefully built into its walls.

The reception clerk was a tall youngish man, not hostile but not friendly, not offensive but not *in*offensive, in a veiled way. He never looked at me over the next days when he took my key. He seemed impatient, not directly but not *in*directly.

He told me wearily that a room on the Place du Forum, which I had asked for, would be very cold at this season. At my request he showed me one, and then two others at the side and back of the hotel. He was right: the radiators were turned off for the winter, on the front. I decided to settle in a room on the first floor, with a little brass plate on the door, *Chambre Jean Cocteau*. (There were others down the hall: *L'Empéreur, Edith Piaf, Jean Marais, L'Archevèque,* etc.)

Inside my room, pleasant with a big bed and *toile de Jouy* wallpaper, there was a framed photograph of Cocteau and a beautiful male companion at a banquet, probably downstairs. I looked at it. I looked at the big bed. They slept in it, too. It was comfortable.

The armoire was the biggest I ever saw, probably twelve feet high. Inside it was like a little room. Outside it was handsome, with pewter hinges and locks and plaques. It was grotesque. I liked it.

The bathroom was nice, too, roomy and old-fashioned, with cracked white and blue tiles, and a separate toilet with a chain and a wrought-iron tank high above. Good hot water. Ample light.

I walked here and there, taking my bearings in the town again, after I'd put things away. It got dark soon. I bought some carnations, red and white—they cost 1.50 francs apiece, instead of the 20 centimes or so I was used to in Grasse and La Bocca! I bought a bottle of cognac, four fine tangerines, and some grapes, for a possible emergency.

I went down to have a light dinner in the hotel, since I'd seen that the Vaccarès next to the Nord-Pinus was closed for the season (*Michelin* said February!). But so was the hotel restaurant and bar. Damn, I said. Why did you not mention this when I wrote for reservations? Damn. I asked in my mild way where I could go. "Oh, a dozen places," the bored young man said nonchalantly, not looking at me. "Jean will indicate them whenever you wish." "I am hungry *now*," I said. *"Jean!"* he said, and a handsome, weary-looking man about seventeen appeared from somewhere and we went out onto the icy sidewalk. He was shivering in a thin dirty white jacket, and his long blond hair blew into his eyes. "Go down to Les Lices, the big boulevard," he yelled into the wind. "Turn to the right. They're all there, quantities of them!" He ran back into the warm foyer.

Across from the Restaurant Vaccarès, on the other side of the Nord-Pinus, is the Hotel du Forum. It has the same number of rooms, the same prices, but no old piece of Roman wall in its façade, and for vaguely sentimental reasons, that (like the bronze statue of Frédéric Mistral in the Place) had decided me to stay at the older hotel. That first night, I walked once around the little square and then up the Forum's steps, and instantly wished I were no place but there, even without Cocteau's ghost in the armoire or nearby. It was friendly.

There was a big fire in the living room–bar. Electric Christmas decorations went on and off in a bothersome way, but there was a nice homely crèche in the corner. I read a copy of *Le Provençal* and had a good drink and listened to a little boy, plainly of the family, explain the crèche to his visiting uncle. There were sounds from the kitchen, and up-stairs somebody was practicing on the piano, very skillful advanced stuff. I was comfortable, as I could never have been in the "lobby" of the Nord-Pinus even if the restaurant and the bar had been ready to welcome me.

In the small dining room, well and snugly decorated, a workable fire burned on the big grill. There was one waiter, perhaps thirty-five and among the best I have ever watched, constantly attentive but never obtrusive. When one client was called to the telephone, he immediately brought two plate heaters to the table, etc. There were a few single men, *en pension,* and they were served with real elegance. There was a large fat couple. Two old men, short and with the au-thority of position and probably of affluence, ate well in a corner. They spoke Provençal most of the time. When they spoke French, one of them had an American accent and in-flection, as if he had lived in the States a long time.

I ate a plate of the famous *saucisson d'Arles,* which really I do not like any more than I like salami, except perhaps on a picnic. But it was served with a pile of delicious chilled rad-ishes and a pat of butter marked *Forum,* and the waiter set a tall black jar of olives on my table. The long spoon had a lit-tle twig of fresh olive leaves tied to its handle. Then I ate some good braised endive. Then I ate a large wedge of apple tart, one of the three or four best of my life. I drank a half-bottle of Tavel.

I walked a little after the good supper, and decided to stay on in the Cocteau Room but eat mostly at the hotel next door, where I would not feel subtly unwelcome as I did at the Nord-Pinus.

The next day, my head ringing happily with all the night's BELLS, I walked a lot more and went to the big CHRISTMAS MARKET, and here and there. In front of the Town Hall, I

listened to two Gypsies play beautiful guitar MUSIC (see
Notes). Far across town I found the Brasserie Provençale,
which I'd seen mentioned in *Michelin* and then on my way
from the station in the taxi. One woman in a pastry shop
showed me how to get there when I felt lost. "It's a fairly
good place," she said, to encourage me.

It was empty when I went in, but soon filled with many
men, mostly young in groups, with older ones eating alone,
reading *Le Provençal,* like me. I'd seen so many fine *coquillages*
in the Market that I asked if I could have some mussels. The
woman owner looked quite baffled, and then said that some
could be brought from across the street, but was I sure I
meant mussels and not oysters? I said I was sure. Then we
decided on not one dozen, not two dozen, but eighteen.
Then I looked at the menu and said I would like some *pieds-
paquets.* She said warningly, "You know that is *tripe!"* I said,
"Yes, I know." She kept on looking baffled. I added to the
general puzzlement by asking to have an order of gin and an
order of red vermouth and no ice, to mix by myself at the
table. By this time the whole family (a little boy and an old
man playing cards, and two young girls helping during
Christmas vacation as waitresses) watched me anxiously—
and I went right on, because I knew I was almost meaning-
less, almost invisible. There was no hostility, no resentment.
I was not really unwelcome, but on the other hand I was not
welcome.

This seemed true everywhere, almost, in Arles. It was
partly because it was not the season for outsiders, so that the
citizens could enjoy each other as if the few tourists were not
there at all. Everywhere the family had moved into the open,
in little shops, in CAFÉS, hotels (see Notes). The Christmas
decorations were part of the family life. The family crèche
was not there to show off to the rare customers but because

the *family* was there, enjoying the space and comfort that is sold by the square inch during the season. I knew that the crèche the little boy at the Forum was showing his uncle was for his *family*. Perhaps that is why the Nord-Pinus seemed hostile? Its foyer had an artificial tree, rather pretty. The chairs were soft, and the brass was polished. But there was no reality, no clutter and warmth, no *family*. There was the tall almost-rude clerk, and now and then Jean in his dirty white jacket, and a remote small elderly maid who worked until noon. Jean was the clerk's pretty-boy. But it was not a "family."

Another reason for my feeling subtly unwelcome in Arles was that I must depend upon people to feed and house me and the Arlesians are closed PEOPLE, remote, in spite of their reputation for robust gaiety (see Notes). They have a haughty toughness about them, with possible anger and suspicion not far back of their outward courtesy. And when I went into a restaurant or a bar, I was given a table when I asked for it, and I was brought what I ordered to eat and drink, and when I asked for the bill, I was given it, but there was seldom even a pretense of interest in whether or not I liked my table, my meal, whether or not I wanted to drop dead right there. Good evening, yes, no, goodbye.

Of course this was not always true; I was given an occasional fleeting but not perfunctory smile. I think the waiter at the Forum had an interest in my welfare that was not completely professional.

I wandered again. I went to the XIIIth International Salon of Santons in the old town house where Mistral spent his Nobel Prize money to start the Muséon Arlaten. It was interesting. There were a lot of children looking baffled by all the Baby Jesuses in one place.

I felt tired and cold, but stopped at the Town Hall on my

way to the hotel because I saw a group of *tambourinaires* go
in. There was a crowd outside, waiting with photographers,
the cars all beflowered for a couple of weddings. One group
came out, the bride pretty, the groom handsome, the men
wearing huge white carnations. I went into the great vaulted
foyer. Another bride stood in the stone-cold air, a plain girl,
and I hoped she wore winter underwear. The groom was a
tiny man at least twice her age, as thin as a mosquito but less
hungry-looking. People surged in and formed a line behind
them, and they went up the fine stairs to the marriage office,
after the flustered bride figured out how to manage her bou-
quet, her rosary, and her long stiff skirts. It was sad and
pointless, and made one wonder: Why? How much?

A big door was open, off the main hall, and some sort of
dedication was going on, I think of the opening of a show of
Provençal photography, with a table in the middle for wine.
People looked dressed up, and the *tambourinaires* waited in a
corner. I would have liked to hear them, but I was very cold,
and not invited anyway. (Nobody would have minded . . .)

I rested under Cocteau's feather puff. For a sou I'd have
stayed there. I talked sternly with myself, put on a new face,
and stopped on the way out at the desk: Jean was there and I
feel more at ease with him than with his boss. I told him I
was a little desperate about food. He wrote the name of a restaurant, L'Assenage, and I knew where it was because in the
morning I had searched out the municipal theatre and read
several restaurant signs, mostly saying *Annual Closing*. It was
empty but open, and gradually filling when I left in time for
the play I'd bought a ticket for in the morning. I sat close to
the GRILL (see Notes). I drank a vermouth-gin, a kind of
game by now to see what it would be and how much it
would cost. (This one was generous, and cost 6 francs. They
ranged from undrinkable to delicious, puny to goblet size,

expensive to exorbitant, everywhere in Provence from village pub to grand-luxe bars.)

The *crudités* were really so, except for the bowl of cooked rice, routine in Arles near the Camargue: carrots, *céleri-rave*, red cabbage, all shaved, and radishes, and a bowl of good thickish vinaigrette. The waitress grilled a piece of lamb on the hearth—asked me how I liked it done. I drank a small rosé. I had to leave too soon. The waitress was vaguely dismayed. I'd return, I said.

Les Nonnes, presented by the leftist Southeast Cultural Center, was the kind of earnest theatrical effort that makes one wonder. A general gloom lies like dust everywhere in a dingy provincial theatre, especially in cold winter. I would have left at the entr'acte, but was not ready for bed so soon again.

It was strange, to walk home. The Christmas lights strung across all the STREETS gave a white glare, almost without shadows (see Notes). I felt a little shaky and old, and crossed the silent intersections cautiously, with vague thoughts of stumbling and lying unseen until morning in the icy gutters. Ridiculous, I said.

By the next morning I was plainly counting hours, not daring to count days, until I could leave, go away, go *where?* I dawdled in the room, and ate more breakfast than I wanted, because it tasted good and I felt hungry.

St. Trophime was locked when I went by at noon, and it was *Sunday!* What if I had needed sanctuary? I felt peevish. All the *bar-tabacs* were closed, even the one supposed to be open seven days a week, so I could not buy a paper. The light was thin, and the air very cold. On the Boulevard, the brasseries were filled, at least in the front windows, by solid couples out for their Sunday *apéros.* I went into one, and sat with a vermouth-gin as long as I could stand feeling thin and invisible among so many fat people. Then I went further toward the back for some lunch. The waitress was a tall skinny blond girl, very worn and with a lovely impudent profile which sat oddly on her air of bitter experience. I ordered a demi of rosé, a very good one from a small vineyard near Les Baux, and a *salade Camargaise* and roast chicken. The salad was good, of tomatoes, olives, ham, chicken, and of course rice. The chicken was not well enough done, very bloody, but there were good *frites* with it, and a small lettuce salad. I drank an espresso, loitering.

It was a good afternoon. I walked to Les Alyscamps. Down on the caravan square (no market wagons, no nomads), many games of *pétanque* went on. The men all wore Sunday black and brown. The hard earth was sandy-grey, and the trees, some of them with enormous gnarled trunks, were silvery and bare. The only color was from some neat green and blue trailer homes. The Youth Hostel was closed.

Until just as I left Les Alyscamps, I was the only person there besides the old guardian and his dog Pimpette. I walked on as slowly as the cold air allowed me to. Inside St. Honorat the light slanted through the dirty faded windows. I felt fine, quiet, almost cheerful among all the empty sarcophagi: little, enormous, mostly plain. I wondered how they were sealed, to hold in the first hundred years or so of rotting flesh. By now they were pure. One side chapel, at its first step, had a white marble marker in the floor, with three crouching dogs and a pair of scissors still showing on it. Why? I wanted to ask the guardian, but when I went out he was busy with two late tourists. Pimpette yapped busily.

I stopped again at the brasserie on Les Lices, to thaw myself. The crowd was younger and noisier, and I sat in a window and watched the Sunday strollers try not to walk faster than usual to beat the wind.

In the morning I had planned to have a good friendly supper at the Forum: the tureen of hot soup on a little warmer, perhaps a grilled chop, certainly more apple tart. I would order a red wine for a change. But when I found the first of several *tabacs* closed, and went across the Place to the "new" hotel, there was by its brass push button a small card in French, English, German: *Restaurant closed.* I felt bleak. So after my second drawn-out stop at the smoky mediocre brasserie I walked back to St. Trophime. It was open, but dim and shabby, with no crèche. I looked in the few lighted windows of small dull shops, and went across town to the Rhône: Once I heard some good hot gospel rock from a tightly shuttered house, and the sound of talking and laughing.

Coming back toward the hotel I stopped at the one little pastry shop I saw open, and bought a heavy-looking sausage roll and talked for a minute with the comparatively friendly woman there, about weather of course, and then the gastronomical hazards of being a stranger in a town closed for the winter season. She knew of one place that might be open: L'Assenage. I went on back to the Nord-Pinus, and took a hot bath, and the little supper tasted pleasant, after I put the fruit on the outside windowsill to chill and warmed the roll on the radiator, and made myself a brandy and tap water.

I felt angered, but in a remote way. When I had come in with my paper bag of supper, the tall young man was for the first time more than almost civil (he was never exactly *un*-civil). He asked me in a roundabout rather mocking way if my work was going well (the maid and Jean came in for bed and tray while I was writing). I said it was, but that my problem was finding a place to eat. (I *wanted* to add that it was unfortunate that I'd not been told that the hotel's restaurant was closed.) He laughed scornfully, and said as he walked away, "Oh, that doesn't matter! You're simply on a diet—good for your health to stop eating!" You rat-bastard, I thought in a controlled and somewhat bored and automatic way. But halfway through the pastry roll I forgot my anger. Sleep was good, wrapped in goose down and the sound of bells.

The next morning I walked across to the Forum, because I saw different notices on the menu board: it would be *open* that night! I felt lightsome. I went to the Musée d'Art Chrétien. I paid the *gardien* in his little warm glass cage and a girl, plain but nicely rounded and neat, asked me with a fairly "good" British accent if I was going down to the Roman galleries. If so, she wanted to go with me. I agreed, feeling amused and *je-m'en-fichiste* and perhaps welcoming of company. The girl was nice, not effusive or silly. We went together into mysterious warmth, the never-changing UNDERGROUND (see Notes). The lights were artful, and of course we grew used to them. And it was a peculiar experience to be there under the old city. There was no sound except for the full rushing of a *source,* and then diminishing drops from it into lower galleries. The air was dry, with a metallic polish to it, perhaps in the mind. I did not feel at all uneasy as I would have on top of a tower, and when we came up the girl went one way and I another, courteously.

I walked down Les Lices and had a slow drink at "the" brasserie, sitting in the glassed sunlight reading Maigret. There were no people to watch. Then I went to the place where a sad billboard said *Ici Se Habla Español*. It was bleak and shabby. The waiter on one side was exhausted, with broken feet. He motioned me without even a flicked lip muscle to the other side when I said I would like to eat. I sat at one of the six or eight tables with the usual paper mats on them, and my waiter was young and doomed to low-grade jobs, very unprepossessing physically, although I saw him laugh once, back at the bar, and he had a flash of pure joy to him, like a child.

I asked for *crudités* and a cheese omelet and a demi of rosé, and read more. Next to me a family of *pieds-noirs*, all blue-eyed and pale except for one dark boy with a Spanish accent, spoke what I think was Algerian. Later two young salesmen ate *pieds-paquets*. Across the big ugly room young people, mostly girls, drank beer or espressos at a few tables.

I heard chair legs scrape, and looked up from my book to see if the mute sickly old waiter was going to let people eat on his side. But almost at once a quick rhythmical whimpering began. Was a child ill? The sound went on, and the owner came wearily from behind the bar, took a look, went back for his wife. She showed more emotion, and clutched her breasts. A young man sat down heavily at the edge of the circle of girls bending over, and looked as if he might faint or vomit, and I wondered if he'd seen some kind of fit, the stiff foaming kind. But the sound was not right for that.

The few other customers went, looked down, went away again with pale faces. The boss's wife called for an ambulance. The soft measured whimpers changed to a steady gentle mumble, almost like speech. One girl hurried into her coat. A red ambulance, Secours Routier, whipped around and in front, and the sick girl, all of this within five minutes or so, was on a litter and gone, and people went soberly back to their tables. I watched her from across the room as she was lifted from the floor to the stretcher and then carried out. Her mumble had stopped. She looked beautiful: young, peaceful, and above all, pale. Had she taken poison? Had her heart failed her? Was she dead? I think she still breathed. I'll never know. I think that she was unconscious before she uttered a sound.

I returned to my Maigret. It was as if I were a fish in a bowl, watching another world through curved glass. The girl's first moans meant something, for I have heard a whipped child sob that way in final exhaustion. But I felt no pain to absorb, and could not guess possible grief. My curiosity, in other words, was numb. Now I can hear some astonishment in the first whimperings, and I shall always see the purity of her unconscious face on the stretcher.

The food was very bad. I was hungry, too; the wine was all right, but full of shards from its cork, which the distressed young WAITER had broken (see Notes). When I went out, the old one with the bad feet held open the door for me and said, *"Bien! Bien!"* as if to get rid of the last customer who had heard the girl.

I walked a lot, finally out to the Musée Réattu on the great river. It is a beautiful place, beautifully tended, with a fine permanent collection of photographs of Provence, always something new, repairs always going on. The Rhône rushes by. That day it was bitterly, brutally cold, and the concierge looked strangely at me, and with some relief, as I finally left the old stone townhouse.

I thought about places, at dinner. In some, one is at ease. I was, in the Forum. I almost breezed in, and the waiter breezed out to meet me, and I hung my coat on a rack as if it was familiar instead of the only time I'd done it. I sat at a table reading, with a drink. The other people, near the fire on the hearth, were two young ones kissing and murmuring at the end of the room. The dining room was fine. I asked myself why I'd turned my back shyly to it, as soon as I sat down and thought. But I had. So I read now and then, listened, ate. Two more couples came, and two men alone, and two women together. People whispered in spite of the discreet and excellent radio music and the kitchen sounds. It was a good place, like a balm on some unidentified sore or wound. I decided some things about Arles that were doubtless borne on the wind that now howled between my two places, my chosen table and my chosen bed. The next day I would move north to Avignon, where a kinder hostel awaited, but for this sheltered moment I was freely warm and alive.

I I Notes

BELLS. Very early in the mornings, after midnight that is, I could hear five—perhaps four, because two of the clocks or steeples rang two or three. The first one on each hour was the town clock, near to my window. Sometimes when the wind was right it sounded almost on top of me, in my guts: the three first quarters, on two notes, then a ponderous deeper note. This took quite a time, for the elevens and twelves. And every quarter hour sounded, 1·2 for fifteen minutes, 1·2-1·2 for the half hour, and so on. The next-nearest bell may have been on St. Trophime—almost in my room at times. It sounded only the hours, one minute after the town clock had finished and, of course, with another tone. Then in the quiet of the early day I could hear two other bells, sweeter and far away, on the hours or in chorus.

The tones outside my window were harsh and not *true.* They pleased me only because I love bells in a town, any town. But they were literally *flat,* as if they were gongs or cymbals being struck, and not curved hollow instruments.

They had a powerful and jarring vibration, which sometimes set my teeth to hurting when I was not even aware I listened. Still I liked them, since they were bells.

Two or three times a different deep old solemn bell tolled, probably from St. Trophime. It was plainly some religious signal, as for a funeral. And at odd times every bell in town, in my hearing anyway, rang at once—Saturday midnight, Sunday morning at seven, and Monday too, one night at six. Perhaps it was something to do with Christmas week. And once there seemed to be a definite pattern, like change ringing except from several steeples instead of only one.

This auditory awareness is considered an assault by many people who think nothing of the noise in an American city. They are, by assumption anyway, driven half mad by an intrusive bell ringing in the night, when constant police and fire sirens do no more than reassure them. The bells of Arles must be a torture to such wanderers from their familiar decibel-tolerance. Fortunately for me, I drew reassurance from them, no matter where they came from to my warm downy bed in the Nord-Pinus, and their night pattern soon grew to be a part of my own.

CHRISTMAS MARKET ON LES LICES. It was one of the most extraordinary I have ever seen. In Marseille, on the streets off the Canebière, it seems a daily thing. One can duck in and out of it. There in Arles it flowed along both sides of the "Grand Boulevard" to celebrate the holidays, and I was swept-pulled-pushed-*thrust* into its mainstream as helplessly as an empty plastic bottle. I bobbed along. I knew I would end somewhere. The pores of other dispassionate bodies kept me warm. I was unaware of my cold feet, and never saw them or any others for the mile or so I walked on each side, if I can say we actually *walked.*

Up toward the theatre, when I got sucked into the flow, there were racks and piles of all kinds of clothing—sheets, caps, shoes, complete outfits for all sizes and sexes, shapeless pinafores, glittering gold sequin tunics, shoddy modish pants suits for fat women. There were piles of "genuine imported tweeds," and brocades and mattress ticking. It was dull to look at, but the people shuffled along warily, sniffing out good buys for Christmas, school, work.

Somehow I got across Les Lices, heading the other way. I must have been pushed across with a surge of people when a policeman held up his white mitten. It was all food, in endless stands on both sides of the packed walk. I have never seen so many different kinds of sausages, meat *pâtés* and rolls, cuts of horse-cow-pig, dead rabbits dripping blood into little paper cups tied over their noses, bunches of wild birds hanging like feathery grapes, more wild birds naked and tiny on white enameled trays. I have never seen so many great wooden buckets of olives of every kind and size and color. There was one tub of green olives mixed with little pickled onions and slices of sickly-looking bitter orange. There were olives stuffed, smooth, wrinkled, shiny, dull. And there were tubs of all kinds of pickles. And never have I seen so many spices, in packets-boxes-jars, aromatics from Provence, pepper from far places.

Then there were dozens of stands of nothing but grains: rice of countless kinds and qualities, ten different types of couscous, pounded wheat and millet. There was a formless section of unattractive dry sweet cookies of peculiar shapes and colors, and great glittering tins of hard candies. At one modest stand I asked for a 2-franc sack of honey drops, and said in a foolish way, "Is it Alpine?" and the young man said, "Of course! Please try one!" and he held out a big plastic bag to me. He had a nice smile, and was stamping his feet

to keep warm. The honey drop was good. I felt warmed by
him, too. He was not doing any business. His little sacks
were lying there in the pale cold light, filled with herbal
cough drops, mint tablets, my honey. He looked more like a
farmhand than a market man, and I shall no doubt remember him now and then until my mind dies.

There were vegetables, on and on. Perhaps I have never
walked past so many unattainable beauties. I was hungry,
and I thought of what I could do, if I were home, with the
crisp gleaming glowing brilliance of all the lettuces and en-
dives and purple eggplants and tiny turnips and strange
twists and pats and whorls of live freshness. It was beyond
my grasp, except spiritually, for any nourishment past my
eye, occasionally my nose. I was hotel bound.

All along the surging pushing alleyway between the
stands were women crouching in front of baskets of lemons,
or holding out handfuls of garlic. They did not even have a
plank and two boxes for a little table, like the boy with the
honey drops. And there were thick clots of people waiting
for slabs of hot nasty-looking pizza at stands with stoves and
fancy ovens: pots of sausages boiling and steaming, piles of
split rolls stuffed with pink diced ham. And there were
stands with kettles of hot oil where strange Tunisian sweets
bobbed, to be fished out onto greasy papers and doused with
bright yellow and pink syrups. The ground was littered with
half-eaten snacks, and wind caught up the papers now and
then, in a hollow in the mob of people.

I found myself across the Boulevard again, in a surge of
laden women and men dragging children. There were endless rows of live barnyard fowls crowded into pens. Huge
geese ambled about on long cords, and turkeys lay on their
sides with their legs tied, their heads up like plumed snakes.
More bunches of dead field birds, and pheasants with their

plumage dimming, hung from racks. And there were rows of
potted plants, Christmas trees, clumps of mistletoe, and a
wide walkway up to the Théâtre Antique with tables and
chairs, old clocks, swords, dueling pistols, tile washtubs,
piles of shabby books, portfolios of prints, a trunkful of rags
of silk and damask.

Back down onto Les Lices, there were the inevitable
ghosts who sell knife sharpeners, carrot slicers, magic glue
that will mend *anything*—then more clothes, so dismally
shoddy. . . .

My feet hurt, through their general numbness. All the
brasseries were jammed with men waiting to reload their
stuff after the Market. They drank standing, and the air was
blue. At the tables beautiful young Algerian and Gypsy men
played cards and drank orange sodas. I stumped along the
cold pavement covered with trash, and it felt good to turn
off Les Lices, out of the ruthless surge of the dark crowd—
the black eyes, black clothes. . . .

Later that day, in perhaps two hours, I went back to the
Boulevard, and there was not one scrap of paper, one
smudge of greasy water, to show the hundreds of stands, the
thousands of people that had pushed and eaten and spat
there for several hours. The wind lifted a little dust in front
of the empty Hotel Jules César. Across the wide street, on
the town side, the cafés were empty. I went into one. It still
smelled of *pastis,* or perhaps it would anyway. It was warm,
and quiet, and I sat drinking a brandy and Perrier and wondering about the human belly and bowels.

Never had I seen so much to eat-wear-devour-suck-tear-
kill-ravel-sew—and suddenly I thought of the long double
line of open tables and vans *behind* the two main alleys, toward the country, with a tang of salt, and with more fish and
shellfish than I have ever dreamed of, dripping down onto

the cold pavement, bubbling, crawling, trying to hop or writhe away, sloshed now and then to stay gleaming, hacked alive according to one's uses, some flesh marble white, some bruised or bloody red. The flea-like *crevettes grises* waved their hairy legs in tiny impotence. There were a few elegant live lobsters. Most of the oysters were small, not costly big ones. The mussels were little, dark purple. There were millions of sea urchins slowly moving their spines. A man picked up a pale *supion* (a small, delicate cuttlefish), pulled out its bone with thumb and finger, tipped back his own head to let it slide down his throat, tentacles first, and he chewing as it went. It looked easy, but not enticing—rather crisp, to bite along, like a new eraser at school?

I wondered where all the fish and shellfish went, in Arles, for even in the few eating places still open, there was absolutely no sign of selling them, nor had I even seen a store with fish on the counters. There were a lot of tubs of tiny shells and fishes too small to bother to eat whole. Of course there was wilted sea lettuce everywhere, great beds of it, and the whole look and smell of the Market there, even in the hard cold, was sharp and salty, very good.

There was one short orderly demonstration against the Burgos trials in Spain—perhaps two hundred well-organized young people with a banner I never did see to read, and a few red flags. Behind them straggled a hundred mixed older people, mostly men. They chanted, *"À—bas—le fasCISme."* People paid no heed at all, that I could see—no scorn, no sympathy.

Everyone was alone, concentrating. I went along, not pushed or shoved but unseen in the concerted need to provide for Christmas, for school clothes, for something good to eat. There was no gaiety about marketing, if there ever was any in Arles: Christmas was a serious problem, one to be faced with tough realistic courage, and not some crazy pagan festival as it would be farther south, in Aix or Marseille. People were not freezing, at least outwardly, as they surged along Les Lices past all the goodies, but they did not smile.

MUSIC. The Saturday before Christmas, when I finally left the Big Market on Les Lices and headed toward the Place de la République, there was the sound of guitars. In front of the Town Hall I could see a knot of young men, dressed mostly in black, and wearing black hats. Two women behind me began to hurry toward the group, perhaps in case it meant a funeral, but when they saw that the men were dark like Algerians they said, *"O alors!"* in dismissal, and turned back toward the Boulevard.

The music grew more insistent. I seemed to melt into the ring of youths, so that now and then the musicians looked straight into my eyes, through me, as far as fishes look through water, not at all, infinitely. A third man stood tensely near the two players, and now and then put back his head and cried out in a strange beautiful wail that was not like anything I had ever heard, not Flamenco, not Arab, but still familiar and right.

The music was good. It had authenticity and power, and as far as I could tell it was being played because it had to be, there and then, for indisputable reasons never explained: not for money, certainly, nor for any apparent ceremony. Later I read in the paper an ad for a nightclub where "The Three Gypsy Brothers" were going to perform for a Christmas *réveillon.* Perhaps this was a rehearsal at the side of the small square lined with ancient massive stone buildings. The music made it logical, with its strength and resonance.

It was extremely intricate, like some of the recordings by Manitas de Plata, technically far beyond me, but with a con-

trol and a rhythm that spoke directly to the stones, to the
air. I felt stirred, and my mind laughed.

The leader was theatrically handsome, dressed in gaudy
stylish clothes: black, tight, flaring, pinched, with impecca-
bly white shirt, high collar touching the ears. He had a
moustache as thin as a knife-cut, and his lips were carved and
scornful. He directed the others with little grunts and
moans, and with his intense eyes, while his face stayed almost like stone.

One younger man was tall and svelte, with a darker skin
than the leader, and handsome too. To my ear he played
beautifully, but the older man was fiercely observant and
critical in an almost mute way, and they seemed in perfect
agreement. The third boy carried his guitar, and stood at the
edge of the bunched crowd. Once he let out a soft wailing
song, a few bars, and the leader gave him an impatient glare
and then flashed his eyes back to the one playing with him.
They faced one another, almost touching their instruments,
and their hands went too fast to follow.

The crowd was all male, mostly under twenty except for
one man about forty who was probably Northern or
English, shabbily dressed and obviously knowledgeable
about the music. Once he looked at me in a detached way
with blue eyes, and then he was like the leader, as remote as a
fish. I was not a female, not even *there*—his fellow traveler.

The music pounded and pressed into the cold air. Suddenly I knew I must walk away from it, from the silent
crowd in its cheap modish clothes, from the two willowy
boys, one waiting and one being swept along by the leader.
He whipped sound until it crackled around us, seemed almost to stop, and then rushed ahead with a look of con-
tempt lifting the thin scar of hair above his beautiful lips. I
almost staggered into the hall of the Hotel de Ville. I could

not look again into his blind eyes; he was probably the most absorbed human being I ever saw. He was coupled to his instrument like a fine stallion to a mare, and as unaware of anything but his own rhythmic necessities. I walked into the great vault of the marriage hall refreshed and different, if dizzied.

That was the realest music, in Arles and perhaps ever.

It was good, too, the first night at the Forum, to hear that piano being worked at, upstairs in the hotel. There was a radio, which one of the sons turned up and down from the bar now and then, the way young people do. It was inoffensive, and better than the plain sound of the one waiter's footsteps and the crunchings of a few clients!

And one day, Sunday I think, when I walked on toward the Nord-Pinus after going to Les Alyscamps as slowly as I could in the cold to make the time pass, I went down a steep street from the Public Gardens behind the Théâtre Antique and from an elegant house came a very good sound of gospel rock, surely a recording. It was fine, very gutty. I slowed as much as I dared, in the bone-cold wind. Then it stopped, behind the closed shutters. It came from the ground floor: perhaps teenage children of the concierge? There was no other sound but the wind.

And that was all the music I heard in Arles. It was too cold for beggars to sing, if they ever do in Arles.

CAFÉS. There were dozens of them, small and smoky and crowded with men, especially at night. On the Place du Forum there were four or perhaps six. The first night, when I found the hotel bar and restaurant closed, I thought it would be fun to have a vermouth on the square. But it was very cold (in the summer I could have sat outside), and every pub looked *private,* so that I knew that if I went in, the loud talk would stop for a time, and a man would come and swab off my table, and then gradually the voices would rise again but not in the same way until I left. The air everywhere was heavy with smoke. There would be the smell of *pastis* and cold leather and sweat, and an impatience with my intrusion. So I walked on.

There were several fairly big, indeed barn-like brasseries along Les Lices. In the summer the terraces must be lively; they were wide, and probably crowded with tourists, and half the young men I saw wandering in twos and threes could well have jobs in them, doing *"limonade."* The one across from the Hotel Jules César (*Fermeture Annuelle,* which was fine with me, since I have no good memories of it, over some forty-one years!) was the best maintained. It seemed popular, with a mixed crowd of aimless young men, their girlfriends, businessmen, on Sundays elderly *bourgeois* couples out for a weekly drink after church, and families in from the farms, eating enormously of mediocre food.

The *ton* diminished fast as one went along the Boulevard toward the municipal theatre: smeared windows, weary broken waiters. The first day I walked down that way, it was during the Big Market, and every café was crowded with slender dark men smiling while their women worked in the countless stands. The next day, two or three of the brasseries were closed, with their chairs tipped over the tabletops behind the greasy glass. Once I ate lunch in one, and the clients were sparse and poor in purse—and very ill fed.

And as far as I know, there is no alternative in Arles, no compromise between the tight little neighborhood bar and the big ugly brasseries along Les Lices. Of course, they all manage to put out two or a hundred tables in the summer. But I saw them when they were run solely, if at all, for the "regulars." They were very personal, plainly for the people who needed them daily. The two big brasseries I went into treated me with carefree attention, not really courteously but not rudely. And I can see how, in such circumstances (a closed-off town, asleep between bouts of *tourisme*), somebody like me needs a good small hotel bar. If there had been one open in the Nord-Pinus, I almost surely would have gone into it once or twice a day, in spite of my lasting dislike of the whole place. It would be a fairly easy change of pace, after a day of looking at Roman carvings and shop windows.

PEOPLE. I think the ones I saw were mostly of the lower-middle and lower classes, except for those few elderly *bourgeois* drinking their post-church *apéritifs* on Sunday in the "best" brasserie, and the audience at the theatre.

Les Nonnes, given by the leftist Southeast Cultural Center, was the kind of play that makes one shrug about the relative values of current success. And about acting as such. And about stage décor. And lighting.

The audience was *bourgeois:* rather dissipated-sophisticated-country-gentry trying to keep up with local attempts at culture. They wore casually stylish informal clothes, and knew each other and went out to the nearest bar at the entr'acte and came back with the studied and rather rude nonchalance of people who feel as if they belong to a different club from the rest of the audience—which indeed they do—different accents, hair, manners. "The rest of the people" that night were young, rather obviously the town's "freethinkers" hoping for a good modern piece of theatre: after all, the playwright was a Cuban, and therefore a Communist; he was half Negro and therefore all-knowing; he was anti-Christian so therefore the play would be shocking, etc., etc.

But except in those two places, the ugly café and the shabby old theatre, and partly because of the closed season, I

saw only people of the working level, and of all ages. I noticed that there were few oldsters. I think this was mostly
because of the hard cold. I saw a few old women, in black
shawls of course, bent over in the exaggerated spinal curva-
ture of people who have for generations picked grapes and
cultivated the earth with short tools. . . .

In the vigorous years, I suppose between twenty-five and
forty, the people were short, and broad. The men had wide
shoulders, as did the women, and they all had a stocky look,
part bone and muscle and part fat. They were like the famous little sausages of the town: solid, meaty, *gutty*. They
wore their heavy dark clothes in a tight way, as if they were
literally stuffed into them. The men still looked light on
their feet, as if they had once been part of the amateur box-
ing clubs or the bands of youths who train for small roles in
the *corridas* at Les Arènes. The women were tough and hard,
but I could see the soft alluring girls they had been so fleetingly.

On the streets, on Sundays in the brasseries, these people
wore their children like badges, with real pride. I felt that at
home they were firm and even rough, but in public the
handsome sturdy little boys and girls were treated like familiar but still honored guests. If they wanted an edifice of ice
cream and Chantilly and chocolate sauce instead of the apple
tart suggested, they ate the former, after firm quiet protests
on both sides, larded with affected little grimaces and eye
rollings from the children. (The boys were as coquettish as
their sisters in their task of involving the neighbors in any
such contretemps, to make the parents lose face.)

In the few public eating places open, I saw children. It was
as if they could for one time of the year, when there were no
tourists, be where life ran full tilt, instead of split between
the family café and the rooms upstairs. There would be a lit-

tle boy (less often, a wee female) solemnly playing a card game near the café stove with an uncle, a grandfather. It was *manly*. The game looked like a modern version of Authors to me, with suits of four books and so on, but in terms of lunar conquests instead of literary. Nothing disturbed these long slow games, although a few older men might drift by, give a quick downward handshake to the uncle or grandpapa, pat the little boy's head. (As a *player* in a café, he was not required to stand up politely, etc.)

At the Hotel du Forum there was a good feeling that the big family had directly but fairly thoroughly taken over the whole operation. In the corner of the pleasant room which during the Season is a *salon de thé-bar,* there was a nice crude crèche, and the youngest son showed it to a visiting elderly relative, with whom he later played cards. I wanted to tell him how nice I thought it was: the camel of one of the Magi was smaller than the Bébé Jésus, as seemed right, and instead of putting the half-body of the Éveillé in a lighted window, his truncated *santon* was simply tucked into a little pile of cellophane grass near the manger, where he waved his lantern dangerously. It was all as it should be—as it would have been with any little children arranging it for Christmas. I wanted to say this, or at least a thank-you, but there was an intimacy between the boy and his old uncle that I dared not intrude upon.

Several times, in the two dinners I ate in the Forum, a tall nice-looking boy of perhaps sixteen came into the ex-*salon de thé* and put logs on the fire. I wondered if he was the one practicing on the piano upstairs. He may have been a little arrogant and vulnerable (*"Deuxième en lycée, beau et intelligent—parents, hôteliers—ambitions d'être avocat,"* etc.). He would make a handsome man. . . .

The other young males in the town, at least on the cold

streets of that season, were taller and more meager than their parents. They went mostly in pairs or trios. They wore smartly cut clothes of last year's fake English-Mod style, with tight pants, pinched waists, flaring collars and lapels. They walked up and down Les Lices on Sunday, hands in pockets so that their hips and genitals were sharply evident, like San Francisco gays but with a different twist and message. They wore their hair fairly long, intricately waved and lacquered over their coat collars. They spoke a language unheard but intimated by grimaces and leers of understanding, and an occasionally hard mocking laugh. They held on to, and belligerently, a recently discovered *machismo*. I felt that it was holy to them, forever burning like the Grail: they were finally *men,* and they had possessed at least a girl or two and therefore they knew and owned the world. In due time they would be engaged, through their families, to some female of their own or a higher level, and they would become more serious, heavier of outline. Meanwhile they were like roving cocks, pecking behind the hens of Les Lices, crowing and rustling their beautiful feathers.

The hens: they seemed to be a skinny lot, dressed shoddily in imitation "high style," girls of fleeting prettiness, working in shops and offices, lonely and on the prowl for almost any boy who might *possibly* be seriously amorous, or easy to trick into a forced marriage by pregnancy. They came out in little groups when offices closed at noon and six, laughing together as if with a shared secret, going together to a brasserie for an espresso in hopes of splitting from the others to join a boyfriend or a pickup. They were not prostitutes. There was a special desperation about them: they mostly did not couple for money, and they tried with naïveté and an awkward inexperience to arrange their lives as, a few years before, their families would have done for them. Some of them would bring it off, and grab many a helpless boy against his parents' hopes, and almost at once they would become square-set and dominant like their mothers-in-law and the mothers they had defied.

A few of the girls I looked at would end on the streets, in other towns than Arles—or on the municipal stretcher, like the pretty one who fell whimpering but unconscious between two tables the day I was there. She was probably drinking a tiny coffee, to keep her nymph-like figure and save money for a pseudo-smart costume for Easter. She would have gone back behind a counter until six, then got home in time for a hot supper and a row with her parents, and then perhaps made love for a few hours with her helpless lover.

There was a characteristic detachment about the young people. It reassured me to feel this in an enclave as small and tight as Arles: it would be the same in Chitry-les-Mines as in Lyon, a kind of shying-off—young animals afraid of what they sensed ahead; they were not much aware of a mistrust and resentment of people older than themselves, but they insisted on being *apart* for their own dances around the candle flame.

There was natural cruelty in them, the kind that earlier they had practiced toward a weaker school friend or a fly or cat. By now it was directed toward a more defined goal, as when one night about eleven-thirty I walked through almost deserted streets from the theatre to the Nord-Pinus. On the Place de la République, completely still, I skirted the steep steps up to the façade of St. Trophime. I knew I was in a hypersensitive phase, over-aware of things like heights to look down from, steps to stumble from, so I was walking with induced attention. As I minced along a narrow unsure step halfway up from the street to the carved stones, a car with perhaps six boys and girls tore past as close as possible to the

bottom of the steps, with a great and immediate roar, and
exactly as it passed me, tottering up there, several of the kids
let out an abrupt terrible shriek. I jumped in my skin, something I do very seldom. My adrenals surged in a flash, and I
felt hot and angered, and perhaps a little jaunty, for I waved
to the swerving careening insolent car. Everything was silent
again, except for me, and I wondered about the need for
human mischief. That had been a Till Eulenspiegel gesture,
in a dull small French town. It had satisfied some basically
sexual need for overt defiance, revenge against whoever had
condemned the culprits to their current servitude. All that
was ahead of most of them was to turn heavy and short-
breathed, plain, resigned. I raged for them, and went on to
my sepulchral lodgings buoyed by the hope and wish that
one of the people yelping suddenly like a banshee to startle
me would escape the Arlesian trap, the world trap, long
enough to know other quick satisfactions, if not slow ones.

I think I have not spoken of other Gypsies I saw, besides
the guitar players. There were many of them, because Arles is
so near Les Saintes Maries-de-la-Mer, the place of pilgrimage.
Of course, the Algerians could have been Gypsies, now and
then—mysterious flash of the eye, half-smile baring the
white teeth, set of head on neck. Some of the men were un-
mistakable, especially if about twenty-five. They had an almost flaming arrogance and beauty, and once in the pushing
crowds just before shops closed, at the corner of the big
square, I caught my breath at the sight of a man moving
quickly past the people. I'll never see anything like him
again.

One day, on the wide sidewalk of Les Lices which in summer is covered with café chairs and tables, a woman was
standing alone by a shop window. She was so dramatically a
Gypsy that I almost laughed: slim, dark, dirty, beautiful. She

wore her hair long and tangled. Her skirt had the full soft swing of any fancy-dress costumer's best offering. Her filthy beautiful feet were tiny and bare, in very high heels. She wore a lot of lipstick, and of course much "typical" gold jewelry. She was impossibly right: *La Gitane!* Perfect typecasting.

And she knew all her cues and lines, so that I was immediately and helplessly clutched by her, hypnotized by the rush of her insistence, which I knew could rise to shrieks and insults if I did not "cross her palm with silver." She gave me the whole act, from first whine for a piece of money, *any* piece, for the love of . . . and in charity. So ponderously, fatalistically, I undid my purse and pulled out a franc. "Oh— you are kind—you are good—let me reward you—" and she dragged at my arm and told me of how she could help me. I smiled at her. She kept saying, "Don't be afraid—have no fear," and I said flatly, perhaps challengingly, "I'm not afraid. I know some Gypsies." I said this more than once, but she kept harassing me, in a low rattle of supplications to take off my glove and let her see my left palm. Why not?

I pulled off my thick mitten, and she seized my hand with her icy little claws, and said some nonsense about life-line, travel, illness, and then smiled brilliantly at me and told me to put a silver coin, *any* silver coin, in her hand. "Don't be afraid!" she kept saying in a hurried daring way. Then I said, *"NO."*

Apparently I do not want my future bandied about. I seem to have a strong aversion to fortune-telling as such, just as I have to hypnosis in public (and perhaps in private?). She understood me, and dropped my hand, and gave me another wild flashing smile. "All right, *ma belle!* You are a nice girl. Be happy! See you sometime," she babbled to me, and she almost dove away.

I turned down Les Lices. As far as I know, she vanished like smoke from the broad empty sidewalk, but I could feel the bony coldness of her little crab-like hands on mine, long after I had warmed myself in the café. And she was the most beautiful female I saw in Arles. I hoped in a detached way that she and the man at the corner were lovers.

GRILLS. It was interesting to find them used in many fairly unpretentious restaurants that advertised: "All meats cooked on the open fire." It is a pleasant "new" style, which I imagine the American taste for barbecuing has helped, during the tourist season. In herb stores there were mixtures of Provençal aromatics for grilled meats and fish, which seemed to sell well, and at L'Assenage a large jar of them stood on the high hearth near the fire. I found that they got between my teeth, but tasted and smelled good.

One of the best things about the new style was that it demanded an open fire, which in that wintry season was highly pleasant to sit near. At L'Assenage, and I think in many other restaurants in the region, it was part of the décor, and the waitress used it casually in her job, pulling more coals forward as needed, pushing the small logs back.

I ordered a cut of a *gigot* of lamb I saw waiting near the grill. She asked me how I liked it and I said, "Rare." She poked some coals nearer to the edge of the hearth, which was about three feet high under a long mantel, and perhaps four feet deep. She sprinkled the meat heavily with dried herbs, and put it on a light three-legged grill over the fresh glowing coals. In about thirty seconds she turned it over, sprinkled it again on the other side, and then turned it only once more in about ten minutes. It was delicious: juicy, simple, with no need for salt or bastings. She did it in flight, really, while she served about ten other people.

I noticed that chicken, in large pieces, was grilled in loosened foil packets, moved about now and then with long-handled pincers. At the last minute of roasting, the packet was opened onto a large hot plate on the hearth. Sometimes the chicken, once done, was put directly on the coals to singe and color. There was a jar on the hearth where extra chicken juices were poured, and then they would be dripped over the vegetables the assistant brought. It was simple, but intricate in its simplicity.

I suppose all this could be done with fish: the foil, the marinade. It seems impossible that it was not. But that time in Arles I never saw or smelled anything from the nearby sea, except in the great Christmas Market and the one time I demanded fresh mussels. . . .

At the Forum the open grill at one end of the dining room was disappointingly half behind a high service counter. It was in steady use, and sent out good sounds and smells. I never ate anything from it, but some steaks I saw looked good, and they were prepared nonchalantly by the waiter as part of his job, without any pomp at all. I suppose in a crowded time he might need a helper.

It is interesting to see this primitive form of cooking return to the dining hall, after so long a time relegated to picnics and Boy Scout jamborees. It must be boring to the chefs of *la haute cuisine:* no place for subtle sauces, for inventions . . .

STREETS. They are narrow and crooked, except of course for Les Lices and, probably, the ones in the new suburbs. The Arlesians drive through these in a giant game, so that when they can find two or more blocks in a straight line they go into a screeching high speed, very loud, with usually a scream of brakes at the end. Late at night they add almost any corner to the game—two wheels on the ground, most of the time. It is permitted to get two wheels onto the almost nonexistent sidewalks, any time of day or night. There is no apparent law about horns, and when a delivery truck or an empty car blocks the street, noises of protest are violent, loud, and yet basically quite friendly, since everyone has been in the same fix countless times.

In any city where the pedestrians are used to red and green lights in their own areas, they often cheat and run across or through them, with general immunity. But in Arles, this seldom happens: the townspeople recognize themselves, as drivers, when they happen to be on foot! They look in all directions. They are extremely cautious. Above all they listen. If there is a recognizable roar of a car within any possible area of several blocks, they *wait*. This is unusual, I think, especially in a small French town. But they know that any fellow Arlesian behind a wheel will go at top speed and make unpredictable turns.

The noises from this kind of game are loud: the quick revving of a car whenever an open space of more than fifty feet offers itself; the wheezing scream of brakes; often yells and curses. It is exciting, and the Arlesians play the whole thing with melodramatic enjoyment. Surely they practice, from the minute they can be juvenile passengers! They remember such and such a street, where between five-thirty and six-fifteen at night, the most crowded hour, one can still build up a speed of more than 75 km.p.h. in less than 300 meters, unless a feckless old woman or a dog adds another bit of excitement, and when at the right-angle turn at the end one has an equal chance of making it at 55 km. on two wheels (preferably after 11:00 p.m.) or of meeting another car head on.

The street below my windows was narrow and more straight than curving, from the little Place de la Cour to the

Place du Forum. There were narrow sidewalks that diminished to nothing and then existed again. Along the side of the Place there was a heady stretch of perhaps seventy-five yards, for which any Arlesian in his right and sporting mind got up all speed, with special backfiring if possible, to add extra drama. All this, resounding up from the cold walls and pavement, made my nights lively, as well as bell-bound. Never once, though, did I hear the sound of a human scream or thud or crunch, nor even that of breaking glass or metal or, most surprising, a siren either of police or of ambulance.

One night for a few hours when my perceptions seemed too aware for comfort, I found both the bells and the wild abrupt roars of automobiles almost too loud. I suppose it was an expression of my general apathetic frustration: the cold, the wind, the dismal restaurants, the general air of proud detachment. Mostly the noises interested me, and I feel sure they were part of the whole nonchalant yet surly bravado of the people, a kind of audible cock-snoot. . . .

THE UNDERGROUND. It was a strange experience to go down into the underground Roman galleries with the young English girls, not so much because of the lighting, which eyes gradually adjusted to, as of the sounds, and perhaps the peculiarly dry air. Arles is a humid town, and down under the streets and buildings, in the somehow cushioned (soft, feathery) quiet, what one breathed seemed completely artificial. It was like being in a gigantic mask of oxygen or non-oxygen. There was no feeling of panic or entrapment, that I was aware of. There was hardly a sign of lichens or moss on the walls. In two places the ground was wet from dripping water, which fell into contrived pools, far deeper, with a hollow sound. The floor was oddly hollow to the ear, as if it were thin stone laid over planks, which of course was

impossible. The girl and I, at her request, talked impersonally in stilted French. She had read Graves's *I, Claudius.* I
suggested Yourcenar's *Memoirs of Hadrian,* and she seemed
surprised that it was written by a *French woman* (instead of
an *English man?*). Our voices sounded ridiculously fresh and
puny in that place so dark and dry and old.

Upstairs, the beautiful sarcophagi looked ornate, pretti-
fied, after the bare stones laid so skillfully on and on, below,
and the unornamented arches, the practical ditches and
drains made for grain, for sleeping soldiers.

I don't like tunnels and caves. But I would not have
minded staying down there. Not alone. Not too long. I
know increasingly that I do not suffice unto myself, always.
But in the galleries I would be my only enemy, as always: the
place itself was not evil. But the girl said shyly to me as she
left that she could never have gone down by herself. . . .

WAITERS. Somewhere in a Simenon about Inspector Maigret, a waiter was recognized as such because he wore soft
shoes of fine leather. Waiters do, was the premise. They have
sensitive feet, and are very kind to them. In Arles, at the
brasserie across from the Jules César which was probably the
town's best, there was a young waiter who wore probably
the most painful wretched shoes I have ever seen anyone try
to walk in. I noticed them because I wondered why, in a
person perhaps twenty-five, there were so many deep pain-
lines in the face, such a shuffling limping walk.

He was thin and lopsided. His face was pallid, and his hair
was a dank ugly pale brown, too long in the wrong places.
His shoes were either brown or black, plainly secondhand
and unkempt, and they had once been high-heeled, now run
over so that his feet were half out on the floor. He wore one
untied, and when he had a moment to stand still, he eased

first one foot and then the other, and bent his ankles out to help the muscles. It was painful to watch. I felt sure that his feet were not only filthy but discolored and covered with calluses, corns, scars. And from his face, so doughy and deep-lined, hot twanging wires went down and rubbed against the floors as he shuffled over them with trays of food and bottles and glasses. He was plainly an old hand at his job, deft and fast, and most of the customers knew him. Simenon was right again, and I knew the wretched young man, so careless of his feet, would not live to be an old waiter, even an ex-waiter. . . .

In the other brasserie I went to, there was a dour elderly man (elderly like fifty-six, for often third-grade waiters seem ageless from twenty on) who had the same hopeless shuffle, but whose shoes were solid if light, and well polished. He took care of the drink-side of the big ugly room, jammed on market days and probably all summer, and on the eat-side there was a very unattractive boy of about sixteen, dirty and clumsy but willing to go back for a forgotten knife. Once, at the long high bar at the service end of the room, I watched him laugh, in a merry child-like way. And when the girl on the drink-side fell to the floor and then was taken away in an ambulance, he stood watching her with sheep-like curiosity, and held a carafe in his hand in case water was needed—no great pity, no horror, but a tacit acceptance. The older waiter stayed impersonal, and as soon as the stretcher was gone he pushed all the chairs and tables back into line, so that people would not see that there had been trouble.

In the little L'Assenage, where I ate hurriedly before the theatre, the serving was done nicely, impersonally, by a member of the family. They were all young. They must have invested a lot of money in the Camargues décor, and their menu was simple and good.

The best waiter I had watched for a long time was at the Forum: about thirty-five, the kind of man who in Provence could be native or Italian, a chauffeur, a gangster, an artisan, not a farmer. He did his job expertly, without any obvious show of interest. He was quiet, deft, attentive, not mechanical but not really human. I could have been difficult or too docile, ugly or friendly, and he would have shown exactly the same detached skillful politeness toward me. Now and then, because I was bored, I tried deliberately to make him aware of my needs as a *person*. I asked for advice about a wine, for instance. My question was answered as briefly as possible, with absolutely no sign of interest either in it or in me for asking it.

In the countless little cafés in Arles, the owner usually took care of the few tables, at least in winter, and most of the customers stood at the counter. I suppose a lot of the young waiters were working the ski country. And the short tough wives-cousins-daughters-in-law were useful. They joked a little in a taciturn closed way with the familiar customers. They were not giving off any merriment. People in Arles do not have happy natures—at least in the winter! They frown and scowl a lot. There is a kind of surly belligerency in them. They are, subtly, ready for a fight, looking for a slur, an insult. The legends are violent and sad. The mistral is a cruel part of life. The bullfighting, *la corrida,* is the formalized rhythmic death-pattern. The violent heartbeats of the drum and the Gypsy guitar are held together by the insistent breathing, very shrill, of the pipes. Yes, I think the place is filled with suspicion and haughtiness, over-defensive. I have not read about this, and may be wrong, *quite wrong.* I give my own feeling as an observer. I met Arles head on, in a cold lonely wind, and my inner winds had blown me there, and it was hard, but did no harm at all to anyone that I can know of, in the twisted mysterious little town. And I am not sure if the shuffling sad waiters are a part of the *raison d'être* of Arles—its defensiveness, its need to be bent and pained. How could I know? But why would a young man plainly skilled in his job let his prime asset destroy him so early? A good waiter babies his feet, and it seems wise to me. Is there a strong self-destruction there? Is it perhaps in defiance of the brutality of life, all that cold wind blowing the seeds away, the trees bent, the ground sucked dry and poor?

—*Marseille, 1971*

AT SEA

Preface

Nostalgia must always be a strange bedfellow, but an increasingly familiar one as we grow past the first years of pick-and-choose. In the case of the views of freighter life that follow, it seems natural that they stay together, instead of being slotted in their chronological rhythm. This bunching is not based as much on wistful remembrances as on a realistic look at some disparate happenings at sea that by now are plainly part of my own nostalgic pattern.

In the first one, which happened on the Italian *Feltre* somewhere off the west coast of Lower California or perhaps San Salvador in 1932, the flash of perception of great human dignity was shaking, and it will last all my life. That whole strange "sea change," which I wrote about in *The Gastronomical Me,* culminated in the night of the Captain's Dinner, with the sight of the carefully preserved sugar image of the Duomo di Milano being eased one more time up a sleazy narrow stairway to the deck. How could the tired old chef face it and us once more? I felt desperate for him and for his dogged pride, but he was much stronger and wiser than I. He won again, because he had learned not to doubt.

In the second and less sentimental report of being on a freighter, Dutch that time, everything was dated twenty years later in private and recorded calendars, and although my own emotions may have been as knife-edged as before, I was more disciplined to divert them. In this case, I was more concerned for the two little girls I traveled with, my daughters, and we were setting out on the first of several adventures. It is interesting, at this distance in reading, to see how odd were the new words we took for granted. By now most of them are strange again, except perhaps for Hudgee-pudgee: sometimes I play a variation or two on its delicious soggy theme. . . .

The third inclusion in this peculiar trilogy is what might be called a "sport" in a litter of otherwise normal pups, but it is not to my mind the runt of the batch. It is about another Italian ship my younger sister Norah and I went on. (She was very much on the *Feltre* when I was . . . a fine and often desperate companion.)

It might be good, here, to state that in my experience Italian vessels are not the most commendable in commercial navigation. Nevertheless, and knowing this full well, Norah and I have often seemed impelled to sail on them, to try them one more time. Perhaps our reasons are perverse. We are drawn to the ambiguous filth and the uncertainty of returning to a continent we would prefer not to hurry back to: our own. We are drawn by the taunting suspicion that this time there might be elegance, suavity, everything that we have almost laughingly sought out, and never found, in liners and tubs run either officially or covertly by the Italian government.

Whatever the reasons, we have foolishly returned to them. The last time we did so, tongue in cheek but still hoping, was because we wanted to dock in Cannes, from

New York. Instead, we were diverted because of political
troubles to Palermo, and then on to Naples, in several
extra days of squalid splendor. . . . First class on a transatlantic princess instead of classless on a Canal Zone tramp!
It was a costly mistake on all our parts, and after the crew
had been calmed down enough to head for Buenos Aires
without shore leave, while all the families and girlfriends
stood waving impotently from the quais, the ship steamed
out and we headed wearily for a long dull air trip through
Rome to Cannes. (I mention this simply to add to my as-
sertion that it is perverse folly to put even one foot onto an
Italian deck, "in this day and age.")

Well . . . in 1954 my sister and I brought our children
home from some years in France, on an Italian freighter.
We knew it was careless and impetuous of us. We were on
the reclaimed Liberty ship for more than seventy days, instead of the scheduled thirty-four. When we stopped in
Cádiz and planned to skip ship, without luggage, we found
that the terrified captain never docked except on Sundays,
when all the brothels were closed, and that passports were
locked away with the crew's papers until Mondays. In
other words, we were prisoners, *there,* until San Francisco at
least.

The story about Israfel is as much a straight report as the
other two things about freighter life, although it is not in
their form. Perhaps what they are saying is that although
people can no longer roam on cargo ships ("The container
is our guest, and the passenger is a pest . . ."), we have fellow travelers in several worlds.

It is probably wise not to look hard for them in our
present wide-bodied jets-buses-trains-cars. Currently, people
in transit tend to pull into themselves and turn remote and
dry. This is called self-protection, and certainly I have
found that in public transportation I am apt to speak little

and feel rather shriveled, and in private vehicles limit my relationships discreetly.

What can we substitute for long slow looks at other voyagers? They are there. They are here. Are we being told not to be human anymore, since it is foolish and wasteful?

So these three views of an intimate contact with my fellows, my teachers, seem to focus on one thing, that we are all at sea. And that is why a possible evocation of other times took over, goaded perhaps by nostalgia, so that I have put them together instead of in chronological order.

I
THE CAPTAIN'S DINNER

M.S. *Feltre*

The Captain's Dinner was strange. We were off the coast of Lower California. The water was so calm that we could hear flying fish slap against it. We ate at a long table out on deck, under an awning between us and the enormous stars.

The Captain looked well in his white uniform, and smiled almost warmly at us all, probably thanking God that most of us would leave him in a few days. The waiters were excited, the way the Filipino boys used to be at boarding school when there was a Christmas party, and the table looked like something from a Renaissance painting.

There were galantines and aspics down the center, with ripe grapes brought from Italy and stranger fruits from all the ports we'd touched, and crowning everything two stuffed pheasants in their dulled but still dashing feathers. There were wineglasses on stems, and little printed menus, proof that this masterpiece of a meal was known about in Rome, long since.

We ate and drank and heard our own suddenly friendly voices over the dark waters. The waiters glided deftly, perhaps dreaming that they served at Bifli's instead of on this fifth-rate freighter, and we drank Asti Spumanti, undated but delightful.

And finally, while we clapped, the chef stood before us, bowing in the light from the narrow stairs. He wore his high bonnet and whites, and a long-tailed morning coat, and looked like a drawing by Ludwig Bemelmans, with oblique sadness in his pasty outlines.

There was a silence after our applause. He turned nervously toward the light, and breathed not at all. We heard shufflings and bumps. Then, up through the twisting white closeness of the stairway, borne on the backs and arms of three awestruck kitchen boys, rose something almost too strange to talk about.

The chef stood back, bowing, discreetly wiping the sweat from his white face. The Captain applauded. We all clapped, and even cheered. The three boys set the thing on a special table.

It was a replica, about as long as a man's coffin, of the cathedral at Milano. It was made in white and pink sugar. There was a light inside, of course, and it glowed there on the deck of the little ship, trembling in every flying buttress with the Mexican ground swell, pure and ridiculous; and something about it shamed me.

It was a little dusty. It had undoubtedly been mended, after mighty storms, in the dim galleys of a hundred ships,

better but never worse than this. It was like a flag flying for
the chef, a bulwark all in spun sugar against the breath of
corruption. It was his masterpiece, made years ago in some
famous kitchen, and he showed it to us now with dignity.

—*Hemet, 1942*

II
DUTCH
FREIGHTER

M.S. *Diemerdyk*

People who travel on freighters may do so accidentally for the first time, as I did in 1932 from Marseille to Los Angeles on the *Feltre,* later bombed and sunk. Thereafter they do it deliberately, or never again.

They either loathe it and know that they cannot stand it again, or they return like opium smokers to the pipe, never halfheartedly, and almost always with a deliberate plan, a kind of rhythmic pattern, for the long, slow, sleepy voyage. Either they must have plenty of time and no other pressing use for it than to spend some of it in a little ship, or they must have almost no time at all and an imperative hunger to spend it in this chosen way, moving to the tides' movings and the stars'.

Freighter travel is never forgotten. I was greatly reassured to prove this, lately, when I rode some five weeks on two oceans, two seas, a canal, a couple of bays, and a river, after having been land-bound for more than a decade.

It is true that I pampered myself somewhat, suspecting that my old skill might be too rusty for comfortable practice. I took a clean, efficient little ship toward Europe instead of a grubby if more romantic one headed for the South Pacific, and I chose the easy month of August instead of the obviously more exciting season of an equinox. I was cautious, and slid out under the Golden Gate Bridge in a mood that was definitely timorous.

The minute I *knew,* though, that it would be days and weeks before I touched land again; that I was there on that little Dutch freighter for good or bad or even hell-and-high-water; that if I died on it I would still be a long time from the dust I should return to; that if I lived decently on it the Captain would like me and that if I lived indecently on it he would not; but that in any and all such cases it was basically my own choice—the minute I knew all this again, I was at home.

I slipped unprotestingly into the first trance-like sleepiness which always engulfs me when I put to sea, and which tapers off almost imperceptibly until I land again. It is true that I walk and even talk at the proper times, but inwardly there is little difference between having eyes shut or eyes open; and my first encounters with passengers and officers and general shipside protocol are even less real than my endless untroubled dreams.

Dutch crewmen seem unusually understanding of such mildly neurasthenic procedures, perhaps because they are said to be sons of a phlegmatic nation, and there is no better place to try one's first steps again, one's first deep breaths, than on the scrubbed decks and in the hospitable neat air of a little steamer named anything ending with *-dyk* or *-dam*. From the Captain, coldly and implacably invisible when duty called and very jolly indeed when it did not, to the most impish deckhand or oiler, the men seemed to accept my private reasons for my public behavior just as philosophically as they did the other passengers', and made us all feel, very comfortably, that we were really not much more bother than the tons of canned fruits and precision tools that weighted down the holds and held us to such an even as well as profitable keel. My own actions were steadily somnambulistic, but they caused no more astonishment than if I had stood on my head before every meal, just outside the dining-saloon door, as did a gym teacher from British Columbia, or had dropped my monocle into my full soup plate every night, as did a permanently and politely dead-drunk lecturer from Amsterdam.

Of course, there are always a few mavericks, who get on in a daze and will get off in a state of frustrated ennui. Most of them will never, as God is their witness, let themselves get roped into another tedious crawl over any ocean on this world.

For instance, there was on our little freighter—as there always is—a passenger who either could not or would not accept the fact that for several weeks it would be impossible for him to read the morning and afternoon papers for exactly forty minutes after breakfast and twenty minutes before dinner. He would stand fuming and scowling, plainly miserable, before the two typed sheets of radio news Sparks pinned up each noon on the bulletin board. One was in Dutch, of course, and one in very British American, and the passenger was sure that there were several vitally important bits of news in the Netherlands report which were being deliberately withheld from him as a one-language Yankee. He would waylay a steward or a Dutch passenger and stand suspiciously comparing what he could read with what was being translated.

I felt genuinely pained for him, partly for his present misery and partly because he would never achieve real supercargodom. He had come aboard knowing, but never actually accepting, such irrevocabilities as that the Spokane dailies cannot be delivered, limp from their presses, a thousand miles northeast of Cuba. He would go ashore convinced that it could have been managed somehow.

In the same way there was, this time and always, the passenger who fought a gallant fight for the last twenty-five days of the thirty-three-day voyage to have fresh eggs for breakfast. She was well-read enough to know that very few modern ships travel with chickens aboard, as in the days of Drake and Magellan. But every morning she hoped anew, and assured her table steward that she must have *fresh* eggs, and almost every morning after the first week at sea she sent back what she had ordered with the unbelieving statement that it was *not* fresh at *all*.

Gently, the head steward, a very clever man indeed and one of infinite experience, ordered little omelets and unnamed scrambles for her instead of the undisguisable soft-boiled eggs she struggled for, until by the time we were heading for the North Sea she was eating highly seasoned dishes that would have seemed impossibly exotic to her in San Diego or Vancouver. The last morning, though, when we all ate an early breakfast and wore our hats and clutched our new passport holders and watched the docks of Antwerp slide by the portholes, I heard her say with a note of dauntless disbelief, "I *do* insist on having my eggs fresh-fresh-*fresh*." And she was right: she did insist.

Another common phenomenon of supercargodom, something which even ten years of land exile had not changed for me, was that I soon sniffed out, through the fog of my private snooze, the familiar hunger for new words. It is something shared by all real travelers and can give as much pleasure to a twelve-days-and-all-expenses adventurer as to a raddled old countess who has spent nine tenths of her life on A Deck, from Hong Kong to Montevideo with stop-offs at will in Plymouth, Skagerrak, Vladivostok.

It takes only a couple of days in Honolulu to enable a Stateside housewife to spend the next ten years rattling off directions to her decorators about *lanais* and *hookalumais*— which she learned in what she knowingly refers to in four, not three, syllables, carefully accented, as Hah-*vah*-ee-ee. In the same enjoyable way, a few days in Paris, especially if helped along by a French Line crossing, can bring out almost voluptuous garglings and rollings of good flat Illinois *r*'s, so that saying *"Trente-trois rue de Rivoli"* to a taxi driver can sound much like the after-treatment of a tonsillectomy.

Even more so, four or five weeks on a Dutch freighter can do fine things to this linguistic *amour-propre* we all wear hidden somewhere until the magic new phonetics brings it to light, and I felt reassured to discover that it was as true in 1954 as it had been decades before, on the *Feltre,* and the *Santa Cerrita* and the *Maréchal Duffroy,* and ... and ... and ...

Very shortly after I went aboard, I learned that, in good Dutch, the barman is called the Buffetchef, pronounced *Puff*ishay (naturally), and that the chief steward, always an equally good man to know, is called the Hof-Meister (*Huff*-Maystuh). Shuttling from one to the other with no pain, it was inestimably satisfying to be able to murmur to the first in supercargo Dutch—which sounds even Dutcher after the

second or third small glass of Genever gin—"Ein Bols"
(Ayn Buhlsh, of course), and then to request knowingly
from the second a large bowl of Hodgepodge for lunch.

Hodgepodge is perhaps peculiar to ships out of Rotterdam. Certainly I have never seen it in the same form on land,
in Holland or even in France, where it might possibly be
called Hochepot. It is a thick, greenish-grey, lumpy, delicious stew of vegetables and bits of unidentifiable meat and
sometimes slices of sausage, to be served in soup plates and
eaten with large spoons and, if possible, pieces of fresh
brown bread for pushing and sopping. Needless to say, it is
pronounced, by any old-timer—which means any passenger
who has been more than forty-eight hours aboard—*Uhdgee-
Puhd*gee. There is something very satisfying about rolling
out this word when it has been preceded by a wise modicum
of Genever and a few twinkles from the poker-faced, warm-
eyed Puffishay.

Cakes (Keks), which apparently are as necessary to the
end of a Dutch sea meal as Bols is to the beginning, are
based on a batter which is yellow, spongily heavy when
baked, and increasingly nutmeggish as the voyage progresses
and the fresh *fresh* eggs grow less so. Keks can be anywhere
from half an inch to three inches thick, sliced in fingers or
rounds, cut in squares, diced or crumbled when stale, and
quite possibly used as ballast in a nautical emergency, and
they are interesting chiefly as an indication of how the baker
feels.

For instance, before our baker's last land-whirl in Cristobal
and the long haul toward Antwerp, we were titillated at
dinner by his version of a dainty slab named Gâteau
d'Amour. The next night, and the only time he let us down
in some five weeks, we had to be content with tinned fruit
cup and vanilla wafers, but twenty-four hours later he had

pulled himself together enough to produce his basic batter again, stripped of the love-cakes' whipped-cream doodads, starkly burned on the starboard side, and entitled Celebration Crumbcake.

And of course the Esperanto of pastry cooks, easy enough to decipher after one or two sorties as supercargo, makes it completely unsurprising to find a cherry on top of anything called Jubilee, or tooth-shattering morsels of nut brittle scattered here and there with the menu cue Noisette, on any ship from a transatlantic liner to a freighter. This lingo is international to the point of banality, and cannot possibly give quite the semantic thrill to a traveler as the ability to recognize, as well as mouth, the word Goudasprits.

Ah, those lovely, dry, flat, whirly Goudaspritses, our baker's one deviation from his occasionally faltering but always narrow path of Kek-Kek-Kek!

They meant, on his emotional chart, a period of high-barometer insouciance, with low humidity so that they would stay moderately crisp and unflabby, and a subtropical zing to the air. On the days he served them, the bread too seemed more delicious, and passengers who ordered American Utt-Keks for breakfast reported them to be comparatively airy, which is to say that they were not more than three quarters of an inch thick, each weighing somewhat less than a pound per Kek. Goudaspritses meant, in other words, a general lightness aboard, even in their pronunciation, which according to the Captain was imposssible for anyone not born in Holland. (We compromised to our own satisfaction, if not his, by gurgling as genteelly as possible when we said "Whgh*ooooo*-da-shpritsh," but there lurked always in our linguistic consciences his firm comment that we simply did not have enough *juice* to speak good Dutch.)

Something that happens at least once on every respectable

freighter out of Rotterdam or into it is a Nassi Goreng for luncheon.

Britishers aboard feel about it much as they do about any-thing even vaguely curried, which a Nassi Goreng is not, and they bandy reminiscences larded with *pukka* and *boy*. Reticent withered Dutch ladies, relicts of traders in Surabaya in the old days, grow almost gay again and chat of Rijstta-fels, which a Nassi Goreng is not quite. And everybody eats too much and sleeps all afternoon, for the feast is not only tantalizing to several of the senses, but it must be floated down on a heady flood of beer.

A Nassi Goreng is served in an almost hysterical way by every available hand on board, including a few ordinarily in-visible oilers squeezed into leftover white jackets. This may be one reason why it is definitely a ceremony performed only when the sea is flat and empty and the ship is on its auto-matic compass or whatever it is that takes over when the bridge can be left to its own devices.

The Hof-Meister, somewhat glassy-eyed from the general emotional temperature and several amicable Genevers, stands straighter than usual at the pantry door, focusing be-hind his thick lenses on every one of the loaded platters that whip past him. The stewards, generally a relaxed and merry squad, are frowning, with beaded lips and unaccustomed clattering and crashing. The tables look overcrowded with tall bottles of mango chutney and short bottles of red and black sambal, and soup plates at each place, and the largest size of dinner plates beside the forks, and big stemmed glasses, and the clear green of the Heineken beer bottles.

There seems to be no set pattern for serving, once the rice is there to act as a kind of foundation in the soup plates. The rice is always browned with minced onion, steamed, and then baked slowly, so that it is a little crisp. And then over and around it, and piled on the dinner plate too, is what really amounts to a gastronomical mishmash of grilled and roasted and fried fishes and meats, in chunks and slices and on skewers: chicken, lamb, kidneys, herring, this-and-that. There are even very flabby fried eggs. And on top of all these things, and around them and alongside, go the more or less familiar "condiments" like chopped roasted peanuts and shaved coconut, steamed raisins, pickled fish, shaved spiced cucumbers, little hot peppers, one or more kinds of chutney of course, grated raw onion . . . on and on. And then, to pull things into focus and to bring real happiness to the world-wanderers who want to go home laden with nonchalant little anecdotes in any language at all besides their own, there is the final fillip, about as subtle as a flash fire in a munitions dump, of sambal.

Sambal, once tasted or even sniffed, can never be compared with Tabasco, or Louisiana hot-sauce, or the *salsa picante* of Mexico, or even the watery, oily, treacherous *sauce forte* splashed cautiously over an Algerian couscous, for it is so much more so that it makes them seem like sweet lemonade or milk.

It is black or it is red, and connoisseurs choose one or the other and shake it with knowing discretion here and there over the general confusion on their plates, at a Nassi Goreng, and then wait happily to fall by accident upon one drop of it, when tears will brim their eyes and they can reach blindly for the beer.

Sambal is, I think I can say without being contradicted, the most thoroughly and incredibly hot flavor in the world. How and why it can somehow, over and above the enjoyable torture it causes, make the basically unattractive clutter of a Nassi Goreng even more entertaining and appetizing than it manages by contradiction to be, I do not try to explain. All I can say is that it is pronounced, surprisingly enough, almost as it is spelled, that it can be found wherever a few old Java hands are gathered together, and that it can add inestimably to the culinary reputation as well as the vocabulary of anyone who has ever added to either, generally, by a trip on a little or big Dutch ship.

So can a Nassi Goreng, of course, even without the red and black sambals!

After five weeks spent contemplating the horizon, the navel, and the Dutch face, things taste better, and memories are good, not sour: the night the Puffishay cried a little because at Panama City he had learned that three weeks earlier his wife in Hille Doornkamp near The Hague had felt a cold coming on; the afternoon a glittering flying fish landed by the engine-room door and Cor of the crew dipped on it like a bird and threw it back into the blue water before it could even open its beak-bill mouth; the morning the Canadian judge came on deck without his orthopedic boot and played a game of deck quoits which everybody pretended not to watch too anxiously, nor cheer with tears too plainly sounding.

There is a kind of sharpening of what wits are left us, on a little ship's slow slide over many waters; and although it demands a certain amount of bravado to attain supercargodom, once done and admitted it is done forever, and like me you can go aboard in San Francisco or Baltimore or Corpus Christi any time at all in your life and get off a few weeks later anywhere at all, and find yourself wide awake again, and stronger and fresher if you want to be, and with a richer, indeed broader, tongue.   —*St. Helena, 1955*

III
ANNOUNCEMENT
FROM ISRAFEL
M.S. *Pluto*

The ringing at my door was abrupt and insistent, and when I opened it I knew quick as a flash of light that an angel was there.

This flash happens perhaps once or even a few times in a life. Confronting an archangel occurs less often, if at all, but by now I have met two shapes of the plain ordinary kind, which sets me a little apart, as I recognize with both pride and meekness.

An angel can be any member of the celestial hierarchy, especially of the lower orders. It does not need to wear wings, although this is a fond belief of many Christian and otherwise orthodox artists who can paint feathers better than feet, which are often covered by folds of thick cloth.

I suspected that Cleveland might qualify, when I first met

him. He had a direct impact of innocence, the way Melville's
Billy Budd does, and the way my other angel did.

At first Cleveland did not look directly at me, into my
eyes, because he was a black from Georgia and I am a white
woman, and he had been taught not only to avoid a white
woman's eyes at all costs but to shun her presence like rot
itself, the rot of bone-brain-and-sinew. He had been blan-
dished by whites, of all sexes, because he was beautiful, but
he rightly felt most comfortable, as even angels need to do,
with people who sounded the way he did when they spoke,
whether with body or soul.

I am much older in years than Cleveland, and I felt all
right, at ease, about sending out from myself what welcoming I had. Gradually he got it, and by the time we had
worked for a few months on his attempts to pass some military and civilian requirements, he was looking straight at
me, and then he began to smile, rarely but well, with a special sudden shine.

He was trying to join the Marines. His older brother had
done that, to stay out of jails and gutters and suchlike, and
Cleveland wanted to for the same reasons. But he kept
flunking, failing, not passing. He worked hard, and I have
seen his lamp on at night, up at the Ranch bunkhouse, and I
have watched the crystal sweat run down his cheek, to pass
the tests: Marines, driver's license, all that. He could not. In
the middle of a good coherent session about why the law
says that before you turn a truck to the left you get into the
left lane and give a signal for the left-hand turn he would
burst into a real belly laugh and say in his soft voice, like
velvet, "Why answer a thing like that? That's stupid."

He was right, of course. But there is a kind of moat, without any drawbridge, between him and what is currently
called Reality.

With time, then, I felt that Cleveland had finally accepted me as a non-menace, racially: I did not want to rape or seduce or wound him, as had happened to him before, even in Georgia, and I already suspected him of what I met for the final time at the door.

He had a black friend called Jim, up at the bunkhouse. It was easier to meet Jim as a person than it was Cleveland, and I was glad when they came to the door together. Jim is big, in a more towering but fatter way, and he knows a lot more about things like how to serve a glass of wine and how to smile when lying or hating. He has to, in order to survive, because he is probably mortal, whereas what I had long guessed was plain when I saw the two of them there: Cleveland is not. He is the angel Israfel.

He stood in such a blaze of innocence that I felt staggered, and touched the wall behind me to stay steady, and said in a kind of uncontrollable whimper, "Oh . . . oh man, you look so beautiful, so sharp!" I was stupefied.

Jim laughed his best hearty hohoho, the kind he does for white people when he is protecting them rather than himself, and handed me a little note, and went quickly away toward the car that idled in the drive with the Boss at the wheel, and I stood smiling at Cleveland, who gazed gently at me.

He seemed taller than usual, with a wide-brimmed black hat set loose and soft on the back of his head. He wore a black high-necked sweater, and a big heavy necklace of silver and turquoise that hung low on his chest, over and between his firm subtle breasts. His pants were of a light cinnamon brown, of thick ribbed velvet. Everything was soft, tight, to show the supple young strong body boldly. Here I am, it said, I am Cleveland . . . Israfel.

I thanked him for coming to say goodbye to me, although

I had already refused to do this the day before, when he
walked down politely to talk once more with me before he
left for Georgia. "I never say goodbye," I had said firmly,
and we shook hands and I felt a deep sadness to see him walk
up the hill, his head already down a little the way he had
learned to hold it in a chain gang when he was sixteen. So
now, in the cool bright morning light, I was foolishly saying
goodbye, and once more we clasped hands and I said again,
"Friend," and he said, "Yes, friend," and I was so dazzled
that my heart seemed to stop, with all that light around him.

The car was waiting. Jim was already in the back, his face
remote. The Boss did not beep impatiently, as he would have
any other time. Cleveland walked away a little and then
turned back, as if he were listening.

"Stay this way," I said involuntarily.

"What that?"

"I said, 'Stay this way.' " What I meant was: Stay out of
jail. Stay sober. Stay away from the police. But how foolish I
was, for I knew all the time that nothing, no evil, could
possibly touch him.

He smiled in a very old kindly way at me, and said in his
grave voice, "Of course. Oh yes! I'll stay like this."

Nobody looked back from the car as it headed for the air-
port, and I went into the house feeling insecure, shaken,
with an inner flutter, as if something incomprehensible had
happened. I was emotional, with a vague need to cry a little
but no experience in doing so. The beautiful strong black
youth had sent out such powerful waves of purity that I was
physically dizzied.

I moved dreamily about the house, steadying myself, and
it was an hour or so later that I remembered the little note
from Cleveland that Jim had given me. Before I read it, I
made myself remember the other angel, Claudio. I thought

of the two of them, and was awed to have seen that many in my lifetime.

Claudio was one of the crew of a strange ship, the *Pluto* or some such name, that plowed and wallowed surreptitiously between Trieste and Seattle, through the Panama Canal of course, and with many unscheduled and unpredictable stops, depending on both the official and the secret cargoes: fighting cocks, plaster Virgins, human beings in flight, fragile flasks of caustic acid, now and then some drugged racehorses. . . .

Once my sister Norah and I, and her two older sons and my two daughters, all aged between seven and twelve, and the fifteen-year-old daughter of a French friend, boarded this little ex-Liberty ship at Genoa, to leave her in San Francisco several weeks after we had been promised to arrive there. She was captained by a once handsome, once brave wreck of a once-man, and crewed by ghosts drawn mostly from Italian prisons on the promise that two years at sea would shorten their sentences by a dazzling lot; that is, two in the hold of freighters like the *Pluto* equaled ten or more in the governmental bagnios.

The men were probably the most evil set that any of us would ever be closely aware of, but they were protective of our differentness, our basic naïveté. My sister and I knew, of course, of some of their reasons for being called convicts: rape, sodomy, political plottings and confusions, a snitched loaf of bread. We came to recognize their personal smells, at least of the ones who took morose care of our grimy cabins and served us bad-to-frightening meals in the tiny airless "saloon," and we could understand them because we soon felt smelly, too.

Norah had to keep a closer watch on her two little boys than I did on my three potential females, especially about

guarding their trips to the head and the shower room. We
sensed, and the Captain warily agreed, that the men had almost forgotten about women as such, and could only find
some kind of release with other men, of no matter what age.
This seemed to be encouraged by the Captain's practice of
docking at every port on Sunday when the brothels were tra-
ditionally off bounds, so that shore leave was unnecessary
(*"Jamais le dimanche . . ."*).

The crew paced and snarled in their trap, and until Norah
and I caught on to the trick we felt almost as frustrated, because for the first few weeks we thought that we must get
hold of our passports and skip ship with the children, even if
it meant throwing ourselves on the mercy of the nearest
consul. (We had spent all our money waiting for two weeks
in a hotel in Genoa for the *Pluto* to leave Trieste, during one
of Tito's finaglings with the Italian government.) The Captain, possibly half mad from prison camps and such, locked
all papers in his safe over the weekends, which is to say
whenever we were within swimming distance of shore. With
no money and no papers, my sister and I dared not expose
five children to the police of Cádiz or La Guaira or even La
Unión! As for the men, they were too hopeless to summon
extra courage.

And all that and much more (How about some seventy
refugees packed belowdecks from Yugoslavia to Venezuela?
Most of them slid down into the foul harbor water in the
night, and we heard them gasp and then paddle away. There
were some who were dumped silently into the Caribbean:
the old and very young too dead to flee further . . .), yes, all
that and almost too much more made Claudio super-real to
Norah and me, because he stayed so pure.

He was tall and beautiful, with the rounded muscles that
can turn soft with time, and light brown hair that always

looked like clean silk in the tropical sweaty filth we lived in, and blazing blue eyes, mostly cast down, that were like a physical shock when they looked straight into ours. He was a Renaissance angel, designed to make some kind of heavenly announcement.

He was the youngest of the *Pluto*'s crew, and the most coveted. He belonged to the biggest brute on the ship, an enormous man who controlled all the supplies, and therefore our lives. I saw his Store once or twice, and it was barred like a gorilla's pen, and only he held the keys to it. When he went in and out, two or three of his slaves guarded him against the crew, and were given a little tin of fish, a rind of cheese, as they protected his gross bulk toward the galley. Claudio was almost always with him, but Norah and I knew that he was there only because the storekeeper had to seem to be in possession of what the others needed almost as much as they did food.

We grew to believe so fully in the purity of this strange being from some other atmosphere that we *knew* (we were all a little off our heads, in our own ways . . .) that the corrupt bully who was so obviously mad for Claudio would never touch him, nor would he ever let any other wretch on board get near him. As long as Claudio seemed to belong to the purser, the storekeeper, the crew was powerless, and probably this strange protection obviated unthinkable feuds and revenges in the stinking bunk rooms, which we found out were built so low, to make more room for cargo and refugees, that even a short man never stood upright except on deck.

So the purser used Claudio the way a lion tamer uses whip and kitchen chair, to keep vital order. Norah and I, perhaps as females, knew that he was almost exploding with need for the beautiful boy, but that he was sly and self-protective

enough to hold to his vow of chastity, like a lustful priest
who reaches for a someday cardinal's hat. With Claudio as
his helpless doxy, the crew would have gone wild and so
would he. With Claudio as his innocent unsullied shield, we
all stayed inviolate.

It is hard to know what comes first in our three basic
needs for protection, food, love. In a dreadful way the *Pluto*
protected us, because if it split at the seams, which it might
well have done, we ourselves would be done for. The gigantic purser puttering behind the bars of his cage, among all
the barrels of wormy mildewed rice and spaghetti and the
tins of polluted herring and bright-pink mummified Argen-
tinian beef scraps, supplied us by professional guile with a
kind of nourishment. Claudio perhaps gave us more than
plain love, which means a kind of serene confidence that we
would all keep on living, and reach port.

The way I got to see the food cage was that I demanded
from the trembling Captain, still spiritually waterlogged
from six days and nights he had swum twenty years before in
the Mediterranean, after his first ship was bombed out from
under him and he was captured by the British, a pass to get a
bottle of brandy from the stores. Norah and I had decided
that we would use it on the children. The water was rapidly
yellowing and turning thickish, like a very weak *pastis* in a
bad café in Marseille. We figured that if we lined up the little ones, first thing in the morning, and gave each of them a
tumbler of the nasty stuff with a stiff shot of alcohol in it,
they might fend off lurking bacteria. We did, and they did.

But it was curiously chilling to find that the brandy,
which I got under guard (the purser, Claudio, and a rat-like
Angelo who was also bosun and ship's barber), was heavily
doctored with cascara sagrada, capsicum, and various other
purgatives and aromatics. It bore a fairly reputable name. I

asked the Captain about it, after one horrifying nip with Norah, and he told us that in case of the always potential mutiny the crew would take the Store first, and seize all the liquor in it, and that this liquor was guaranteed by the "fairly reputable" fabricators to knock unconscious or griped or writhing or sick as a dog anyone who downed more than three ounces of it.

Norah and I were careful about our morning dosages into the vile thick yellow water we handed to the five scrawny children, who waited dutifully for it every morning in my cabin, still marked "Five Gunners" from its World War II days, and perhaps that anti-mutiny potion got us on shore again.

One time my sister and I were sitting on the deck of the *Pluto*'s little superstructure, looking aft. We felt more listless than usual, and would have liked to sip cold white wine. We could hear the children playing one of their endless desperate games: Scrabble or Camelot, perhaps Parcheesi. Below us there were no more furtive scuttlings of almost naked refugees, slimy with unaccustomed tropical sweat, waiting for the signal to slip overboard: we were perhaps ten days past La Guaira and then the Canal, heading north, and the last of those unknowns had left forever. But once we had sat dockside for almost a week there in the Venezuelan port under Caracas, to rid ourselves of the rich cargo into the dark waters, while the crew waited in invisible irons belowdecks and in the silence before dawn we listened to the disease-filled workers along the quay cough and cry out. We watched languidly as sparkling Liberian freighters docked alongside us and gave cocktail parties, all the black officers in their starchiest tropical whites.

During the weekend some rich men from Caracas, portside, had pretended to ready their beautiful deep-sea fishing cruiser for a sortie for marlin or whatever is sportiest in those lukewarm waters, but instead they occupied themselves with a bevy of exquisite girls from a convent, like butterflies at first in their Givenchy cottons but before long bare and bedraggled, and numbed, hopefully, by the drinks that a huge black musician kept flowing from a silver pitcher, between his stretches of music. He played a kind of steel guitar, and a kind of bongo drum, and sang a kind of bastard Trinidad-Guadalajara beat, for two days and two nights. The craft grew quieter and quieter, except for him, and late Sunday the girls were discreetly carried off and dumped into two Rolls-Royces headed for Caracas and the convent. And all the time our five children played Scrabble or Camelot, perhaps Parcheesi, and Norah and I had sat listlessly waiting for something, just as we did ten days later, as the *Pluto* rolled sluggishly up the coast off Nicaragua, perhaps.

We leaned against the hot metal wall of the bridge, looking aft into a thick greyish brilliance of noontime, and heard someone singing, in a high true voice, and below us moved Claudio, carrying two big buckets of swill from the galley, to dump into our feeble wake, where hopefully the next tide would shove the stuff toward the mouths of tortoises and tunas ... or perhaps porpoises, although that is doubtful because of their high intelligence.

I would like to remember that Claudio was singing a few bars from something we knew, but that would be false, and all we did know was that he was singing.

This suddenly, and for both of us at once because we had been together so long through so much peculiarity, was almost too much for our carefully maintained control, and we knew that we were a hairsbreadth from trouble: we would cry or be sick, and upset the children, and not be able to guard them to the toilets and pour out the medicated brandy. We lay carefully against the wall, and then began to talk about Claudio, and doing it kept us sane, or at least functioning with some dignity.

He is untouchable, we said. He is stainless and intact. He is like the young man who was an Emperor's lover but never soiled by lust. The buckets of garbage, the passions below-decks, the stench and dead nameless refugees and all the evil cannot touch him. He is Israfel. (I remembered the name, that strange blazing day, and much later I read that in the Koran Israfel is "the angel whose heartstrings are a lute, and who has the sweetest voice of all God's creatures.")

Claudio walks like a superior being over the salty iron decks of the rusting hulk of a sneaky unlicensed freighter, and his is a celestial dismissal of the present heat and smell, around him and below, and a message upward. Norah and I hear it, and lie limp and astonished at its purity. No more words. Our minds are purged, through with searching for such fripperies as *meaning*. . . .

Claudio walks in serene confidence to the stern, heaves the swill into the wake in two practiced movements, and bangs the battered old cans together in a rhythm for whatever he is singing. Then he looks up and sees my sister and me, lying there helplessly against the ship's flimsy wall, and he smiles the most violently and shockingly beautiful smile I have ever seen on any human face, if such it was.

It was impossible even to sign in the air to him, so awed were we.

He came along the deck and out of our sight, his face peaceful and the buckets swinging easily, and finally we collected the children and went below to eat something, in order to stay more or less upright, but we did not speak of

Claudio again, until some time after we got to San Francisco. We were not scared to. It simply was not necessary, for Norah and I knew what we had witnessed.

That is why I was blinded to see Israfel again, and I wished my sister could be with me. He stood in front of the open door, pure in his tall black supple body. He was a dazzle of silver and blue necklace, wide black hat far back on his head like a halo, bun-colored velvety trousers, all poised easily as if to fend off any evil, to enwrap any good and carry it away singing.

His guardian angel Jim handed me the crumpled note, and Cleveland made the courtesies he had been taught and shook hands with me in a brisk ho-hum way, and then gave such a smile that I fell back against the wall. His face lit with an intensity of love and understanding, so that it seemed like dark molten metal, and his large brown-black eyes were red, coals in a stoked furnace or perhaps more lava, the kind rubies spring from.

It was clumsy, stupid of me to stutter what I did, something like "Stay this way." It was because I was shocked with astonishment. Here was Claudio again, the angel whose heartstrings were a lute. Here was Cleveland ... Israfel ... again. Where were they going? And where have they led me?

"Behold, I send an Angel before thee, to keep thee in the way," is written in the Book of Exodus.

When I finally read the little crumpled note, I knew that I would not need to repeat it, for it was a kind of Announcement of where I might some day see Israfel again. Of course I should talk more of it, to make this a well-rounded account instead of a straight report, but I prefer not to. It can stay inviolate, like its messenger.   —*Glen Ellen, 1974*

THE
WIND-CHILL
FACTOR

A Problem of Mind and Matter

 Preface

And here is the story or rather the report I wrote about a few days and nights on the dunes of Long Island, when I learned that I could survive, at least something like Sound and at least for a time longer than was really needed.

It seems odd, by now, that I wrote in the third person, because it is one of the most directly personal accounts I have ever given of something that has happened to me. I think that I probably felt I should detach myself as deliberately in the report as I had done while the winds blew.

Certainly it was no longer a question of professional timidity, as it was when I wrote my first article for publication and sent it off to the house organ of the Southern California Automobile Association, as I have described in the preface to "Pacific Village."

I still believe in both kindliness and justice, but have no patience with self-deception. When I filled out the notes I had forced myself to make during the winds, I was like a pale invalid, unable to identify with the immediate past. At least, that is how it now seems. Unless I look at the story I do not even remember what name I gave myself. And while the winds blew, I knew that I had no name at all.

In Sag Harbor, though, when I confronted the emphatic discipline of telling a straight story of the far past, it was much harder to write without prettifying, smudging. I had made no notes as things progressed on Painter Avenue in Whittier. Perhaps it is fortunate for older people that children seldom keep hour-by-hour reports of their own storms. They do not yet know how to deceive themselves.

There was doubt in the woman's mind about whether it would be wise of her to try to make some notes about her experience at once, or let the long blizzard go through its sixth noisy night. Perhaps putting onto paper what had happened to her could make things worse, invite another such experience, and she was not sure how well she would handle it, or more truthfully if she could survive it.

Her name was Mrs. Thayer, and she was living alone in a friend's cottage, ideally installed for a solitary good few months on wild dunes toward the tip of Long Island. The house faced the ocean, and except for the earth's rounding she could have looked east to Portugal and south to Cuba. In the rooms heated by electricity things were cozy and fine, until an uncommonly sustained blizzard moved onto that part of the planet, and onto the tiny spit of sand, like a bull covering and possessing the cow, the warm shelter.

Mrs. Thayer finally had, or went through, or lived past, a most astonishing experience in her life, on the fifth night of the storm.

By then she was used to adjusting the thermostats in each of the five heated rooms, and turning them up in the bathroom when she could no longer put off a shower, and then down in her bedroom once the electric pad had warmed her guts. The house had a kind of private weather station on one wall, and the barometer and thermometer worked among all the other gadgets that did not: the meters for wind velocity and wind direction, the tide clock, something called a durotherm hygrometer. The ship's bells sounded later and later, and finally went silent. Now and then a delicate needle spun meaninglessly in one of the brass puddings with their crystal crusts, as the blizzard yowled above and around. Mrs. Thayer found that she looked at them fairly often, as if to keep track of what might really be happening, and noticing blandly when the barometer dropped in a few hours from 30.15 to 28.60, whatever that might mean.

She also accustomed herself to listen through the static on the kitchen radio to mysteriously progressing reports about ice conditions on New York and Boston streets, and how much garbage lay on their sidewalks. She herself had no such problems, for the little car in her friend's garage would not start, even if she had wanted to hold it on the road into the nearest village and, because she lived alone, she made so little rubbish that it was all right to put it tidily in an unheated corridor until the wind stopped. Another problem in the cities was animals, who must of course befoul the snow, since few four-legged people have adapted themselves to flush plumbing. Mrs. Thayer was, for the first time in most of her lives, without such a friend, which may have added to the severity of her experience on the fifth night.

The wind, which had during the first two days shifted capriciously this way and that, finally settled into a northwest blow, steady but fiercely insistent. It bent the grasses almost flat on the dunes, and when occasional dry snow piled up in corners, it soon soiled the sculptured drifts with yellowish sand from the implacable surf. Waves changed from long piling rollers to mighty beasts wearing spume four times their height. The sound of them, and of the gale that pushed them sideways, took possession of the house.

Mrs. Thayer found, after the third night, that as she slipped into good sleep she would feel for a few minutes as if she were being rocked, moved, gently tipped, by what was happening outside the tight little shelter. She knew that she did not actually feel this, but she accepted it as a part of being so intimately close to the majesty she lay beside.

The air grew steadily colder, and the woman alone there in the dunes (the natives knew better than to build anywhere but inland in such brutal country) closed off rooms she did not need, and limited herself to the kitchen, the bedroom, the toilet. Everything stayed cozy for her, with no apprehensions: if the electricity went off, she would wait for people who knew she was there to get to her somehow, before the place grew too cold. . . . Almost nonchalantly she did not think about such things, even when the telephone went dead for a couple of days. It would ring clearly, and there would be only a wild squawk on the line. She suspected that her own voice might be heard, and would say in a high firm way, "This is Mrs. Thayer. Everything is all right. I am all right. Thank you." It was childish to feel rather pleased and excited about the game, but she did.

The night of the fourth day she ate a nice supper at the

table in the warm kitchen, and adjusted thermostats here and there and tidied herself for sleep, with parts of at least six books to read first. In bed she turned on the electric warmer, and succumbed late but easily to sleep, perhaps at one o'clock in the morning. She felt well fed, warm, and serene.

A little after four an extraordinary thing happened to her. From deep and sweet-dreaming sleep she was wrenched into the conscious world, as cruelly as if she had been grabbed by the long hairs of her head. Her heart had changed its slow quiet beat, and bumped in her rib cage like a rabbit's. Her breath was caught in a kind of net in her throat, not going in and down fast enough. She touched her body and it was hot, but her palms felt clammy, and stuck to her.

Within a few seconds she knew that she was in a state, perhaps dangerous, of pure panic.

It had nothing to do with physical fear, as far as she could tell. She was not afraid of being alone, nor of being on the dunes in a storm. She was not afraid of bodily attack, rape, all that. She was simply in panic, or what Frenchmen home from the Sahara used to call *le cafard affolé*.

This is amazing, she said. This is indescribable. It is here. I shall survive it, or else run out howling across the dunes and die soon in the waves and the wind. Such a choice seemed very close and sweet, for her feeling was almost intolerably wishful of escape from the noise. It was above and against and around her, and she felt that it was invading her spirit. This is dangerous indeed, she said, and I must try not to run outside. That is a suicide wish, and weak. I must try to breathe more slowly, and perhaps swallow something to get back my more familiar rhythms. She was speaking slowly to herself, with silent but precise enunciation.

She waited for some minutes to see if she could manage

the breathing in bed, but her heart and lungs were almost out of control when she got unsteadily to her feet, tied her night robe around her, and went into the little toilet. There, it took a minute to get her hand to turn on the light, for she was wracked with a kind of chill, which made her lower back and thighs ache as if she were in labor, and her jaws click together like bare bones. She remembered that in her friend's mirror-cabinet was a bottle of some variety of aspirin, and with real difficulty, almost as if she were spastic, she managed to run water into a mug and swallow the pills down her throat. If you cannot swallow, she said flatly, you are afraid of your enemy. She felt sick, and won this tiny battle of holding down the medicine at great moral cost, for by now in the astonishing onslaught she was as determined as an apparently insensate animal not to submit to the steady roaring all around her.

She dared not look at herself for a time, but walked in a staggering way about the warmer parts of the cottage, recalling methods she had studied, and even practiced, for self-preservation. There was one, taught to her during a period of deep stress, in which one takes three slow small sips of almost any liquid, and then waits a set period, from five to fifteen minutes, and takes three more, and so on. She devoted her whole strength to this project, as if life depended on it, which it may well have. She carefully heated some milk, and when she could not open the bottle of Angostura which might have taken the curse off its insipidity, and she sensed that she might break the little bottle with her almost uncontrollable hands, she poured in two big spoonfuls of sugar. It was a revolting brew, but she drank about half the mugful of it over the next period of carefully repulsed frenzy.

The wind had become different. Its steady pressure of sound had changed to a spasmodic violence. Snow was stinging against the northern and western storm windows, and Mrs. Thayer already knew that the doors on those sides were frozen shut. It did not matter. A door to the outside place where people changed bathing suits in the summer began to bang hard, in irregular patterns. It is unhinged, she said with a sly grin. It did not matter either. The whole thing she must work on was to keep herself inside her own skin, and she was the only one there to do it, and with real sweat she did.

She pulled every trick out of the bag over her long life with neurotics. She brushed her hair firmly, and all the while her heart kept kicking against her ribs, and she felt so sick that she could scarcely lift her arm. She tried to say some nursery rhymes and the Twenty-Third Psalm, but with no better result than an impatient titter. She sipped the dreadful sweet milk. She prayed to those two pills, called Quick Relief for Nervous Tension on the radio, to help, to help fast, never to cure of course of *course*, see your physician for persistent muscular discomfort. . . .

If I permit myself to think in my present terms I am done for, she said in rounded words and clearly punctuated sentences, in a silent voice that rang like Teacher's in her head, like Father Joseph's, like Dr. Rab's. It is a question of moral energy, she said. Subconsciously I am admitting that the storm is great and I am small, and for a time or possibly forever I have lost the balance that human beings must maintain between their own inner force and that of Nature. I was unaware of what the wind and the ocean were doing to me. I have been respectful and awed, but too bland. Now I am being told. Told off. Yes, she said, I am admitting it. But do I have to bow any deeper, cry Uncle, lose everything?

She went on playing several canny games like this as she moved feebly about the rooms. Heavy curtains moved in the

fierce air, and she gradually added long woolen socks and a
leather coat to her strange coverings, but managed as part of
her dogged rescue work to focus enough on a mirror to arrange her hair nicely and put on firm eyebrows and a mouth
that looked poutish instead of as hard as she had hoped. This
is simply going on too long, she said like a woman on the
delivery table, and added more lipstick.

For a time, as the aspirin and the warm milk seemed to
slow down her limitless dread (Dread of what? Not that
the roof would fly off, that she was alone, that she might
die . . .), she made herself talk reasonably to what was
puking and trembling and flickering in her spirit. She was a
doctor, or rather an unwitting bystander caught in some
kind of disaster, forced to be cool and wise with one of the
victims, perhaps a child bleeding toward death or an old man
pinned under a truck wheel. She talked quietly to this helpless shocked soul fluttering in its poor body. She was strong
and calm. All the time she knew cynically that she was nonexistent except in the need thrust upon her, and that soon
the patient would either die or recover and forget her dramatic saintliness when the real ambulance came.

"Listen to your breathing," she said coolly. "You are not
badly hurt. Soon you will feel all right. Sip this. It will make
the pain go away. Lift your head now, and breathe slowly.
You are not really in trouble." And so on. Whenever the
other part of Mrs. Thayer, the threatened one, let her mind
slip back to the horror of an imminent breaking with all
reason, all lucidity, and then out the door it would be final,
the kindly stranger seemed to see it in the eyeballs and the
pulse as she bent over the body, and spoke more firmly:
"Now hold the cup. You can. I know you can. You will be
all right."

This got monotonous, and in fact it was embarrassing, to

have the two things floating inside her, as she tried consciously to go with the sounds of the gale instead of letting her consciousness accept them weakly and undermine her. Finally she said rudely to the kind creature (a fellow passenger?) who had been trying to give her some help, "Go away. I *will* be all right." And the other part of her shrugged and withdrew, knowing there was nothing more to do, knowing that she would not have been dismissed if Mrs. Thayer depended on her any further.

The next step was to try to read. But the poor soul found it hard to focus her eyes on the print, and when she did it was on sentences picked hit-or-miss from this page or that. There was one from an anonymous book called *Streetwalker:* ". . . to admit fear and weakness to any living soul . . . would be to reveal my unfitness for the life I have chosen, and, since no other is now possible for me, to reach the limits of despair—and God knows what would happen then."

I am being played with, Mrs. Thayer said angrily, and with great care put the book back in its shelf-place and then was reading, in a controlled way, while her heard thugged along and she felt wambly all over, "This is the day for each of us to assess our own strength, in utter silence to plumb the depth of our own spirit." What in God's name was she looking at? She saw coldly the title, *Second Thoughts* by old man Mauriac, and all her admiration of a lot of things in him turned into fuming jelly, and instead of putting back the book neatly she tossed it on the floor, and started to walk about the little house again.

Its secret balance, the stuff like the fluid of the inner ear, was centered now a little below her diaphragm, and she walked with special care, in order to keep the whole place from crushing like an egg as the giant thrashed.

Her father had talked often about a couple of years he'd

once spent as a reporter in North Dakota. He said that farm women went stark mad there for one good reason, and that was because in their lonely cabins, when they could see out the window, the snow would always be blowing horizontally. Always. It sent them mad, that sideways snow on and on. It was not the wind, for them. The sideways snow did it.

Mrs. Thayer knew. The sound of the wind, for her, was going sideways, exactly on a line with the far horizon of the Atlantic, for days, nights, perhaps five or a week or anyway much too long. It was in her bowels, and suddenly they were loosened and then later, also to her surprise, she threw up. She told herself dizzily that the rhythm of the wind had bound her around, and that now she was defying it, but it kept on howling.

The pills worked, helped by the warm drink. The human parts of her body helped. The mind did not fail her, and she knew all the time, or at least brought herself gradually to believe so, that she would never have run out like a beast, to die quickly on the dunes. Once she stopped roaming and lay down, feeling purged and calmer, but the minute she was flat on the bed she heard the wind pressing against the wall beyond her head, and it was as if she were locked in a cell and in the next one a giant lay in his last agony, breathing with a terrible rage and roar. She got up and brushed at her hair again, and then walked with a decreasing stagger about the little rooms.

In a couple more hours everything was all right inwardly with her, except that she was languid, as if she had lain two weeks in a fever. The peculiar panic which had seized her bones and spirit faded fast, once routed. She was left wan and bemused. Never had she been afraid, that is, of tangibles like cold and sand and wind. She was not afraid, as far as she knew, of dying either fast or slowly. It was, she decided precisely, a question of sound. If the storm had not lasted so long, with its noise so much into her, into her brain and muscles . . . If this had been a kind of mating, it was without joy.

Gradually she was breathing with deep but not worried rhythm as she lay under a cover on her bed. The wind still thrust at her, but she sensed that the giant was in that state of merciful lull that rewards old scoundrels in their final throes: he was not choking and hitting out at her. She got up carefully, and did several small things like polishing her fingernails, and then poached an egg in some beef broth and ate it. She felt as hollow as an old shell, and surprisingly trembly. She slept for two hours, out like a drunk.

The whole peculiar experience was still in her mind when she awakened. Why did it happen? Was it a question of decibels, of atmospheric pressure? Had her ears, which like every other living human ears in the world were different from any other living human ears, simply been too long assaulted by the pullulations of the violently moving air about her? Where was *she*, then? Could she survive such an obvious dare again? Why must she? All of this puzzled her, and she found herself hoping like a child that the air would be calmer, and soon.

She permitted herself the weakness of one gentle tap on the barometer, and felt no real dismay when its thin fluttering indicator went down a little more. If there was any message in it, perhaps it said that since Mrs. Thayer had lived through the past hours, she would never know them again. It is probable, she said, that if I must, I shall bow, succumb, admit greater strength.

There was no point in thinking much about this, in her

weak lackadaisical state, so she wrote a few notes to herself, not caring if they might bring on more wind or not, and went to bed. And during the late afternoon, while she dozed with a deep soft detachment, the sound abated and then died, and she was lost in the sweet dream-life of a delivered woman. —*Bridgehampton, 1973*

THE
CHANGEOVER

Preface

All this story needs as an introduction, I think, is that it
happened in the early sixties and that it is not a story. It is
what I perhaps mistakenly consider a report, a *reportage.* It
is straight plain telling.

I went up to Reno from San Francisco after a long illness, to
break a pattern of convalescence. Most people go there for
amorous or marital or financial reasons, but I went to get a
divorce from myself, the sick or malingering self. It was early
spring, and I felt like a refugee from the clinics and the test
tubes.

On the train, which I took in Oakland, across the Bay, I

looked with deliberate interest from my window as the land and water slid by. I liked the movement of heading into something unknown, although the cars crowded with people already stripping themselves and stretching out for the long sit-up ride to Kansas City were not attractive. Men took off their coats and shirts and hung them above their heads on the luggage racks and put their feet out into the aisles and turned off all but the little blue night-lights, so that from the end of the car it looked like the scene of a large accident, with bodies sprawled grotesquely in the dimness. In the seat across the aisle from me, an old woman settled into her feathers like a tired hen and then rustled slowly through a paper bag until she found a hard roll. Holding it with both hands, she chewed on it sleepily, half dozing.

I staggered through the cluttered aisles to the club car, and after a martini I went on to the diner. I ate simply and well, and everything tasted mildly exhilarating, the way it should when a person stops being ill and suddenly is not too afraid to be well and vertical again. Reno came along fairly soon after I had walked back through the tilting, lurching cars, over all the legs, to my assigned seat. I pulled my coat and makeup box off the rack, and we slowed down.

I had gone through Reno once before, a good many years ago, on the same train, perhaps, but heading West. Then, I was sitting in the club car with my husband, and just before we got to the station a kind of squeal went up and the train seemed to tip to the left, like a rowboat, with the weight of people peering out of the windows, piling over each other to see the bright lights. This new night, as I climbed out of the train, I recalled that strange feeling of excitement of so long ago in the travelers from the Midwest gazing at the sinful city of gambling and divorce and high life. With that one quick look up the main street of the little town, they were breathing and touching vice, and without any danger of infection. On one side of the train had been darkness, empty and unheeded, and on the other, for a quick flash—like a peep show—was a glimpse of a gaudily lighted street banked with neon and arched by an electric sign. It was dramatic, so quick a brightness after the long rocking ride across plains and deserts and through mountain gorges. As I got off the train, I wondered if it was still that way.

Out in the cold grey station, it was complicated to get two suitcases that had been checked into the baggage car in Oakland. A polite sleepy porter turned up finally and managed it for me, in spite of locked doors and dark rooms and a general air of disuse about the place. He and I seemed to be the only people who still believed this silent building was a railroad station. He carried my things out to the empty street and put them beside a lamppost. "You be all right here," he said gently. "I call for a cab. Take some time but be along."

I stood there passively under the thin light. The air, too, was thin, and cold. I felt doggedly detached about the whole dream-like procedure, and only an Olympian curiosity when two very thin men, dressed in shabby, decent clothes, came silently down the street toward me, pulling along a baby coyote on a piece of string.

"Hi there," one said in a meek voice. "You ever see a real baby coyote?"

His companion leaned over, miming, to pat the little animal, which was sitting down as if it had walked a long way, and the talking one said, on cue, "He's real nice. Tame as a kitten."

"How old is he?" I asked.

"Maybe couple weeks. You want him? Five bucks."

"Not tonight. No, not now," I said, and without even shrugging—almost without a sound—the two men went up the hollow street again with the little wild puppy trotting behind them at the end of the piece of string.

I was not thinking one way or another, about Time or anything else, but a cab did come, although I never saw the sleepy porter again. On the way to the hotel at which I had made a reservation, suddenly there was a flash of almost audible light, and, sure enough, I had not forgotten the street of neon and thick gaudy signs with the arch blazing over it. I was in Reno, symbol of sin, of quick divorce and quicker marriage, of unlicensed license, and the hotel lobby seemed a normal projection of the flash-by of the street from that earlier train window—a glitter and glow under the low ceiling, with hundreds of slot machines crashing and flickering and ringing bells, and chaotic decorations twirling in the air to say that even if Time meant nothing, Easter and daffodils and bunnies were next on the calendar.

There were rows of tables for roulette and whatever other games are played on tables, and the people around them were mute—an old Ernst Lubitsch movie of Monte Carlo. It was the slot machines that seemed alive—certainly more alive than the unsmiling men and women who stood woodenly in front of them, not even blinking or twitching when lights flashed for a jackpot. Plump little cash girls packed into white satin shirts and black slacks moved through the voiceless crowds, changing bills into dollars, dollars into nickels. Very loud mariachi music blanketed us raggedly.

In one corner, hidden, was the hotel desk. A trim young man in tight frontier pants and high-heeled boots carried my bags there, and then, when I had registered, he crowded me into a minuscule elevator and we shot past a few floors smoothly. In the room, he did a kind of precision dance of turning on lights, flicking his eyes here and there over ash-trays and such, showing me how to adjust the heat, taking the tip. At the door, he smiled warmly and drawled, "Y'all have fun, now."

The room was from a hyped-up motel, somewhat elegant. I sniffed it like a cat, and was there. In the bathroom were packets of aspirin and a hangover remedy, and courtesy samples of hand lotion, and free shoe polishers. The drinking glasses and the toilet seat and even the telephone by the bed were marked *Sterilized for your protection,* and there was a little package of buttons and threaded needles on the television set. One wall of the room was glass, and, below the balcony outside, the Truckee River rushed backward and ducks fought the high water and clutched at the banks in the colored, shifting lights from the lobby, a few floors beneath me.

I began to feel more like a person. I flicked the TV on and off, and then the radio on and off. I read through all the folders on the desk about what was at my fingertips—my beck and call—and what I could eat in the various dining places and when, and mostly what I could drink. For an odd sum like $7.84, or perhaps $14.23, I could have almost instantly a hospitality kit containing fifths each of vodka, scotch, bourbon, rye, gin, ice, and my choice of setups, brought to my room by a smiling cowboy.

It seemed ridiculous to me to pass up the one chance of my life to take a long cool look at the ground floor of this place. I felt that my vision was ready, cleared by illness. I would never again, if I lived here a thousand nights instead of one, be able to see it as I would this night. I called for room service.

The same bellboy who had shown me to my room came, almost as if he had been outside the door. He was neatly

232 ·   AS THEY WERE

strong, and short in spite of his heels, and as impersonal as a geranium in a pot. "Y'all want me?" His smile was a really nice one.

I asked him if he thought it would be all right if I went downstairs by myself, to look around.

He figured me financially, logistically, alcoholically, sexually, in one quick look. I passed. "Y'all's safer here than in your own home," he said. "Once you get accustomed, this place is real fun, and no harm done. They keep an eye on things downstairs. Go right ahead."

I said, like a docile child, "Thank you very much. I really didn't want anything else."

He beamed kindly at me and said, "Just go right on down," and closed the door on a silhouette of slim solid hips and tiny gleaming boots.

Back in the incredible lobby, I felt stiff and shy. I wandered from one aisle of slot machines to the next, trying not to stare too much, not to goggle as the automatic people pulled at the handles and fed in coins and then did or did not scoop up more coins and feed them back again. I told myself that I was invisible, but very soon I knew that I was not. I was being watched covertly by the small plump girls wearing sailor caps marked *cash,* and by the tellers on their raised platforms, and by the nonchalant plainclothesmen chatting here and there. Probably the cowboy had told them that I was loose in the place—not because I was going to drink too much or even play too much or pick up a man or a girl but because I was a strange one, not yet identifiable. I was not dressed like the rest, basically. I was alone. I might perhaps be a suicide? I had no perceptible rendezvous arranged, in or out of the hotel, so if I was a go-between, between what and what? The eyes were on me.

I decided to go right on drifting, and gradually I knew

where the rest rooms were (they were large and comfortable, and a woman in Levi's and a shabby catskin coat was writing postcards in German script), and where the coffee shop kept open twenty-four hours a day, and where a boy in a high white bonnet made hot roast-beef sandwiches twenty-four hours a day for the gamblers, who forgot whether it was time for what—breakfastlunchdinner. There were people eating orange-juice-coffee-poached-eggs-on-toast, with the preoccupied shaving-lotion look of suburban commuters at 7:22 a.m. At the bar, to which the main aisle through the slot machines led, people were meeting for a cocktail, the women looking very wives-of-suburban-commuters in short brocade sheaths and pearls and mink scarves, and it was long after midnight instead of 7:22 a.m.

Behind the bar was a small stage, somewhat above the bottles, and first there was the blasty mariachi band I had heard when I came into the hotel and then, with a special blink and blare, there was a small jazz combo of four men, with a girl singer. They were Navajo Indians, with an impervious disdain behind their show-biz smiles but dressed snappily and playing fairly well.

Feeling weary, I sat down at one of the small tables between the active part of the lobby and the bar. Around me were several other single men and women, but there did not seem to be any open interest in pickups. I ordered a double Gibson from the motherly waitress. I felt curious about how a drink which I consider an apéritif would taste at that incongruous hour, in that unbelievable place, with no meal to follow. It was good, and I enjoyed it slowly.

The m.c. of the Navajo band was clumsy about being Indian, and angry. He made one too many jokes about it, and told one too many too long stories, and gradually I realized that in the aisle leading to the bar two groups of six or eight

young men had gathered, not one-arming but just standing
there. They were blond and sharply dressed, and they were
getting ready to make trouble with the increasingly racist
man at the mike—prearranged trouble. The men in the
combo were watching, as they beat and tootled, and the girl,
who was perhaps more Mexican than Indian, and almost
white-skinned, was watching, too, from behind her trite,
sexy singing. All the eyes that I had felt on me before were
fastened now on the two groups of boys gathered closer and
closer to the bar, the bottles, the stage.

The m.c. told another barely funny story of how the Indian would be here to live on his land again after the atomic
bomb had taken care of the white man, and the boys slid on
in—and with them, as gently as the flanges of an oyster or
the spreading hood of a cobra, the security men in their
well-tailored business suits moved in, and the boys, tense
with racial hatred and envy and whatever else it may have
been, moved on out and away.

The music kept on, but the young sweating m.c. mopped
his face and let the girl singer take over and handle the act,
and disappeared. The people at the bar and the little tables
kept on drinking. I ordered a single Gibson, and felt that I
had just taken the last step to safety from a plank stretched
across boiling oil. The mariachi players came grinning on-
stage, and a fat *castrado* yelped and whimpered through
"Guadalajara." It was time for me to go.

Upstairs, I was painfully hungry. The discreet meal on the
train was a century behind me. The folded cards and menus
on the Formica desk said I could order almost any dish at almost any time, and by now I knew that downstairs day and
night did not mean what I had always thought. Why should
I not call room service and ask for scrambled eggs and a glass
of milk, a bottle of beer, a split of champagne, or perhaps a

hospitality kit? If I poured some milk or beer or wine—or even a double Gibson—into a saucer, maybe the little wild dog would come and lap it up. Far below the balcony, the Truckee still flowed backward, uphill. There were no ducks now, clutching at the banks against the swift water.

I adjusted the heat, turned the TV and the radio on and then off, and decided that I did not want to see the smiling cowboy again, ever, even bringing me nourishment with his good smile. The sun would be along soon, and meanwhile I knew that I was not ill anymore. The divorce had been granted. I had complete custody of myself.

—*St. Helena,* *1962*

GARE DE LYON

Paris fairs and expositions, always attempted and sometimes realized on a grand scale, have been beset, at least in the twentieth century, by strikes, riots, floods, and other natural and man-made hindrances to such minor goals as opening on time. In the same way, they have left something strong and beautiful behind them, whether tangible or in men's minds and hearts.

In 1937, for instance, there was the Internationale. Strikes were an almost stylish necessity of life in those quaintly distant days before all hell broke loose, and the fair lagged in summer heat while opulent or simply eager tourists marked time in the cafés and museums; outlandish buildings were put up and torn down and picketed and sabotaged. I was there from Switzerland to meet my parents, who loved great fairs, as do most Midwesterners reared on St. Louis and Chicago and even San Francisco shivarees, and my father was excited by the violent scornful unrest in that year's Parisian air, as he had never been at home by giant mechanical toys like roller coasters.

We walked every day in the purlieus of the Exposition, to guess when a pavilion might possibly be opened or bombed. At night we looked at the lighted revolving statue of bright gold in the U.S.S.R. exhibit, but Father did not want to visit it, for vaguely political reasons. Once we went on the Seine in a *bateau-mouche,* and he was thrilled when every window in the Citroën plant was filled with striking beleaguered workers saluting us with raised fists. Nothing like that at home!

But from that fair, which never really came to life for us who waited, rose one bright star, the Guernica mural by Picasso. It was there. It was on view. It was well guarded. It was moving and terrible, and we went perhaps five times to look slowly at it, close up, far off, not talking. It was a difficult experience for my father, but one he faced with an almost voluptuous acceptance, so that we began to return compulsively to the long room where the painting unrolled itself. There were piles of rubble and discarded tools on the unfinished paths outside the building, but inside people walked silently up and down, finding parts of themselves in Guernica, even from Iowa and California.

Backwards to 1931, there was a fair called the Exposition Coloniale. As far as I know, some of it opened more or less on schedule, at least in time to assemble peculiar exotic hints of the imminent collapse of French attempts to keep their own sun shining around the clock on territorial land grabs. What else could it try to demonstrate? Why else would a reputedly thrifty nation spend hundreds of thousands of francs re-creating African villages and Indo-Chinese temples for visitors to gape at? From now in Time, it all seemed then to have some of the luminous gaiety of a terminal cancer patient's final defiant fling. I lurched about on camels, and watched silent blacks squatting in front of their phony huts

to carve cabalistic masks. Everywhere there was a heady perfume of leather, of raw silk and wool, of unknown spicy
foods. As in the Internationale that came so few years after-
wards, the Coloniale had a dappled green magic, under the
summer leaves, and left behind it more than its rare polished
woods and supple cloth.

But both those fairs seemed unreal. They were *there*, in
spite of strikes and riots and general political uncertainty,
but where are their physical traces? Where is the cardboard
Angkor Wat by now? The painting of Guernica still exists,
but where is the long shady building that harbored it?
Where is the golden statue that revolved seductively, almost
lewdly, above the Soviet pavilion? In the end, where are the
dreams and wars that spawned all that pomp?

It was perhaps different in 1900. The hunger and shame of
the Franco-Prussian War had been half forgotten by a new
generation, and the Dreyfus Affair seemed temporarily under
wraps. Paris needed and indeed deserved a circus. Architects
were appointed, perhaps subconsciously, who could evoke all
the rich weightiness of the Third Empire, before the late and
current troubles, and they put together some pleasure domes
for their fair that still enchant us: two palaces, the Grand and
the Petit; the bridge across the Seine named for Alexander
the Third; best of all, to some at least, the Gare de Lyon.

It happened before my time, and the French accounts are
understandably vague about how and when that World's
Fair finally ground into action. It seems natural, by now,
that the enormous glassy station was formally inaugurated a
year late, but it is still there to prove that in 1901, on April
17, the President of the Republic and countless international
notables gathered in it to declare that the Gare de Lyon was
indeed a reality.

No doubt other very solemn things have happened there

in almost a century, like treaty signings and top-level hanky-panky connected with both railroads and people, and municipal banquets, but it is hard to imagine that they did not contain a certain element of enjoyment, in that magical place. Surely the ceremonial toasts tasted better there. . . .

As far as I can know or learn, no other railroad station in the world manages so mysteriously to cloak with compassion the anguish of departure and the dubious ecstasies of return and arrival. Any waiting room in the world is filled with all this, and I have sat in many of them and accepted it, and I know from deliberate acquaintance that the whole human experience is more bearable at the Gare de Lyon in Paris than anywhere else. By now the public rooms on the train level are more plastic-topped, chromium-benched, than in the first days of wood everywhere, with iron and brass fittings. But the porters seem to stay sturdy and aware, and there is a near-obsolete courtesy at the "snack bars," even five minutes before commute time.

For me, it began to come to life in 1937. I was there often, from 1929 on, always one more ant scuttling for a certain track, a cheap train south to Dijon, a luxury train to Lausanne. The station was something to run through. It was a grimy glass tunnel, and I felt glad when we pulled out and headed south.

But in 1937, when I could meet my parents in La Ville Lumière, I grew almost shockingly aware of the station. I went there early that twilight, to wait for their train. On the quai that looked far out under the glass roof and along all the gleaming tracks was a café, part of the big noisy bar-brasserie inside. There were little trees in long boxes, to sweeten the air and catch the soot, and the tables were of that grey-white marble that apparently was created by Nature solely for café tabletops. I sat waiting, drinking a brandy and water, realizing suddenly that I was not in a station, but in a place.

My family arrived, worn after a rough crossing, and it was not for perhaps ten days that I went back. My father was going down to Nice. For the first of countless times I cunningly arranged our getting around Paris so that we would have to *wait* for the train to slide in under the glass roof along the silver track, so that I could be there ... in the place.

It was one of the pleasantest times I'd ever known with a man I'd always respected and loved. We were two people, suddenly. We sat behind the boxes filled with gritty treelings, and although it was only late morning we drank slowly at brandy again, with water and casual talk and mostly a quiet awareness of the loveliness of the great station.

It was not noisy. It was not stuffy. People did not look sad or even hurried. Trains whistled and chugged in and out, slid voluptuously toward us and then stopped. Big boards lit up here and there, high above the tracks, telling people where to go, when. A porter came to tell me that it was time for the gentleman to board.

"This is the way to do it! How can a railroad station be so beautiful?" my father asked happily, and I knew that I had marked off another mile in my life.

Then there was a war, and when I went back to Paris in the early fifties, I scuttled through without more than a shy shamed look at the glassed roof that the Occupiers had found too essential to destroy. I did not permit the station's magic to take hold again until about the mid-sixties, when I went alone to Paris, for the first time in my life: no husbands—lovers—parents—children ... I was on a writing assignment, and I asked to be lodged in the attic of a hotel on the Seine in a room I liked most. My husband and I had planned, before the War and he died, to rent two little connecting rooms there and make a kind of pied-à-terre, a place where we could leave books and be warmer than in Switzerland. This all turned impossible, and when I went back so much later I felt scared, so that I asked to take one of those familiar rooms. And in the other, to my astonishment, lived a person I admired deeply named Janet Flanner. It was fine. My husband would have liked it.

And so it happened that I reported, that summer, to my friend about my love affair with the Gare de Lyon, and she in turn decided to take her own look, her view she admitted had always been sketchy in spite of some forty years in Paris, and with due reflection she reported the whole thing to André Malraux, who then controlled the governmental wires that could declare a French relic or monument legitimately "historical," and therefore supposedly immune to further human destruction.

Malraux had a rare and passionate belief in "the redemptive power of beauty," and seemed to know that a minor living art form is far more vital than a major dead one. From what I have been told, he started at once to safeguard the shabby old restaurant in the Gare de Lyon, so that by now it is a twinkling *Monument Historique,* worthy of all that was opulently cheerful, generously vulgar and delightful, about *la Belle Époque.*

Things were different from my lives before, in the midsixties. The job demanded that I go between Paris and the South quite often, and I was looked at as freakish because I insisted on taking the Mistral train from the station instead of flying. A waste of time, of energy, I was told by my bosses. But nobody could understand how totally renewing of many strengths it was for me to go there at least two hours before

the beautiful train pulled out, to eat a slow breakfast, and
then slide southward through the forests and farms and into
Burgundian vineyards and then suddenly, like an explosion,
into the Midi below Lyon ... and on down, through poi-
gnantly familiar towns like Avignon to the spot past the
Étang de Berre, just before the Quartier de St. Louis in Marseille, where there is a mysterious flash of gold from the tiny
needle of Notre Dame de la Garde.

From then on it was less emotional sailing, with cliffs and
twisted pines and strange villas, until I got to the familiar
little station in Cannes and the resumption of my professional life, but always I felt brave enough for it, after the
private meal in Paris.

The main room of the First-Class Restaurant-Buffet at the
Gare de Lyon seems to run the whole length of what to us
Americans is the second floor. Actually, if one enters by way
of the noble staircase from the inside quai of the station,
there are several rooms of varying importance to the left,
closed and reserved for board meetings and other mysterious
gatherings. Mostly, pundits and tycoons heading for them
use a smaller staircase that goes up under the Clock Tower,
and never set foot in the enormous Restaurant. (The Big
Ben Bar and the cloakrooms are conveniently to their right
as they enter.)

To the rest of us travelers, going up the staircase from the
quai is much more exciting than the handy little "back
stairs," and the huge room sweeps out, dream-like and yet
inviting, and across from us the lace curtains move faintly in
the drafts from the great square below.

Down at the far end, to our right, the Train Bleu is properly hushed and somewhat more elegant, if that is possible,
than what any traveler can expect in the main room, only
tacitly separated from its little offshoot. Service is swift or

slow, according to one's logistical needs, and there is a comfortable feeling of *bourgeois* polish and sparkle everywhere: clean linen and brass, waxed floors, good plain food as well as a few fastuous dishes. Madame Maigret would approve of it. So, I feel sure, would Brillat-Savarin, if it were not some 150 years too late. . . .

It is one of the most amazing public dining rooms I have ever seen, or even imagined. The ceiling is very high and elaborate. The windows are tall, looking on one side upon a goodly part of Paris, and then to the right into and under the endless stretch of grey glass roof over all the tracks that come to a dead stop down below . . . Switzerland, Italy, Spain, the Near East, all France to the south. . . .

The walls, between and above the great lace-hung windows, are covered with more than forty huge murals of every possible scenic delight that the Paris-Lyon-Mediterranean trains could offer their travelers at the turn of the century, mostly peopled by plump Edwardian diplomats in top hats, and famous divas and courtesans in filmy garden frocks or even bathing dresses, all frolicking discreetly against breathtaking landscapes.

By now, the paintings have been cleaned, and their elaborate frames retouched. The lace curtains have been mended and starched and rehung, and the three monumental ceilings with their "crammed and gorgeous" paintings have been pulled back to life in our comparatively clean air, after years of collecting soot from the old steam trains below. And all the elegant *bancs* and chairs, comfortable in dark soft leather, have been refurbished, along with the sumptuous but functional brass racks for luggage and hats, and the tall lampstands along the middle aisle.

Perhaps best, at least for the waiters, is that the endless polished floors underfoot have been strengthened or repaired, so that there is no longer the steady creaking that I first noticed, when I listened there in the sixties.

I am not sure, by now, why I first decided to go to this station two hours before train time. Perhaps I wanted to sit where I had once been with my father. Perhaps I wanted to ready my spirit for the new job in the South. A porter (oh, a fine man, an angel in a blue soft blouse! I remember him clearly: tall, past middle age, oddly protective of me as was exactly right on that day ...) told me when I asked to follow him to the café on the inside quai that he thought I would be better off upstairs, where he would come for me in ample time before the Mistral left. I felt docile, and followed him under the Clock Tower and past the end of the big noisy brasserie-café on the ground floor and up some back stairs, into the shrouded silent corridors of the First-Class Restaurant. I had never been there before.

He pounded on ahead of me with my luggage, and a waiter who knew him came from somewhere past the deserted old Big Ben Bar. My porter went straight down the middle aisle of what seemed like a silent gaudy cathedral to me, and stopped toward the far end, which as I remember was being remodeled for the new Train Bleu section.

"Madame is hungry," he said in a mild way to his friend. "She is taking the Mistral. I'll be back." I felt helpless but undismayed. This was part of important private history, I sensed.

The waiter was surprisingly young to be working in such an awesome monument. He gave me a menu, and I settled myself in the huge sunny temple while he went down to the newsstand where I had planned to sit in all the sooty racket behind a spindly box tree, drinking *café au lait*. When he came up again with two very solemn dailies, I told him that I would like bread and butter, Parma ham, and a half-bottle of a *brut* champagne that seemed quite expensive to me and that is no longer on the excellent wine list. He looked pleased, and scudded off, with the floor under him making a fine high racket in the emptiness.

In 1967 or whenever that was, I felt dismal about the state of bread in Paris, and had not yet found that it would be almost as bad everywhere, and I decided then that the fresh loaf served at the Gare de Lyon was the best I had tasted since before World War II. (It still is.) The butter was impeccable, not something from a tinfoil wrapping marked with either optimism or blasphemy *Beurre d'Isigny.* The ham was genuine, perhaps tasting of violets on the wishful tongue. The champagne seemed one of the best I had ever drunk.

The waiter saw that I was more interested in where I was than in where the grim newspaper editorials were telling me to be, and he stood tactfully beside the table while I asked him about some of the murals. He knew a lot, in a controlled but fervent way that I had long recognized in devotees. Now and then he flicked at one of my crumbs, to stay professional.

Then the handsome, thoughtful, strong, blue-bloused, honest, punctual porter beckoned to me from the gigantic doorway that opened onto cloakrooms and the Big Ben Bar and the far closed doors of a Belle Époque palace, and I left without sadness, knowing that I would return. I turned back at the end of the corridor, and the waiter lifted the bottle of champagne where I had left one glassful, and bowed and smiled. I felt fine about everything, even my job ... generous, warm, floaty.

The next time that I cannily arranged to be in Paris so that I would have to take the Mistral again, I went somewhat earlier to the station. I forget whether there were only two waiters that morning, or whether it was later on, when I suddenly looked up from my habitual little meal and saw four or five of them drifting around the table. Mostly they were young, but there were some old ones, too, and they had decided they knew me, and what they had apparently decided to share with me was horrendous.

The Restaurant, they said, was doomed. *"One"* (*"they"* in our lingo) had decided that it was too old to live. The famous lace curtains were in tatters. The paintings were out of date, and filthy with some seventy years of soot and general neglect and pollution. The floors buckled under the weight of the men's trays. Yes, a promising young chef, probably a madman like them all, had opened the Train Bleu. But who but stunned starved travelers would come up to such a drab old wreck as this? "It is a crime of neglect," they said furiously, very quietly, as they stood around my table. "It must not happen. This beautiful thing must not be condemned to death . . ."

I looked at them, so proud, and at the gleaming glass and silver and linen and at my little meal, and then past all of it to the bedraggled lace, the dim dirty light, the flaking gold leaf above us. I would like to think that I said firmly, "Something will be done." The truth is that I probably whimpered a little as I let the men bustle me down the stairs to the train for the South.

I talked about all this, though, with my Paris neighbor, Janet. I told her about how passionately concerned the waiters were. And it went on from there. And by now the Gare de Lyon is in comparatively fine fettle, no way an aging beauty revived by hormones, but rather a mature female who has survived some unpredictable if foregone setbacks with good health and gracefulness.

Much is going on under the five storeys of the mansarded structure of 1900 (". . . a fairly discreet evocation of the Belle Époque," one government document describes it with equal discretion), and within a few years most of suburban Paris will commute from six deep layers of artful stations being burrowed out, for various environmental reasons. Currently, ridiculous bright-orange awnings in a garishly scooped shape have been placed over the seven majestic windows on the "Paris" side of the Restaurant floor, but doubtless they will fade, and fall off.

The interior style of this giant station is "pure 1900," whatever that may mean. On the ground floor thousands of people push in and out, buying tickets and meeting uncles and going somewhere, and the café-brasserie is always open and crowded. On the "train" side, the little trees in front of the marble-topped tables were sparse or gone when I last saw them in 1974, and the newsstand did not have its old inky glamour. This could be partly because I too was older and Colette and Simenon had stopped churning out their paper-backs, and partly because travelers do not feel as leisurely as they did when I once sat there with my father. By now there are snack-bar counters inside the busy buffet, and people drink and eat hastily. But a graceful stairway still leads up-ward, under the glass sky, and instead of one's being alone in the bright huge Restaurant, there seem always to be some *people*. They read newspapers or talk quietly at odd hours like my own; the place buzzes gently, like a rococo hive, all carv-ings and paintings and gilt.

Conceivably gentlemen throng at proper hours around the

Big Ben Bar, where "all the cocktails of the Belle Époque"
are said to be served . . . along with the British (and by now
international) substitute of whiskey and water for the sweet
pinkish drinks of 1900. (I have never seen a barman there,
but then, neither have I seen more than a few travelers in the
Restaurant at nine-thirty in the morning . . .)

Once in the seventies I ate an early lunch rather than a late
breakfast in the Grande Salle. It was moderately filled with
middle-class people who looked as if they were going somewhere soon, which of course they were. They ate quickly but
seriously, in general the *plat du jour,* and read newspapers or
peeked at their watches, or talked quietly with Aunt Ma-
tilda, who was going to see her first grandchild in
Montélimar. The waiters glided miles and miles on the
gleaming new floors. The incredibly long lace curtains
pushed in and out over half-open windows onto the square,
but there seemed little city noise. The ceiling with its three
enormous murals looked somewhat lower since it had been
cleaned, and the walls glowed richly. I walked about, looking at the paintings I liked best, sipping a "Kir au Chablis,"
and the waiters smiled at me as if they knew we shared a fine
secret, which of course they did not know at all. Or did
they?

I drank a Grand Cru Chablis, three years in bottle, feeling
as extravagant as one of the well-kept women in the glamor-
ous murals high above me, and ate a fine little soufflé of
shellfish and mushrooms. Wood strawberries were listed,
and their mysterious perfume would have suited the sudden
sensuality of the meal, but the waiter shook his head. So I
ate dark small raspberries with the rest of the wine, and
leaned back to look at the ceiling crammed with color, in
carved gilded curlicues, high above the incredible walls cov-

ered with their gaudily leering murals, all gold-scarlet-blue, a gigantic jumble of snowy Alps, fishing boats, trains, women, politicians, vineyards ...

Even in its dingier days since 1901, the Gare de Lyon had stayed alive, I thought beautifully, and had made tired travelers stretch and smile. It had, one baffled but delighted writer said, "great harmony in spite of its decadent extravagance."

Yes, that was it: a strange massive *harmony!*

I thought of my friend Janet, who had grown angry with herself after she went there to lunch quietly alone, a double wonder for a person of her gregarious volatility. She felt baffled about not using, ever in her long years in Paris, more than the quick dashes through the station and onto the quais for trains going south to Lyon and then east and west and on further. She groaned, and scolded helplessly at human blindness.

Often people try to keep secret the charm of a tiny restaurant one thousand light-years from nowhere around the corner, in case there will not be a free table the next time they are hungry for its inimitable broth or brew. But who can hide the secret of a colossus like the Gare de Lyon, where thousands of people rush or amble through every day, according to the trains they must catch or leave or even think about?

Inside, under the misty glass, in the music of wheels and horns and whistled strange signals, there are signs guiding passengers to the toilets, the newsstand, the café, the Buffet, the upstairs Restaurant, the Train Bleu. There is no attempt to hide any of this vital and perhaps aesthetic information.

It comes down, I suppose, to a question of where one really chooses to be, and for how long. This is of course true of all such traffic hubs as railway stations, but nowhere is there one with a second floor like that of the Gare de Lyon, so peculiarly lacy and golden. It has, in an enormous way, something of the seduction of a full-blown but respectable lady, post-Renoir but pre-Picasso, waiting quietly in full sunlight for a pleasant chat with an old lover . . .

—*Glen Ellen,* 1979

NOWHERE BUT HERE

It is very simple: I am here because I choose to be.

"Here" is a ranch on Route 12 in northern California, about two miles from Glen Ellen, where Jack London lived and drank and piled up the reddish volcanic stones of the region into strong clumsy walls, towers, cattle troughs, a dam. He devised a kind of sled drawn by oxen to come here for some of his best rocks, from up in the Ranch Canyon, where they have lain since Mount St. Helena blew its top about six million years ago, about twenty-five miles northeast of here as a tipsy crow would fly.

Some fifty feet south of my house there is a pile of the same rocks that flew through the air during the mighty blow. By now, native trees have grown up through their rich cracks and crannies: bay, madrona, live oak. One of the great rocks landed with its flat side up, to make a fine table. When the foundations of my little palace had been laid, more than ten years ago, some dear friends and I sat there on the other stones, and one of us ran along the top of the new walls, sprinkling a bottle of champagne on them in a ritual of goodwill that was actively religious.

And that was almost surely the first and last time that the flat rock has ever had a tablecloth on it, because I soon observed that the great pile was a perfect cool dark bastion for the rattlesnakes that still consider this their rightful territory. The day of the Blessing, they were courteous, recognizing our naïveté, but soon even my cat decided to stay away from their compound as long as they stayed off ours. We do not bother one another, even with more winy ceremonies.

It probably took a long time for those flying boulders to cool off, but by now they are beautiful and mossy to look at, and to leave alone.

Jack London was a born builder, no matter how untrained, and the man (David Pleydell-Bouverie) who owns this ranch is another, although highly shaped and skilled, and neither one could leave the rocks where they had fluttered down, as in my tumultuous little grove. Where London had his oxen drag their slow heavy loads for many miles, to build a gawky trough or a strangely perfect dam, David Bouverie simply hauled material down from his canyon to construct bell towers and gateways and suchlike. Where London was touchingly uncouth, Bouverie has been almost lightsome in his use of the seemingly limitless supply of solid ash that flew here.

To the east of my house, plumb with two tall stone gateposts that are in turn plumb with the bell tower, I look through and past them toward the mountains that separate Napa and Sonoma valleys. Between my house and the Tower are vineyards, and hidden from me as the Canyon curves back toward Napa there is the Waterfall. It is about 150 feet tall, and in winter I can hear it roar. At its base, behind the curtain of water that falls into a lovely pool, there is a long deep cave where Indians often hid, I'm told, from the white men.

The bell tower is mysteriously correct for this landscape. It is at once monolithic and graceful, unlike most of Jack London's piles of stone, and was built piece by piece by Bouverie and a local mason, of course Italian. It houses a fine bell, which Bouverie sometimes insists is the only reason he built the Tower.

He bought the big bell from Old Man Hearst, as one of the countless rejects from the European booty that now loads the castle at San Simeon. In a capricious joke, it was priced at thirty-six dollars, to be paid on the spot. Years later, one of the Old Man's sons offered Bouverie a hundred times that for it, but by then it was so firmly a part of this Valley, to see from the highway or to hear when the wind is right, that such a sale was unthinkable. It rings almost every day of the year, at sundown: twenty-one strong measured pulls. At midnight on New Year's Eve it is pealed longer, faster, louder. . . .

Ringing the bell, first made to summon monks here and there in a Spanish monastery, is no easy trick. Now and then a newcomer to the Ranch will ask to give it a few pulls, and its uneven stutter is painful. The appointed ringer, presently, is Jason King, going on fourteen, and after a few timid try-outs (ringing a big bell is like painting with watercolors: once it's started, there is no turning back . . .), this lanky redhead is in control, so that even the finality of the end of another day is acceptable in his weighty music. The bell rope is on the east side of the Tower, and hidden from me, but I often smile at the suspicion that my young friend is airborne at the end of it, no matter how seasoned and sure his peals sound.

When Jason, or his father the Foreman, or Bouverie the Builder swings up and down on the long rope, I go like a moth to the candle flame and stand on my East Balcony until the twenty-one rings have sounded. Then I stretch my arms and wave them, as the ringer steps around from the back of the Tower. There is no use to shout to him, for he is deafened in his cocoon of sound waves. He lifts his arms to me. It is a twilight ritual, sprung surely from some atavistic pattern.

On the north side of my house there was, for a few years anyway, a planted grove of several kinds of eucalypti, tall and healthy. Then in about 1974 there was a freakish period of day and night temperatures of under 20 degrees Fahrenheit, for eight days. It started early one morning, while I was staying overnight in San Francisco, and when I got home, everything was frozen tight. The pipes at this ranch never burst, as did most of them in our part of the Valley, but they were solid ice for much more than a week.

By then I'd lived here for several years, and was in close trusting relationship with the other people who lived all the time on the Ranch, whether the Boss was gone or not.

Joseph Herger, who had been Foreman here since the Ranch took shape in the forties, was a doughty Swiss peasant, a milker by trade, who had "pulled tits," as he put it, until he moved onto this 500 acres of wild country and started pulling poison ivy and pulling fence posts and pulling loads of cow pats into the gardens. And right then, in the Big Freeze, he was very ill with some kind of influenza. He lived in an isolated cabin, because he was a loner.

Phyllis Whitman, the Housekeeper, was really in charge of the Ranch when Bouverie was not here. She was and is a strong forceful person, at her best in emergencies, but also admirable at the kitchen stove. (Now she is far away, remarried after a sad widowhood.) And she looked after Joseph from her house in the Ranch compound, while I drove every day to nearby Boyes Springs to get water from a friend's outside hydrant, which by a fluke had not frozen.

I would load my station wagon with every big kettle from the Ranch kitchens and mine, and fill them with a hose and then ease back to the Ranch, trying not to slosh too much over the two cattle guards between the Ranch houses and the highway. (They are made of old rails salvaged when tracks were pulled out to prove that it was more patriotic to buy cars than to travel by train.)

Then Phyllis and I would flush all our toilets. Joe's and mine took only a few gallons of water, since we lived alone. Phyllis needed more, because some of her many children still lived here. That was when I decided firmly that every rural dwelling should have not only a battery-powered radio but a workable outhouse.

And then I would come down here, over the cattle guard and into the pastures and my grove, and try not to listen to the eucalyptus trees dying. They cried out and groaned and sometimes shrieked in the cold, for they were strangers here. The native trees growing up from volcanic rocks stayed strong and quiet, but the tall Australians perished noisily, and it was nightmarish to hear them, as they cracked down from tops to roots.

By the time Bouverie came back from Greece or perhaps Bavaria or New York, the trees had changed from their soft silvery greens to a strange black, and were plainly splitting into two long halves. They were a great hazard, since they could crash every which way in any wind from north or west, and burn like torches with their rich oils. People came finally and cut them down. It was almost as painful as their dying had been. Later lush sucklings came up from most of the roots, but the cattle trampled them. I saved a couple near the house, to catch up with the fourteen that were left, and now they look strong and promising as I smile at them through the north windows.

All this is no doubt part of why I live here.

Losing the grove of course changed the clear perfumed air, the climate in my house, the light on its walls, but it gave me a new view of the northern hills and mountains, past the flat green or golden meadows where aristocratically bred cows wait every spring and summer for their scheduled birthings. (The first bull here, when I came, was old and placid. He was called Maximilian. Since he retired from active duty, a succession of young ones of great race perform their jobs quickly and soon leave for other pastures.)

My house is between the two cattle guards, so that I am somewhat in limbo, literally on the wrong side of the tracks, while the Ranch life goes on under the bell tower and past the sprawling vineyards into its own courtyards and similar enclaves. Brave friends risk the railroad tracks to come down here, and even to go back. And since I need to cook simple meals the way some people need Bingo or Double-Crostics, a considerable number of hungry thirsty allies move in and out of this place where I have chosen to live.

The house is, as far as I can tell, a small gem. It is indescribably well conceived and constructed, so I must content myself by stating that it consists of two large rooms and a middle one for the privacies of life: toilet, shower, bath, washbowl, things that most of us Anglo-Saxons hide in small unventilated closets as if our bodily functions were perforce ugly and shameful.

My bathroom, thanks to Bouverie's forthright agreement with this theory, is large and low, with probably the biggest tub in this region, and a capacious shower and a long counter, all sane and practical but voluptuous. Everything is tiled a pattern made in Japan from a Moroccan design, and one long wall is painted the same Pompeian red as the ceiling, and has a changing pattern of pictures I feel like looking at for a time. I move them at will, and people who use the bathroom often stay there lengthily, in the nice old rocking chair or the shower or the tub, looking at what I've put on the red wall and thinking their own thoughts.

The bathroom is low-ceilinged, but the other two rooms of this *palazzino* are domed, in a fine conception of Bouverie's: random-width and random-laid redwood, never touched with oil or varnish, in a contrived curve (of course of straight lines!) that runs through the whole structure. Gradually the wood is turning darker, but I am almost unaware of this, since I live with it. In fifty more years it may be nearly black, from the strong indirect light of the days, and the subtle gases that cooking and laughing and sleeping people send out. Now and then, in a quick atmospheric shift, it will make snapping crackles, from west to east, in a mischievous but not frightening way.

There is a three-foot drop in the house, between the two rooms, but the ceiling goes straight through so that it seems higher in the western half. In "my" room, where I work and sleep, I look up at it when I am in bed, and its random symmetry cools my mind.

The western room is not only deeper but larger, and the big balcony outside it almost makes another room, and keeps the house cool in blazing summertime. From all this space, I look not only south into the native grove, and northward across meadows to the far mountains, but due west into a low range of wooded hills that are a county park, with easy trails, and then on to the high blue mountains of the Jack London Preserve. And now that most of the Bou-

verie Ranch has been added to the protectorate of the Audu-
bon Society, the only houses anyone will ever see from my
porch on the slope up from the meadows are already built,
down along Highway 12 ... small, inoffensive, and tree-
masked.

And all this may be another reason why I live where I live.

For several years before I came here in 1970, common
sense as well as various good friends had been telling me that
it was foolish for me to plan to spend my last years in a
three-storey Victorian house in Napa Valley, with no more
nubile daughters to act as involuntary slave labor. At times it
seemed that I was trying to run an unlicensed but popular
motel-bar-restaurant there, instead of the welcoming warm
home my girls and I had lived in for a long time, and most
of my peers in St. Helena were either moving away or holding discreet garage sales before they settled into elegant
mobile-home parks near supermarkets.

I did not want to leave the little town. Almost half of my
heart was there, sharing honors with Aix-en-Provence, where
I could no longer live as I would choose (in a second-floor
apartment on the Place de l'Archevêché!). Time and taxes
told me otherwise.

It would have been folly for me to rent or build a little
house out in the hilly vineyards of the Napa Valley, because
of the logistics of marketing and transportation and so on.
The alternative was to find a nice old garage or tool shed in
St. Helena, and install plumbing and wall-to-wall carpets,
and accustom myself to air conditioning and viewless windows, and hope that if I didn't show up for a few days somebody might peek in to see what had happened to the queer
old lady-authoress (found quietly dead between the stove
and the icebox, with a glass of vermouth in one hand and an

overripe pear in the other). The prospect was dismal . . . not so much the dying as the *living* that way.

Then my friend David Bouverie in Glen Ellen, westward in the next valley, proposed that I leave my beautiful old house and build a practical two-room *palazzino* on his ranch. I could use his land, and the little house would revert to his estate when I finally left it, and my heirs would be repaid what it had cost me. All this I did, especially since he proposed designing it for me.

And this *he* did, with all the bold skill of his earlier days as an English architect, and his knowledge of the winds and weather of this country as an American rancher. I said I wanted two rooms and a big bath, with an arch at each end to repeat the curved doors of his two big barns. I wanted tile floors. He did not blink . . . and I went back to Aix for several months to grow used to a new future.

It took a couple of years, once here, for me to feel that this was and would be, perforce and *Deo volente,* my "home." I had never before lived in a new house, and I felt like a guest in a delightful rented cottage, perhaps there to write a book, to hide, to escape. But there were familiar books and chairs and pictures, and Ranch people nearby to keep a kind eye on me in case of worry or trouble. Slowly but willingly I grew into the place, so that I was *here.*

The air is mostly dry and sweet, where I have chosen to stay. During the rains it is soft with seasonal perfumes of meadow grasses and new leaves. By mid-April the cows are back from their winter pasturage, usually heavy with imminent calvings, and they tread down myriad wild flowers into the volcanic ash that makes up much of this valley's earth, sometimes three inches deep and sometimes thirty feet.

Dear friends from St. Helena and even Aix and Osaka

come here, or I go over the high hills on the beautiful Oak-
ville Grade to be in St. Helena again, to walk down Main
Street under its noble old electroliers and see dentist-doctor-
CPA-librarians-winemen. In summer, here, I am a kind of
female Elijah, fed by the kindly local ravens: fresh vegetables
and fruits, all eminently meant for my table, which is seldom
bare. For more than half the year, the air moves in four directions through the little house, and in winter I can be as
warm as I want, with a Franklin stove in each room and an
unending supply of madrona and oak from the Ranch, if and
when electricity runs low. My cat and I like heat in the bathroom, but I am weaning him from this sybaritic attitude, if
that is possible with felines, and plan to get him a little electric pad for the coming winter. I have not yet settled my
own puzzlement about how to enjoy a chilly shower bath or
toilet seat. . . .

It is plain that creature comforts are an acceptable part of
my choice to live here in my later years. Aside from them as
well as because of them, I find this house a never-ending excitement, and I think that this is as necessary when a person
is in the seventies as in the teens and twenties. What is
more, knowing *why* and *where* is much easier and more fun
in one's later years, even if such enjoyment may have to be
paid for with a few purely physical hindrances, like crickety
fingers or capricious eyesight.

My eyes, for instance, are undependable by now, so that I
do not drive. A young friend takes me marketing once a
week. And my legs are not trustworthy, so that I have given
up the walking that can be wonderful here on the Ranch:
the sharp crumbled volcanic soil slides easily and is brutal to
fall on. I move about fairly surely and safely in my *palazzino*,
and water the plants on the two balconies. I devise little "inside picnics" and "nursery teas" for people who like to sit in

the Big Room and drink some of the good wines that grow and flow in these northern valleys. I work hard and happily on good days, and on the comparatively creaky ones I pull my Japanese comforter over the old bones, on my big purple bedspread woven by witches in Haiti, and wait for the never-failing surcease.

How else would I live where I live? It all proves what I've said before, that I am among the most blessed of women, still permitted to *choose.*   —*Glen Ellen, 1980*

A NOTE ABOUT THE AUTHOR

After her beginnings in 1908 in Albion, Michigan, and childhood in Whittier, California, M. F. K. Fisher continued her education at Illinois College, Occidental College, and UCLA, and at the University of Dijon in France. She is best known for her gastronomical writings—in 1937 her first book, *Serve It Forth,* was published, followed in 1941 by *Consider the Oyster* and in 1942 by *How to Cook a Wolf* (all of which were collected along with two later books into one volume entitled *The Art of Eating,* republished in Vintage). Mrs. Fisher has spent a good portion of her life as housewife, mother, and, of course, amateur cook; she has written novels, poetry, a screenplay; for a few years she was a vineyardist in Switzerland; and in the late forties she did a brilliant translation of Brillat-Savarin's *The Physiology of Taste,* which has also been republished. Two recent books are *Among Friends,* about growing up in Whittier and a book celebrating Marseille, *A Considerable Town.* For a long time Mrs. Fisher made her home in St. Helena, California, but for the past ten years or so she has lived near Glen Ellen, in the Sonoma Valley.